WASTE AND THE WASTERS

WASTE
and the
WASTERS

POETRY AND
ECOSYSTEMIC THOUGHT IN
MEDIEVAL ENGLAND

Eleanor Johnson

The University of Chicago Press
CHICAGO AND LONDON

The University of Chicago Press, Chicago 60637
The University of Chicago Press, Ltd., London
© 2023 by The University of Chicago
All rights reserved. No part of this book may be used or reproduced in any
manner whatsoever without written permission, except in the case of brief
quotations in critical articles and reviews. For more information, contact the
University of Chicago Press, 1427 East 60th Street, Chicago, IL 60637.
Published 2023
Printed and bound by CPI Group (UK) Ltd, Croydon, CR0 4YY

32 31 30 29 28 27 26 25 24 23   1 2 3 4 5

ISBN-13: 978-0-226-83016-2 (cloth)
ISBN-13: 978-0-226-83017-9 (paper)
ISBN-13: 978-0-226-83018-6 (e-book)
DOI: https://doi.org/10.7208/chicago/9780226830186.001.0001

Library of Congress Cataloging-in-Publication Data
Names: Johnson, Eleanor, 1979– author.
Title: Waste and the wasters : poetry and ecosystemic thought in medieval
    England / Eleanor Johnson.
Description: Chicago : The University of Chicago Press, 2023. | Includes
    bibliographical references and index.
Identifiers: LCCN 2023037668 | ISBN 9780226830162 (cloth) |
    ISBN 9780226830179 (paperback) | ISBN 9780226830186 (ebook)
Subjects: LCSH: English literature—Middle English, 1100–1500—History and
    criticism. | Environmental degradation in literature. | Climatic changes in
    literature.
Classification: LCC PR275.E59 J66 2023 | DDC 820.9/001—dc23/
    eng/20230830
LC record available at https://lccn.loc.gov/2023037668

♾ This paper meets the requirements of ANSI/NISO Z39.48-1992
(Permanence of Paper).

For Emlyn and Joanie

CONTENTS

INTRODUCTION
Thinking and Talking
Ecosystemically
1

CHAPTER ONE
The Five Disasters Facing
Medieval Ecosystems
11

CHAPTER TWO
The Laws of Waste:
The Bible and the Common Law
37

CHAPTER THREE
Waste in Sermons and Penitential
Manuals: The Unjust Steward
51

CHAPTER FOUR
Winner and Waster:
The Imperilment of the Land
69

CHAPTER FIVE

Wasters and Workers in *Piers Plowman*:
Famine and Food Insecurity

83

CHAPTER SIX

Chaucer's Yeoman's Wasting Body:
Pollution and Contagion

102

CHAPTER SEVEN

The Wasted Lands of the Green Knight,
and the Wasting of Camelot: Climate
Change, Climate Revenge

126

CHAPTER EIGHT

Gardens, Bees, and Wastours:
Political Waste and the Fantasy of Sustainability

150

CHAPTER NINE

Aftermath: From Wasting to
Waste Matter

160

Epilogue

169

Acknowledgments 175   Notes 177
Index 213

INTRODUCTION
Thinking and Talking Ecosystemically

The term "ecosystem" was first used in 1935, as a way of talking about the natural world as broken down into systems of exchange—the material transfer of resources between living and nonliving things.[1] Etymologically, "ecosystem" combines the Greek *oikos*, "household," with *sistema*, which means "a whole composed of several parts or members."[2] So when we use "ecosystem" we are talking about the world we live in as a household. And we are thinking about that household as an organized collection of interconnected parts. When we say "ecosystem," we mean the complex network of living and nonliving things that constitutes the habitable world. When we say "ecosystem," we mean soil, water, plants, animals, gases, ice, rocks, salt, winds, energy, and a host of other things that make the world a place for life, and we also mean how they all work together. We mean a slice of nature that submits to scientific inquiry, data collection, and analysis and that manifests specific behaviors and tendencies. We mean something we can get our scientific methods around, something that can be grasped and studied for how it works.

Throughout this book I use "ecosystemic" where one might expect to see "environmental" or "ecological," precisely and deliberately for its etymological meaning.[3] "Ecology" is the study of the household we all live in; "environment," deriving from French, means, really, our surroundings. The terms "ecological" and "environmental" both have copious attestation in works of ecocriticism and countless adherents among ecocritics, "ecological" perhaps being foremost for highlighting the interconnectedness of humans with other beings and with their surroundings.[4] But in this book I prefer "ecosystemic" because

I want to bring in the ideas of complexly interrelating and interconnected living and nonliving things in a kind of household, *and* I want to foreground *system*—the idea that different aspects and agents and elements in an ecosystem are organized and interdependent. I want to foreground livability and systemic interconnection—the organization of the household—together. And I want to foreground the idea that people, their social patterns, their interactions, and even their cultures intersect with, are structured by, and help to structure the more obviously "natural" environment composed of rocks, sunlight, air, trees, animals, water, and soil. "Ecosystemic," for me, articulates more vividly than "ecological" or "environmental" how utterly bound together the "natural" world and the "social" world are, how mutually constitutive they are, how indeed they organize each other, and how each plays a role in the habitability of the earth as an organized system.[5]

Today the idea of an "ecosystem" almost invariably carries an aura of vulnerability and fleetingness. When we talk about ecosystems, we almost always talk about their fragility, their decay. An ecosystem is not something that will always be there; it is a delicate entity, negatively affected by the encroachments of civilization, technology, energy, and mass culture. It is a household whose management, organization, and composition are insecure, under threat. It is a livable space on the verge of becoming less livable, a house whose management has run amok so badly that the inhabitants need to move elsewhere. But there's nowhere to move.

This notion that our habitable places are precarious and imperiled is, we tend to think, a relatively new one, a lamentable consequence of mass industrialization. The climate-destroying Anthropocene era, emergent but distinct from the Holocene, is generally understood to have originated in the past few hundred years and to be tied to the rise of global capitalism.[6] When I tell people my book is about ecosystemic collapse and ecosystemic thought in medieval England, they are almost unanimously perplexed.[7] This perplexity originates in four questionable assumptions. The first assumption is that medieval Europeans believed they lived in a natural world protected by a providential God who ensured things like food supply and weather. So presumably there was no notion that things could really ever be destroyed, ruined, or polluted beyond livability. The second assumption is less about belief and more about history: medieval people had less cause to think about ecological disaster because the Industrial Revolution had not happened yet, so the natural world was not yet broken. The third assumption is that even if ecological change had been happening, medieval people would have been unaware of ecosystemic danger because they had no meteorological science to help them perceive and track it. And a final assumption—my favorite because it makes this book worth writing—is that medieval people could not fathom ecosystemic precarity and collapse because they had no organized, critical, scientific language for it. They couldn't think it because they couldn't say it. So, to sum up, lots of God, no science, no industry, no language, so no ecosystemic awareness. All reasonable assumptions, but all wrong.

It's true that medieval Europeans believed in God. They did believe nature's functioning was guaranteed by divine will. But the baseline assumption was not that God would be reliably kind and gentle toward mankind. Therefore they absolutely did not believe that, since nature was underwritten by divine will, nature would automatically favor them. Instead, they assumed that ecological change and natural disasters were themselves God's will, manifested to punish their malfeasance. Put otherwise, medieval people believed in anthropogenic climate change—though admittedly in a different sense than we mean now. The second false assumption is that, since the Industrial Revolution had not yet happened, ecological precarity did not exist. But robust and very noxious proto-industries abounded in medieval Europe. The sea coal industry caused horrendous urban air pollution. The shipping industry spread plagues. Changes in agriculture brought widespread soil depletion, soil erosion, deforestation, privatization, and an overall reduction in available arable land throughout the period. The third assumption, that medieval people couldn't perceive these changes because they lacked science, is also wrong. A generation of cold, wet winters destroyed European harvests and starved millions of people. That was noticed, meteorology or no, and ample documents survive that attest to the noticing.

Assumption four, that they lacked a critical vocabulary, is right: medieval people did lack an organized scientific vocabulary for ecological danger. But that does not remotely mean they lacked thought, perspective, and insight. They did what people do when faced with a set of problems for which no organized vocabulary exists: they made art. Specifically, they used the resources of poetic language—meter, rhyme, alliteration, metaphor, simile, personification, characterization, plot, dramatic staging, repetition, and countless others—to devise a system for thinking and feeling their way into intractable and inarticulable problems of ecological peril without making straightforward, positivistic statements. They combined multiple other discourses—law, theology, psychology—each with a particular, if narrow, vantage point on ecosystemic danger, making those discourses flow together as only literature can. Medieval poets invented their own ecosystemic discourse.

Some of this discourse is fairly visible. Interspecies contact, for instance, seems to have been of sustained interest to medieval writers. Great numbers of stories survive about women who turned into wolves, horses that saved their riders or fought other knights' horses in battle, birds that complained to princesses about their own romantic troubles.[8] Medieval people, reading and writing on the backs of slaughtered animals, watching the occasional stitch line slant across the parchment leaf where a bookmaker had to sew together two uneven pieces of skin to make space for a stanza, often meditated on the fleshiness of books, on the corporeality of knowledge.[9] This interest in interspecies contact was not just about animals. Some medieval works of art—both verbal and visual—even allowed for a certain porosity between animal and vegetable life; *Sir Gawain and the Green Knight* is probably the most famous example from medieval England, but there are also stone carvings of human faces with foliage spilling from their mouths.[10] Evidently the boundaries between human and natural were more porous than we might imagine. People were in and of their ecosystems, by turns vulnerable to them and helped by them. However special people held themselves to be in God's eyes, there was a surprising awareness about the contingency of being human in the "natural" world.[11]

Despite medieval people's comfort with interspecies entanglement, it is hard to find full-throated articulations of ecosystemic accountability or ecosystemic interimplication. Scholarship on the Middle Ages reflects that seeming silence: if you look through the vast majority of scholarship on medieval history and culture, there is not much to indicate a sense of fragility, precarity, or preciousness in the "natural" world, or to show how mankind's actions might impinge on them. So perhaps the lack of vocabulary for "environment" and "ecosystem" really does indicate a parallel lack of cultural awareness, lack of thought, or lack of concern for the environment as such. There is no question that medieval people were interested in how human beings might be connected to the world of plants and animals, but did they worry at all about things like resource allocation, pollution, ecosystemic damage, ecosystemic justice, urbanization, or how individuals affect the next generation through their own discrete choices and behaviors? Was there really a concept of ecosystemic peril where there was no robust scientific vocabulary about ecosystems?

The answer is yes. And in late medieval England, where and when this book focuses, that ecosystemic thought coalesced in poetry, and it coalesced around the word "waste." Waste was a useful term because it was popular and familiar, but also complex and shifting. Medieval people latched on to the term as a way of gaining interpretive purchase on a world that was increasingly (and obviously) out of control.

To be clear, when I say "medieval people," I don't mean just poets or some educated elite. Because of its presence in many different registers—legal, moral, sermonic, biblical, penitential, practical, domestic, medical, and poetic—waste was a term known to everyone, even though it tended to mean slightly different things in each of those discourses. Its broad availability and its shifting meaning made it an ideal term for doing complex ecosystemic thinking: it was a familiar concept, but it was ambiguous in a generative way. Moreover, many of the poems I study in this book—as well as the law, the sermons, and the biblical passages—were familiar to at least some illiterate or semiliterate English people, both men and women. Indeed, at the end of the fourteenth century poetry was shuttling between some fairly high-flown registers and some quotidian and popular ones, and it was doing so because medieval English poets had come to understand that ecosystemic catastrophe was *everyone*'s problem. Poetry, that is, was doing advocacy work, not just inkhorn philosophizing. So I believe that waste was a conceptual node with deep and far-reaching cultural

6 : INTRODUCTION

roots, and when I talk about medieval English people, I mean more than just the educated classes.

WASTE IN THE MIDDLE AGES

To modern readers the claim that "waste" was a keyword of early ecosystemic thought in medieval England may not sound very surprising: we now think daily about waste, garbage, pollution, and the overall detritus of industrial production in our conversations about environmental crises. We think of waste matter as the objects or substances that have outlived their function in human society but that linger within it or at its margins as unwelcome detritus. But "waste" in English did not acquire that meaning until the eighteenth century.[12] In medieval England, waste did not mean garbage. It was primarily a behavior, so much so that the term "waster," used to describe people who habitually engage in wasteful behavior, came into currency in the period.

So just what did waste mean in the English Middle Ages? "Waste" was a strange word, with a sprawling range of meanings. As a noun, it meant a particular kind of land—the wasteland (I'll discuss this meaning at length in chapters 2 and 7). But "waste" was most often used as a verb, signaling both overuse and underuse, both hoarding and spending, both criminal behavior and sinful behavior, both consumption and dissipation. We use waste as a verb nowadays too: we waste our time and our breath, our money and our gasoline. But when we do, we almost always mean underuse, or squandering, and we usually signal an action that mainly has consequences for the person who wastes. So if I waste my time, I'm not hurting anyone else. If I waste my money, I'm the one who suffers, not you. Sure, you can waste my time and my money too, but those usages are less common and, more important, if you *do* waste my time, you hurt no one but me. We do not usually use the *verb* waste in a truly ecosystemic sense to mean an action that affects an entire system of things and organisms. Circumstances were very different in medieval England, where the verb waste was always a truly ecosystemic infraction. It always had consequences beyond the wasters themselves, consequences that were ecosystemic and environmental.

We will find waste-based ecosystemic discourse in a wide range of places. We will find it in medieval English legal documents—both case reports and statutory laws pertaining to the use and abuse of real estate. We will find it in the Bible and in commentaries on the Bible. We will find it in Late Antique Christian philosophy and in medieval responses to those philosophies. We will see it also in medieval penitential manuals. We will see ecosystemic thought in municipal records, plague narratives, historical chronicles, surgical manuals, and political documents. But the most important archive of concerted ecosystemic thought, as I have said, is poetry.

Late medieval English poems decisively showcase an awareness that agriculture, labor, nature, economics, social relationships, and the resources of the soul are not just related, but coextensive. These poems present a vision of an ecosystem with precious few boundaries between the notionally internal world of the human body, the human soul, and the notionally external world of nature, human social relations, and the marketplace. These porous boundaries between body, soul, social world, and economy reveal a deep sense of precarity as well as preciousness in the minds of medieval poets when they thought about their place in the world. And to think through these ideas, they think and talk about "waste."

WHY MEDIEVAL WASTE, WHY MEDIEVAL POETRY?

Parsing how waste became a focal point for philosophies and literatures of ecosystemic interdependence, ecosystemic precarity, and social ethics, I hope, will shed some light on the blind spots in contemporary ecological thought. In particular, I hope it will urge people who are already desperately concerned about interconnected ecological crises—global warming, ocean pollution, food contamination, pandemics, and energy shortages, for instance—to think more carefully about how psychology, medicine, social interaction, generational planning, wealth management, property usage, and even the very idea of ownership are all intimately interconnected to ecological danger. Ecosystems are not just the "out there" of the "natural world." As medieval people recognized, the environment encompasses our thoughts, our words, our money, our energy, and our social patterns as well as the rocks, trees, and streams that surround us.

Finally, I want to address why we would want or need to understand a specifically medieval and specifically Christian idea of ecosystemic vulnerability. The bald fact is that many contemporary climate change deniers, many advocates of the "drill, baby, drill" orientation toward ecological resources, many who believe the earth is here for people to use willy-nilly forever, many who believe they are more entitled to the goods of the earth than other people might be, many who believe that waste is not an immediate concern, many of these people come from Christian vantage points. Some of them, for example, understand the Bible's notion of "stewardship" to entail certain ungainsayable rights and indeed obligations to use fully all resources that the earth offers up. There is a misunderstanding of Christianity at work there.

Pope Francis has tried (and so far, failed) to correct the notion that humans are entitled to use and exploit the goods of the earth to the fullest extent they wish: "Although it is true that we Christians have at times incorrectly interpreted the Scriptures, nowadays we must forcefully reject the notion that our being created in God's image and given dominion over the earth justifies absolute domination over other creatures."[13] Pope Francis named himself after Saint Francis of Assisi—a medieval theologian and social activist—for a reason: medieval people were quite clear that dominion did not mean "absolute domination." Despite the slowness even of scholars to recognize this, medieval people were clear about on it: having dominion does not mean exerting domination.[14] My hope is that seeing this awareness so clearly and pervasively realized in Christian texts more than six hundred years old might possibly prompt at least some people to change their views on the notional right of humanity to dominate the earth.

So even though this book is scholarly in its central ambitions, I have endeavored to write it to be user-friendly enough so that at least some nonacademics, those who care about the history of ecosystemic thought and who might be searching for new ways to reach out to climate change deniers and talk openly with them, may get something out of it as well. As a result, I've given a little more plot synopsis and context for some of the literary works than is typical of a scholarly book. I've also sequestered some theoretical and scholarly problems and ideas in the notes, so that those they interest will see them and, I hope, be provoked by them, but so that those who want to focus on the broader argument will not be overwhelmed. I have also tried to write in an accessible tone and style.

As for its more specifically academic audience, I have written this book in the hope that it will appeal not only to scholars of late Middle English literature, but also to ecocritics from other disciplines—history, art history, philosophy, theology, sociology, political theory, engineering—and to literary scholars from other periods—Early Modern, to be sure, but also Industrial and Postindustrial periods. My general belief is that understanding the ecophilosophies of earlier eras can only hone and sharpen our own.

A caveat. As I have said, this book centers on medieval Europe, and most of its chapters focus even more narrowly, on medieval England. I wish my expertise extended more widely and that I had another twenty years to work on this project, so that I could write about proto-ecological thought in other regions of the world and do a massive comparative study. But I leave that for other scholars, and I will read their books with keen attention, and with gratitude.

CHAPTER ONE

THE FIVE DISASTERS FACING MEDIEVAL ECOSYSTEMS

Many scholars of the European Middle Ages bristle at the notion that "medieval" should be a lexical shorthand for a rough and difficult life. After all, the Middle Ages bore witness to miraculous artistic creations, significant intellectual movements, and some truly progressive, inclusive cultures. In medieval Spain, Cordoba had running water, supplied by an aqueduct, as well as a culture of religious tolerance among Muslims, Jews, and Christians for many generations.[1] Notre Dame was built in the Middle Ages, and it has graced the Parisian skyline as a testament to medieval art and engineering for eight hundred years, despite its being badly damaged by fire in 2019. Alchemy, much maligned in popular culture both now and in the Middle Ages, was a meaningful forerunner of empirical science.[2] Many things about the Middle Ages were marvelous and impressive. If I had to live in any era and city other than twenty-first-century New York, I would probably choose twelfth-century Palermo.

If I were a man. And Christian. And wealthy. And trilingual. With good genes for eyesight. And teeth. And a preternaturally strong immune system. Because life really *was* difficult in the Middle Ages, in a whole host of ways. "Medieval" *should* signal peril when applied to contemporary social and geopolitical situations.

But what twenty-first-century people don't usually mean in using "medieval" as a slang term is an ecosystemic crisis. However darkly we perceive medieval reality, our perception is that the environment and its many ecosystems were doing a lot better in the Middle Ages than they are now. How could they possibly *not* be doing better? The Industrial Revolution hadn't yet happened, global trade was not the juggernaut it is now, fossil fuels were not used at anything approaching the scale they are now, and there was no plastic to fill the oceans. Sure, in 1400 you might die of an infected splinter, you were fairly likely to die in or shortly after childbirth if you had enough children, and you would certainly die if you had a chronic medical condition like diabetes or cancer, but you could generally let your baby eat grass without fearing she might ingest lead or toxic fertilizers. You could sail the ocean without seeing garbage islands float by, and there was no such thing as plastic pollution of the ground or the groundwater. You certainly would not passively ingest pharmaceuticals from the tap water, and not just because you hadn't any tap water (unless you lived in Cordoba), but also because there was no pharmaceutical industry. And there was no global warming to worry about.

That being said, it is also true that the ecosystemic crises we find ourselves in now resonate with the ecosystemic conditions of the Middle Ages in surprising and uncomfortable ways. Although there were many arenas of ecosystemic peril and even catastrophe to focus on in the medieval European world, five related crises beset medieval Europeans, some of them particularly acute in England. The first was land shortage stemming from erosion and privatization. The second was climate change, along with, third, food scarcity. The fourth was contagion: the Black Death. The fifth was pollution, mostly in cities. People were sick, cold, and hungry, surrounded by pollution, and struggling to farm. Medieval ecosystems, whether rural or urban, were nowhere near as benign as we might imagine.

SOIL, LAND, AND SHORTAGE

Although not because of plastic, heavy metals, or rogue pharmaceutical particles, one of the ecosystems under great pressure in England in the Middle Ages was the soil. The medieval practice of converting woods to fields by felling and uprooting trees significantly altered the relation between soil, water, and plants.[3] Clear-cutting of trees between 700 and 1200 caused shifts in river flow patterns and led to massive erosion.[4]

Agricultural methods in England in the thirteenth and fourteenth centuries engendered widespread soil depletion.[5] The ground beneath the feet of medieval English people was unstable and unreliable, and they knew it: William Langland's *Piers Plowman* concludes with the arrival of Antichrist, who destroys the human world specifically by attacking the soil.[6] Once the soil is destroyed, Antichrist turns to attack the people of England directly. As the poem understands well, there is an intimate relationship between the health of the soil and the health of the people: the soil goes first; the souls inevitably follow.

The soil depletion of the thirteenth and fourteenth centuries triggered a series of grain shortages in the fourteenth century, not just in England, but elsewhere, which were worsened by the population's having grown sharply just before the plague years. As a result, according to historian Richard Hoffman, "the years around and following 1300 do offer clear signs of impoverishment, production failures, immiseration, and food and other resource shortages in many parts of Europe."[7] In contemporary parlance, the fourteenth century saw food precarity and food scarcity. And medieval people recognized that—they knew food was scarce and the supply precarious—without formal scientific understanding, global technology, or having those words in their languages. As I will discuss in more detail in chapter 4, the poem *Winner and Waster* talks at length about how the wealthy's profligate consumption, coupled with the misuse of land resources, creates shortages of food for the poor. *Piers Plowman*, the central text of chapter 5, encourages people to work the land carefully and assiduously; once they become lazy and allow the land to lie unworked and untended, famine comes as a scourge to punish them all.

Further complicating matters of ecosystemic and agricultural precarity, the period from the eleventh century to the fourteenth in England saw an intensive privatization of land—particularly of woodlands, pastures, moorland, wastes, and meadows. Before this time, beginning with Old English law and continuing through the Common Law of the English late Middle Ages, peasants and farmers had full access to those "common" lands.[8] But then things started to change. The first such change was afforestation, in which land was sequestered for the private use of the Crown, usually for hunting or pasturing, and was therefore not available to the general population for farming, pasturing, hunting, or anything else.[9]

The second avenue toward privatization of lands during the fourteenth century was assarting, a practice by which a wealthy landlord clear-cut commonly held lands for private use.[10] Wastelands, moorlands, meadows, pastures, and woodlands were all subject to assarting by wealthy landlords. Although these types of land were not arable, access to them was tremendously important to the local agricultural economy.[11] For instance, the wastelands were rich in mast—the acorns and other undergrowth used to fatten livestock—the meadows and pastures were rich in grazing, and the woodlands abounded with timber and firewood. Furthermore, these areas were often full of peat and underbrush, key sources of fuel for heat and light in the winter months. In the late Middle Ages, nonarable land was often even more profitable per acre per year than was arable land: pastureland, moorland, and even heathland often brought in more cash value than did traditional farmlands.[12] According to ancient custom, these nonarable lands were held, used, and maintained in common by all the local people who sought to use them. All members of the agricultural community were entitled to take profits from them by fowling, hunting, peat harvesting, grazing, and woodcutting, and they were expected to repair seawalls, construct dikes, and otherwise ensure that the wastes remained available for the collective good.[13] These lands thus represented a type of collective landholding in which no single landholder had exclusive rights. The practices of afforestation and assarting that became rampant in the later English Middle Ages undermined that traditional mode of collective holding.

Particularly for the poor, who relied heavily on access to these commonly held lands, afforestation and assarting of common lands constituted a substantial problem: in these lands the poor could no longer hunt, get firewood, or obtain timber for construction or repairs.[14] Say a hailstorm ripped through your village in November and tore a hole in the roof of your cottage. If the common lands around your village were no longer available to you, you could not get wood to fix the roof, nor could you harvest peat to warm your house. There were no lumberyards, and no shops selling peat. You and your family were just going to have to figure out how to patch the roof with something else and hope for the best. You'd have to survive that way for six to eight months. Although "the rich" could and often did succeed in restricting the king's privileges of afforestation by enacting statutes, on a local level few courses of action were available; farmers and peasants had little legal support in fighting the diminishing of their access to afforested or assarted areas.

But that doesn't mean they didn't try. The local peasants and farmers sometimes resisted the restrictions placed on land use by powerful landlords, although their attempts to continue enjoying their accustomed rights were met with criminal prosecution under forest law.[15] The fines and punishments for breaking into new forests or assarted lands meant that acts of resistance were often rebellious and violent. Ralph Hanna has discussed one instance of this phenomenon, in which local peasants grew so agitated about the privatization that a royal justice had to be rescued from their violence.[16] Such spikes of local resistance continued to the end of the fourteenth century.

Resistance sometimes did take place legally, too, through lawsuits and allegations of improper assarting. Even though the courts typically favored the trend toward privatization of lands, peasants and landholders persisted in defending their ancient rights to common lands against what they perceived as unjust assarting. They had some success, as reflected in statutory changes: the Statute of Merton (1236) permitted lords to assart lands only if other people's usage of those lands continued unimpaired. Several decades later, the Second Statute of Westminster enabled tenants to make a claim of novel disseisin—forcible and unjust ejection—in cases where a lord restricted access to common lands by enclosing them. This legislation, however, seems to have been frequently ignored; in 1330 the citizens of Cambridge had to sue for their rights to use the commonly held wastelands surrounding the city.[17]

Indeed, we learn from fourteenth-century case law that statutory attempts to restrict assarting and to regulate afforestation were inadequate, at least in the minds of the common people, who repeatedly resorted to extralegal measures to maintain their rights in lands that formerly were commonly held. Frequently, people simply continued to use the assarted lands as though they were still common. In 1332 a group of people broke into an area recently enclosed by the archbishop of York and tore down a house he had built there. When the archbishop sued the men for trespass, they claimed that his building interfered with their ancient rights of common. In their view they had merely sought to squeeze some profit out of lands they rightfully possessed in common, so they justifiably removed the awkward obstacle—the archbishop's house. Against their claim, the archbishop insisted that he had private and exclusive rights to the land by virtue of his lordship. The suit went on for some time, but the archbishop ultimately won, in keeping with the trend toward privatization of commonly held lands.[18]

A broad practice of deliberately breaking fences or breaching privatized lands by bands of men claiming eviction from formerly common lands continued throughout the century.[19] In 1336, in response to an accusation of violating pasture boundaries, a defendant claimed that the lands in question were commonly held wastelands and that he had long-standing customary rights to take what he did.[20] In 1359 a man was accused of taking excessive iron from his lord's assarted land. He replied that the lands had formerly been common lands, and so he only did what his ancestors had anciently and always done: profit from the commons.[21] In 1382 William Brook and others were accused of cutting trees and taking goods and chattels from the abbot of Whitby. The defendants claimed they took only reasonable goods from lands held in common "from time immemorial."[22] They claimed that this commonalty extended to all the woods, pastures, moors, and wastes in which the abbot sought damages from the court. According to Brook and his fellows, the abbot had, at a time in the recent past, enclosed some of these areas, asserting them for private use. The defendants then claimed that this was an unlawful act to commit in common lands and that they therefore should not be convicted for trespass for having broken in and taken profits from the abbot's enclosures.[23] The abbot, in their minds, was the real criminal—he had ripped the commons away from them— while they were merely acting on their rights in restoring the land to themselves.[24] In the minds of these defendants, they were merely trying to restore their own rights.

Literary history complements legal history in testifying to the distress of English people about privatization. The wonderful but woefully underread poem *Parlement of the Thre Ages* specifically addresses afforestation—when hunting lands are privatized and restricted from common use. The poem begins with a scene of a young man hunting in a forest, killing and skinning a deer, then stashing the butchered carcass in a fern-covered hole while he catches a nap. This man is clearly a poacher. He stashes the meat so he can't be caught with it; as he says, "so that no forester of the land should find it thereafter."[25] He hides the antlers so no hunter can find them, then looks around nervously as the warm sun lulls him and he falls asleep while waiting for darkness to fall before he sneaks out of the forest to take his kill home. This is a scene of food scarcity and food precarity, a scene of a person entering the afforested forest against the law, poaching an animal, and doing everything he can not to get caught and not to have his precious kill taken from him. The poem was written at a historical and cultural moment when the availability of land and its resources was under constant pressure. That pressure was so clear and so pervasive, in fact, that the poem does not even bother to identify the main character as a poacher—his activity would be immediately familiar to almost anyone who read the poem. Poaching was an act of resistance to a deteriorating ecosystem and a means of self-preservation in a place and time of land and food scarcity.

Despite historical and literary resistance to afforestation and assarting, once begun they were continuous processes in the English late Middle Ages.[26] Available common land dwindled markedly,[27] so that very little remained for common use, particularly in the east and southwest of England.[28] Not surprisingly, these assarted areas saw more agricultural wealth concentrated in the hands of a small number of lords than did areas that maintained a higher proportion of wastes as commons, such as the Midlands. In the period this book focuses on, then, there were two major sources of pressure on the land itself: one was soil depletion/erosion caused by farming practices. The other was afforestation/assarting, the overall reduction of land availability brought about by privatization.[29] Fourteenth-century England, then, suffered from problems of resource allocation, food scarcity, and land destruction that anticipated those that besiege the twenty-first century.

CLIMATE AND FAMINE

If land contraction was bad, the weather was worse. First, the so-called Little Ice Age hit fourteenth-century Europe hard. The 1310s had a run of very cold, wet weather that led to serious food shortages, catastrophic famines, and scarcity-related deaths throughout Europe.[30] You'd think that rains would be good for food production and that drought would be the real enemy of agriculture, but in fact the cold, wet weather prompted two consecutive years of crop failure across Northern Europe in particular—in 1314 and 1315. This double failure triggered a seven-year Great Famine, affecting some 400,000 square miles of Europe and over thirty million people.[31] The Great Famine is estimated to have killed about 10 percent of the population of Northern Europe.[32] Let me repeat that, because it should be shocking, and it's easy to let mortality data that are seven hundred years old not penetrate: 10 percent of northern Europeans *died* of hunger during a seven-year famine. One out of every ten people you would have known was dead. *Of starvation.* If one in ten starved to death, a great many more suffered food insecurity and malnutrition: 50 percent? 90 percent? During this famine, yields of wheat and rye hovered around 60 percent of normal in Europe, and yields of oats and barley around 66 percent.[33] In England, in 1316 wheat yields were 55.9 percent of normal. In Cuxham in the same year, wheat yields were 67 percent of normal. A study of Bolton Priory in the north of England showed grain yields about 50 percent of normal.[34] Given the massive shortage of grain, it seems reasonable to estimate that two-thirds of the population experienced significant food stress.

It wasn't just crops that the rain affected. It also destroyed vast stores of fuel—primarily wood and peat. The fuel shortage had many knock-on effects. One, of course, was that there was less fuel for heating homes. Another was a lack of fuel to boil seawater to extract salt; the price of salt quadrupled over the course of just a few years. Because salt was so expensive, the foods that rely on salt—such as protein-rich salted fish and cheese—were suddenly in short supply.[35] At the same time, both because of grain shortage and because of the weather itself, livestock used both as food and in the production of food died off in great numbers.[36] The weather seems to have triggered animal pestilences including rinderpest, a disease of ruminants.[37] The rains and sodden soil caused liver fluke in sheep.[38] In some areas the number of sheep and goats fell by 70 percent during the fourteenth century.[39] Two of the Ramsay Abbey manors in 1319 went from having forty-eight and forty-five head of cattle respectively to six and two.[40] In 1317–18 the winter was so fierce that animals froze to death in their pastures.[41] So medieval people were losing crops, heat, and protein all at once because of changes in the climate.

Compounding the long, cold, wet winters and the food shortages of the 1310s, there seems to have been a period of abnormally intense droughts in the 1320s.[42] Those droughts caused further crop shortages as well as depleting the soil, setting up an ideal situation for severe flooding when heavy rains returned in the 1330s and 1340s, causing erosion and further loss of arable land in eastern England.[43] The country saw widespread coastal storm flooding in these decades and again in the 1350s and 1360s, when the Thames overflowed. Flooding and dike breaches occurred again in the 1370s in the Thames estuary, Sussex, and East Anglia.[44] Between the start and the middle of the fourteenth century, half of the Suffolk town of Dunwich was destroyed by flooding.[45] One town endured flooding so severe that in 1355, corpses were washed up from the local graveyard.[46] Because of flood damage and, in some cases, entire farms' being covered by the sea, large areas of farmland were simply abandoned between 1350 and 1400.[47] Flooding along the Thames estuary was so bad in 1335 that the money spent on repairing dikes and walls that year exceeded the annual average for the century by almost a factor of ten. Three years later a flood nearly as severe occurred, undoing most of the previous repair work and resulting in another year of outsized expenditure.[48] The middle of the 1370s witnessed widespread and severe flooding in Essex, and whole towns along the Thames estuary were ruined by salt water in the last third of the fourteenth century.[49] For instance, the town of Barking and its abbey were so severely damaged by the storm surges of the mid-1370s that Londoners, just a short way up the Thames from Barking, began to worry about the effect the Barking disaster would have on their own livelihoods—the floodplains were impeding the navigability of the Thames, and Barking residents' repair jobs were inadequate and perhaps dangerous.[50] By 1382 there was a real risk that the arable land around Barking would be permanently ruined by the inundation, and the flooding was seriously interfering with the fishing industry upriver.[51] From about 1368 to 1420, there were numerous catastrophic winter floods in Sussex, so that meadows were inundated well into the summer and farmlands nearest the coast were sodden.[52]

The entire period saw winters lasting two or three months longer than normal, making for shorter growing seasons and populations of increasingly desperate and aggressive predatory animals. The food shortages increased the demand for fish; then overfishing led to the collapse of the herring populations off East Anglia between 1360 and 1380.[53] No food on the land, less food in the sea. Thus English people in the fourteenth century saw some of the worst climactic conditions of the past thousand years in Western Europe—events and shortages nearly unimaginable until the past twenty years or so during our own period of rapid and dangerous climate change.[54]

So did medieval people perceive these climactic shifts? Did the weather strike people as unusually harsh? The short answer is yes. As a German chronicler pointed out, "there was such an inundation of waters that it seemed as though it was *the* Flood."[55] William Jordan notes the tragic matter-of-factness in many historical accounts, which explain calmly that of course buildings tend to fall down in floods.[56] The slightly longer answer is that because of the relatively low literacy rates and the paucity of surviving first-person accounts in the period, if we want to find evidence of how regular people, not just chroniclers or annalists, might have experienced and understood climate change, we have to turn to the literary archive, to see how the lives of regular people are depicted in these straitened times.

As I noted in the introduction, when I say "regular people," I mean a wide range of people. Of course I include literate, relatively wealthy people who owned or composed vernacular literary works. But I also mean semiliterate and illiterate people who had heard poetry read aloud to them, perhaps at their local lord's manor, perhaps in some other social setting. I mean the kinds of people—farmers, peasants, women—who found in *Piers Plowman* the political inspiration that culminated in the Peasants' Rising of 1381. My own view is that we, as scholars, do a disservice to historical people when we assume that only the rich, only the fully literate, only the cultured people at a given moment would have had access to literary ideas or to poetry. So in this book my assumption is that, if ideas filter into the poetic archive—especially if those ideas are widely attested in the poetic archive in a particular period—it speaks of a broad cultural awareness of those ideas.

The poet of the fourteenth-century poem *Winner and Waster* worries that, with all the clear-cutting of wooded areas by landlords, there won't be enough fuel to keep people warm in the wintertime. A man would have to walk "ferrere than his fadir dide by fyvetene myle" (farther than his father did by fifteen miles) to get wood to "warmen his helys" (warm his heels) in the wintertime.[57] Although this statement is primarily a critique of assarting and clear-cutting, the worry that underpins it is, of course, cold weather. The beginning of the same poem laments the dangerous weather in yet starker terms, imagining a coming time "when wawes waxen schall wilde and walles bene doun / and hares appon herthe-stones schall hurcle in hire fourme" (when waves shall grow wild and walls fall down / and hares shall huddle together on hearth-stones).[58] Strong storm winds whip waves to wildness, knock down walls, and make hares huddle together for warmth on hearthstones—which they can do because the structure has been so damaged as no longer to be inhabitable by hare-trapping humans. Evidently there was a sense of climate change, a sense that the weather, the cold, the wind, and the ocean itself were growing wilder, imperiling the habitable environment. Medieval English people were not blind, nor were they stupid: they could tell something was going seriously wrong with their ecosystems.

William Langland's apocalyptic poem *Piers Plowman* even more aggressively registers the weather as a significant threat.[59] Langland often ascribes the bad weather to a God made angry by the actions of foolish people. Langland wrote of the terrible windstorm of 1362,

And the southwest wynd on Satirday at eue
Was apertely for pride and for no poynt ellis.
Piries and plumtres wern puffid to the erthe

22 : CHAPTER ONE

In ensaumple, segges, that ye schulde do the betere.
Bechis and broode okis wern blowen to the grounde
And turnide vpward here tail in toknyng of drede
that dedly synne or domisday shal fordon hem alle.

[And the southwest wind on Saturday evening was plainly for our pride, and for no point else. Pear trees and plum trees were blown down as an example to sinners, that they should serve God better. Beeches and oaks were blown to the earth, turning their roots upward, as a sign of dread that deadly sin shall consume us all at Doomsday.][60]

In *Piers Plowman* there is absolutely no question that God caused "this wind," nor is there any question that mankind deserved it. Nature serves at the pleasure of God; if we misbehave, it becomes his punisher, but also the teacher of his intractable people. Nature's punishment is meant not merely to be cruel, but to set an "ensaumple" (example) that people should serve God better. Indeed, for Langland the logic seems to be that people must look carefully into the lessons of current natural calamity in order to protect themselves better against the infinitely more horrible events that will come at Doomsday. Pay attention to the weather *now*, Langland suggests, so that you can avoid eternal damnation later.

But Langland's proleptic worrying isn't only about Judgment Day: he's also quite worried about the intervening time, when the earth becomes increasingly uninhabitable, increasingly inhospitable, increasingly wasted. At the end of a later passage of his poem he says,

I warne yow werkmen—wynneth while ye mowe
For Hungir hiderward hastith hym faste!
He shal awake thorough water, wastours to chaste,
Or fyue yer ben fulfild such famyn shal arise:
Thorough flood and thorough foule wederis fruytes shuln faille

[I warn you workmen—earn while you may:
For Hunger hastens this way fast!
He will awake through water, to chasten wasters,

Before five years have passed such famine shall arise:
Through flood and through foul weather fruits shall fail.][61]

As in the biblical tradition of the Noah story, here Langland imagines a situation where God is so irate with the behavior of his people (here called "the wasters," about which more in chapter 5) that he punishes them with bad weather. Langland's poem imagines an England where the weather is so bad that crops die, there is famine, and agricultural work is scarce everywhere: so "work while you may." He imagines this weather—only five years away—will produce floods, drowning crops. This is catastrophic, but entirely in keeping with the punishments in the Bible.

Langland made his poem in three versions—the so-called A-text, B-text, and C-text. Each differs markedly from the other two, but this particular passage remains almost untouched across the three versions. This consistency matters because it is somewhat unusual: when Langland revised his poem, he revised it intensively, changing countless passages between each version. So this consistency means that, however many elements of Langland's social philosophy and poetic agenda evolved between the composition of his first text in 1360s and of his last in the 1390s, his sense that the weather would come as a scourge to punish the wicked remained unchanged. Langland's apocalyptic scenario is at least in part a meteorological one. This is no surprise given the amount of cold, wet weather he would have seen in his lifetime.

Despite, or indeed perhaps because of, its apocalypticism, *Piers Plowman* inspired a tradition of imitations. One poem, "Piers the Plowman's Crede," imagines a man wandering in search of someone who can teach him the Apostles' Creed. He finds no adequate teacher in any of the monks or friars he approaches, but then he encounters Piers the Plowman, who does ultimately teach him the Creed. More noteworthy for our purposes is the way the poem depicts Piers. At first he is so emaciated that "men myghte reken ich a ryb, so reufull they weren" (men could count every rib, they were so pitiful).[62] His wife is with him, and she wraps herself in extra clothes to protect herself "fro weders" (from weather).[63] They have an infant as well as two-year-old twins who are singing a sad song, crying in one voice, "that sorwe was to heren" (that was a sorrow to hear).[64] This anonymous imitator of Langland reimagines the title character of the poem that inspired him— Piers the Plowman—as a starving man, ill-dressed for the weather, out in the cold with his family. This imitator then goes one step further than Langland had in depicting the weather as a scourge: for this poet the weather is not a threat to everyone equally, nor is it something primarily in the future; the threat is somehow more acute for families, with their young and conspicuously vulnerable children. And the threat is already in full force. Moreover, whereas Langland had depicted hard agricultural labor—to be supervised by Piers the Plowman—as the way out of ecosystemic peril, his imitator imagines even Piers's own family succumbing to climate crisis. In the generation after Langland, things are getting worse, not better, in the imaginations of medieval people.

Another reader of Langland's poem, the anonymous author of *Richard the Redeles* (Richard the uncounseled), likewise registers the danger of the weather, though subtly. *Richard the Redeles* was ostensibly written as an advice poem urging Richard II to find better advisers and supporters and to reject corruption. But the real audience of the poem was transparently the brand-new king, Henry IV, who is depicted only in the most laudatory terms throughout the poem.[65] In its critical advice to "Richard," the poem devises a sprawling system of metaphors portraying Richard as a hunter, while his advisers and the less powerful people of his realm are described as deer.[66] The poet laments that Richard did nothing to help his deer, though they were starving, and that he turned on them, injuring them with "droppis of anger" (drops of anger), harrying them with "stormes that stynted nevere" (storms that never stopped), and plucking the hair from their skins until "the fresinge frost freted to here hertis" (the freezing frost fed on them down to their hearts).[67] Because Richard took insufficient care of his good deer, the young ones failed to thrive and grow strong, so that the "wyntris wedir hem wessh with the snowis" (winter's weather washes them with the snow).[68] This meteorological conceit concludes with the poem's saying, "For well mowe ye wyttyn and so mowe we all, / That harde is the somer ther sonne schyneth nevere" (For you must know well, and so must we all / that hard is the summer where the sun never shines).[69] This is a densely metaphorical passage, but the message is clear. The deer are Richard's subjects, whom he has cared for poorly. The weather is his emotional conduct toward them: the rain is his anger, which comes in unremitting storms. The freezing frost and the winter snows are his indifference and carelessness. The summer where the sun never shines describes life in a country where the monarch is selfish, thoughtless, and uncounseled. Metaphors.

But not *only* metaphors. As any clinical psychologist will attest, people use metaphors to talk about and process trauma. This poet's primary figure for the threat Richard poses to his people is meteorological in a specific way. It is focused on winter: cold, rain, and lack of sun. The imagination that produced this metaphor was born and lived during the Little Ice Age, when cold, wet weather and dark, cold summers were the norm, but no less traumatic for being normal. *Richard* is a poem not just about political catastrophe, but about ecosystemic catastrophe, in which climate disaster heightens the concern and urgency about political misconduct and the threat of a sunless sky would send real and posttraumatic shivers down any reader's back.

Even the most famous eighteen lines of medieval English poetry, the opening lines of Chaucer's *Canterbury Tales*, register the bad weather, though in classic Chaucerian form, they do so with a smile.

Whan that aprill with his shoures soote
The droghte of march hath perced to the roote
And bathed every veyne in swich licour
Of which vertu engendred is the flour
Whan zephirus eek with his sweete breeth
Inspired hath in every hold and heeth
Tendre croppes, and the Yonge sonne
Hath in the ram his halve cours yronne,
And smale foweles maken melodye,
That slepen al the nyght with open ye
(so priketh hem nature in hir corages);
Thanne longen folk to goon on pilgrimages,
And palmeres for to seken straunge strondes,
To ferne halwes, kowthe in sondry londes;
And specially from every shires ende

Of engelonde to caunterbury they wende,
The hooly blissful martir for to seke,
That hem hath holpen, what that they were seke.

[When in that April, with its sweet showers
The drought of March has pierced to the root,
And bathed every vein in such liqueur
Of which virtue engendered is the flower,
Whan Zephir also, with his sweet breath
Has inspired in every wood and heath
The tender crops, and when the young sun
Has run half its course in the Ram
And small fowls make melody,
That sleep all night with open eye
(So Nature pricks them in their hearts),
Then folks long to go on pilgrimages,
And palmers to seek strange places,
To distant saints, known in many lands,
And especially, from every shire's end
Of England, to Canterbury they went,
The holy blissful martyr to seek,
That has helped them, when they were sick.][70]

Chaucer here imagines not just any April, but some enchanted April. An April that chases away the winter and ushers in the sweet winds of the west, bringing lust and pleasure to the hearts of animals and spiritual awakening (and some lust and pleasure) to the minds of men. The sheer quantity of positively connoted words in the opening of this passage is striking: soft, bathed, virtue, tender, young, sweet. There is not a single unpleasant thing about this April. This is not an April racked and ruined by climate change. Not a freezing, soggy April but a gentle, damp, fecund one. The rain is "sweet," not incessant and destructive. This is the perfect April. So why do I claim that Chaucer's writing in any way reflects the pressures of cold, long, wet, miserable winters that we see so clearly depicted in *Piers Plowman* and its heirs? There are three reasons. First, the passage is so relentlessly positive that it seems to conjure storm clouds precisely in seeking to dispel them: the poet doth protest too much about the beauty of the spring. Second, these first eighteen lines make up only one sentence—a rather tortuous and syntactically difficult one—as though the poet is trying to get out a whole vision of gentle nature before someone might interrupt to contradict. Third, the final couplet of this passage contains a perfect full rhyme in Middle English: "seke" (seek) rhymes with "seke" (sick). Chaucer only rarely makes a full rhyme in a couplet; when he does, the effect is to call a great deal of attention to the rhyming words—the full rhyme acts as an emphasis. What's emphasized here is that people go *seeking* saints on pilgrimage because they have been *sick*. There is suffering and trauma in the recent past of these lines. Chaucer's enchanted April is a cover-up for long, brutal, sickening winters. And also, inevitably, for the years of plague that rolled through England during Chaucer's lifetime.

CONTAGION

Probably the most significant ecosystemic trauma of the European Middle Ages, in terms of loss of human life, was the Black Death, which hit England first in 1348, then again in 1360–61, 1369, and 1374.[71] The plague was brutally even-handed: city dwellers died, but so did those in rural areas, albeit at lower rates. Older people died in great numbers, as did the very young, but able-bodied men and women of prime working age died too.[72] Wealthy people died as well as the poor. Priests and clerics died at rates roughly equal to the general population (in some areas slightly higher, presumably because of administering last rites to dying and highly infectious people). The chronicle of Meaux Abbey notes that in the plague the abbot himself died, along with thirty-two monks and lay brothers, and that the abbey was in terrible disarray because of the lack of management.[73] No category of person was spared. By 1374 the main waves of plague had claimed the lives of at least a third of the total population of England.[74] Again, this is worth pausing over: one out of every three people, dead. Some densely populated areas fared even worse: as much as two-thirds of the population of London died within a single year.[75] Two out of every three. The population of Norwich in 1347 was about 20,000; by 1377 it was less than 6,000.[76] Population levels from 1300 were not reached again until the middle of the sixteenth century.[77] The Black Death was an ecosystemic cataclysm the likes of which the world had never seen before and has never seen since. The fatality rate among infected people was somewhere around 80 percent.[78] By comparison, early variants of COVID-19 had a fatality rate somewhere between 1 percent and 3 percent.

Did medieval people understand the plague as a microorganism-borne pestilence? No, of course not. But as an ecosystemic event? Yes. Microbiology and germ theory were nowhere on the horizon; instead, many medieval people, including William Langland, considered the Black Plague (much like the weather) to be the result of God's displeasure with sinful mankind.[79] As historian Rosemary Horrox puts it, "All contemporary commentators were agreed that the plague was an act of God, sent to punish mankind for his its sinfulness and to frighten it into repentance and future good behavior."[80] This sounds like naïve medieval people ascribing reasons for phenomena they did not properly understand. But let's slow down and check our presentist and scientific biases at the door.

Medieval people definitely *did* have an understanding—albeit not a microbiological one—about contagion and infection. People knew, for instance, that proximity to people with plague increased your own chances of getting sick; this is why Boccaccio's *Decameron* tells how a group of young Florentines decamped from pestilential Florence to the countryside. Medieval people understood that diseases were communicable between people; they understood that you actually *could* run away from the disease. They understood that contagion was worse in more populous areas. They understood that one person could bring about the sickness and perhaps death of thousands. Moreover, they understood that animals played a role in spreading the disease. As Boccaccio puts it at the beginning of the *Decameron*:

> Of such efficience was the nature of the pestilence in question in communicating itself from one to another, that, not only did it pass from man to man, but this, which is much more, it many times visibly did; —to wit, a thing which had pertained to a man sick or dead of the aforesaid

sickness, being touched by an animal foreign to the human species, not only infected this latter with the plague, but in a very brief space of time killed it. Of this mine own eyes (as hath a little before been said) had one day, among others, experience on this wise; to wit, that the rags of a poor man, who had died of the plague, being cast out into the public way, two hogs came up to them and having first, after their wont, rooted amain among them with their snouts, took them in their mouths and tossed them about their jaws; then, in a little while, after turning round and round, they both, as if they had taken poison, fell down dead upon the rags with which they had in an ill hour intermeddled.[81]

People caught plague from people. Inanimate parts of the urban environment (like clothes) that touched a dead person could spread plague. And plague could spread between people and animals. Not all that far from the average twenty-first-century person's functional understanding of germs and the spread of disease. Medieval people were, in fact, so painfully aware of the ready transmissibility of the plague that, as Boccaccio tells us, husbands and wives refused to care for each other if one were sick, and mothers at times refused to tend their sick babies.[82] This last was perhaps not as coldhearted as it may sound to modern ears; a mother in the Middle Ages might have had five or ten other children to worry about, so if she died taking care of the baby, who would take care of the others?[83] This was a culture that lacked microbiology but not basic observational skills: the plague was an ecosystemic menace because it was a social menace. Anyone who lived in the same ecosystem—be it a neighborhood, street, household, bedroom, or town—as a sick person was at risk. And the closer you got to a sick person, the greater your risk.

In addition to being social, the plague's ecosystemic embeddedness was in part economic: medieval people understood that the plague had to do with the early and emergent global economic marketplace. Although they did not have that language, they understood that trade routes were the primary path of the disease. The plague came to Italy through merchants from the Near East,[84] a fact Boccaccio registers in the beginning of his *Decameron*, noting that the death-dealing pestilence of Florence had killed countless people in the East in the years before.[85] The Eastern origin of the plague is also noted in Robert of Avesbury's chronicle, which notes that the pestilence first started in the Near East, as well as in a chronicle from Rochester Priory, which notes that "a great mortality" began in India, traveled through Syria and Egypt, and thence was carried to Greece, Italy, France, and England.[86] And indeed, in 1348, when it did spread to England, through the town of Melcombe (now Weymouth) on a ship returning from France, the arrival of the plague was recognized and noted by the *Chronicles of the Grey Friars of Lynn*, which says that sailors coming from Gascony were infected with a pestilence, and that therefore the inhabitants of Melcombe were the first in England to get sick.[87] Indeed, city records from late medieval England show a significant amount of legislation geared to prevent possibly infected foreigners from entering English cities and to regulate those foreigners' behaviors strictly once they were there.[88] So, if you construe the world of trade as part of a human ecosystem, if you construe traders and consumers as part of the environment, medieval people understood the plague in manifestly ecosystemic terms.

Surprisingly little English literary writing directly addresses the cataclysmic population die-off in the wake of the plague—far less than we find on the Continent, particularly in France and Italy. But what there is is powerful. A recent book by David Coley on the four poems of the English *Pearl*-manuscript makes a compelling argument that those four poems (*Pearl, Cleanness, Patience,* and most famously *Sir Gawain and the Green Knight*) meticulously trace out a haunting presence of the plague in late fourteenth-century English culture. Coley finds that *Cleanness* is loaded with plague vocabulary—slightly unusual word choices that resonate strongly with late medieval descriptions of plague and plague symptoms.[89] To me, though, the most compelling and most moving instance of this manuscript's working through of plague trauma comes in the poem *Pearl* itself, which narrates a grief-stricken jeweler's quest to find a "pearl" that has been lost in a garden. Once the jeweler falls into a dream, that lost pearl is found and turns out to be his dead two-year-old daughter. Given that the manuscript containing this poem probably dates to around 1390 and that the years from 1348 to 1390 saw multiple waves of plague, it is plausible—though not certain—that the grief in this poem begins with plague. Like Coley, I read *Pearl* as a poignant and understated meditation on plague trauma.[90]

Tackling plague more directly, *Piers Plowman*, in its apocalyptic ending, describes how "Kynde" scourges a sinful mankind with "sharp sores / like pox, and pestilences," and tells how many people "swooned and perished from suffering death's dints."[91] "Kynde" is usually translated as nature in modern editions and translations, and that translation is fine, but it does sacrifice the important secondary meaning the poem leverages here. Semantically, "kynde" also means "mankind," or "kindred"; in the context of the larger poem, "Kynde" usually denotes God. So the idea that "Kynde" is scourging mankind at once points to nature, to an angry God, *and* to a diseased population of humanity, sickening and scourging each other. Plus, as the word "kind" does now, it carried a sense of gentleness and care. The question the poem works through, then, is how it is possible that a kind, loving, caretaking God could possibly scourge mankind so savagely and sorely, through his fellow man, his kindred. How can we understand mankind to be kind to itself and its fellows when it sickens and destroys its friends and neighbors? There is something deeply and desperately wrong with a poetic world in which Kynde is the point of origin for plague. Or maybe just something deeply and desperately traumatized in the real world in which the poem is written.

Likewise indicating a profound sense of cultural trauma in the aftermath of the plague, Chaucer's Pardoner in the *Canterbury Tales* describes a figure—"a sly thief"—called not Plague or Pestilence, but simply Death, who slaughters people while they are sitting upright, who slays, in fact, "all the people" of the country.[92] Associating this Death more closely with the plague, the tale goes on to say that "he hath a thousand slain, this pestilence," and that the killing is indiscriminate, taking "both man and woman, child, and servant, and page."[93] So in essence this tale personifies the Black Death as simply Death. The three main human characters in the tale set out to slay this pestilential Death, failing to understand, of course, that Death can't die. Instead, the main characters themselves die—though, fascinatingly, not directly from plague, but from scheming against each other, as though Chaucer couldn't quite bear actually to recount a pestilential death. Chaucer's

32 : CHAPTER ONE

mirthful *Tales* bear the signs of pestilential trauma, including a profound aversion to speaking about the plague directly. There is another place in the *Canterbury Tales* where Chaucer carefully reflects on the sociocultural impact of the plague and stages that impact as an ecosystemic one. But we'll save that for chapter 6.

CONTAMINATION AND POLLUTION

In addition to plague, this period saw a significant rise in pollution. As I said before, in the Middle Ages your child probably wouldn't get heavy metal poisoning from environmental exposure, and you wouldn't pass floating umbrellas and toothbrushes as you crossed the North Sea. But just before the fourteenth century, complaints about pollution—particularly in cities—became acute. More and more Londoners began complaining about the foul smell from burning sea coal—a soft coal that produces a great deal of smoke. In 1285 a commission was established to look into the use of sea coal in lime kilns. The commission found that burning sea coal was so noxious as to annoy and even endanger the people living near kilns and smithies.[94] These complaints led in 1307 to a royal prohibition against burning sea coal in kilns; the proclamation noted that people found the sea coal's smoke both annoying and unhealthy, and that the air was "infected" by it.[95] This proclamation evidently didn't work, and another prohibition was issued in 1315. This prohibition seems also to have been largely ineffective, so the burning of sea coal continued apace until after the Black Death decreased population pressure on energy and fuel resources so that people needed less coal.[96] Recent bioarchaeological work suggests that medieval people's health suffered greatly from the exposure to urban toxins and pollutants: medieval skeletons exhibit bone pitting along the sinuses, indicating recurrent respiratory infections; skeletons also show patterns of damage to leg bones that suggest the chronic exposure to pathogens and toxins in the urban environment took its toll by causing periostitis, a condition that would have been painful and obvious to people who had it.[97] City air was dirty in the fourteenth century.

Also very dirty were the streets. Examining borough records from three major medieval English cities—London, Norwich, and

THE FIVE DISASTERS FACING MEDIEVAL ECOSYSTEMS : 33

Liverpool—Lynn Perrigo has shown that streets and walkways were so polluted with household garbage, human excrement, animal offal, and fallen timber that multiple orders and ordinances had to be issued from the thirteenth century well into the fifteenth to try to curb dumping.[98] The recurrent issuing of such orders shows that they failed, so these three cities were left to take more extreme measures, such as appointing "rakers" and surveyors to walk the city, enforcing these codes, removing the bodies of animals, and generally trying to keep the streets somewhat passable. Throughout the fourteenth century city dwellers continued dumping animal remains and even slaughtering animals in the streets and leaving their rotting entrails there. They also often let their pigs roam the streets, though this practice was restricted by municipal ordinances. But even with those ordinances in place—some of which allowed pigs to be taken from stalls and walked into the streets only on one day a week—there was still an enormous volume of pig manure in the streets of urban medieval England. Historian Dolly Jørgenson estimates that in medieval York, in an area of about one thousand households, you could expect to walk through almost two thousand liters of pig manure each week.[99] Walking in a city was *much* less sanitary than it would be today—and medieval people found it so upsetting that numerous accounts talk at length about the terrible smell.

Rivers were also frequently polluted, particularly in larger cities. Like streets, rivers got so bad that ordinances and rules were enacted to prevent blocking rivers with garbage, but to little avail.[100] In a moving if oblique literary testimony to the condition of London's waterways, John Lydgate's *Troy Book* talks about the structure, layout, and efficiency of the ancient (and famously destroyed) city of Troy, linking these elements closely with the presence of the river Xanthus flowing through it:

> And thorugh this toun, so riche and excellent,
> In the myddes a large river went,
> Causyng to hem ful gret commodité;
> The whiche on tweyne hath partid the cite,
> Of cours ful swyft, with fresche stremys clere,
> And highte Xanctus, as Guydo doth us lere.

[And through this town, so rich and excellent,
In the middle went a large river,
Causing great convenience for the people;
The river divided the city in half,
With swift flow and fresh, clear streams
It was called Xanthus, as Guido (Lydgate's source) tells us.][101]

Why does Lydgate fairly drool with admiration of Troy and its river? Troy was the literary-historical progenitor of the British people via a supposed escapee from Troy named Brutus. London, in literary works, was often referred to as Troia Nova, Troinovant, or simply New Troy. With this in mind, Lydgate's seeming obsession with how clean and regulated Troy and its river were seems a plangent musing on why Troy's municipal great-grandchild, London, couldn't get its act together to keep its own bifurcating river—the Thames—clear, fresh, quick-flowing, and useful. Lydgate fetishizes the Xanthus as a pure and noble ancestor for the corrupt and debased reality of the Thames. He uses the glorious Xanthus to highlight his own broken urban ecosystem.

Lydgate goes on to heap praise on the Xanthus, saying it was full of fish, cleverly divided up by workmen so that its entire flow could be directed through "condut pipes," which were designed to fully purge "al ordure and fylthes in the toun, / waschyng the stretys as thei stode a rowe" (all ordure and filth in the town, washing the streets as they stood in a row). Indeed, because of this shunting of fresh, clean river water throughout the city, "in the cite was no filthe sene" (in the city there was no visible filth); and it was all done so ingeniously that no one could ever even see "by what engin" (by what engine/trick/device) the filth was swept away, "so covertly everything was cured" (TB, 2, 741–59). Lydgate's Troy is the fantasy prehistory of the reeking, shitty, garbage-strewn city of London. But it seems a far cry from where Lydgate's London is; before his aria on the wonderful Xanthus and how it keeps Troy clean, Lydgate feels compelled to say not only "as Guido doth us lere" (as Guido teaches us) but also, in the very next line, "as I rede" (as I read). Lydgate registers how far-fetched and impossible this clean, well-watered city seems, and he feels the need to cite his source twice in a row during his explanation. Londoners, he seems to recognize, will have a hard time swallowing this description, given the state of their own river; better trick it out with authoritative backing and note that this is coming not from Lydgate's own imagination, but rather from his reading about the past.

But the pollution that people found detestable in medieval cities was not limited to particulate pollution in the air or garbage in the streets and rivers. A short anonymous fifteenth-century poem called "The Blacksmiths" attests to disquiet about noise pollution in cities. According to this poem, blacksmiths labor at their forges, all covered in smoke and soot, driving people in the neighborhood "to deth wyth den of here dyntes. Swech noys on nyghtes ne herd men neuer" (to death with the din of their dints. Such noise in the nighttime men never heard before). The poem goes on to lament how blacksmiths shout out "Col! Col!" (Coal! Coal!) and blow loudly into their bellows all day and night, "Huf, puf!" and "Haf, paf!" with their hammers clanging down, "Tik, tak! hic, hac! tiket, taket! tik, tak!" All this noise creates a situation in which "no man for brenwaterys on nyght han hys rest!" (no man can rest at night for the boiling waters).[102] Clouded with smoke and steam, shot through with blood, shit, and animal carcasses, but also riven with racket, the medieval English urban landscape was indeed a highly polluted one.

The fourteenth century saw soil depletion, the reduction of available arable land, famines, catastrophic disease, significant pollution, and climate change. Alone, any of these ecosystemic changes could have damaged the livability of the ecosystem—would have disrupted the organization of the household everyone lived in. But these ecosystemic patterns compounded each other, causing steep declines in population and creating eerie ghost towns. Medieval people knew this was happening. They saw it with their own eyes or heard about it from their parents and grandparents or from neighbors. They saw it affect their children. They had no meteorology. They had no climate science. The twenty-first-century need for more and more compelling scientific proof of what we all can feel in the massive weather systems that crawl across the land each year and leave torrential deluge in their wakes was not in play in the Middle Ages. People saw plague, they saw soil loss and pollution, they saw climate change and famine, and they simply assumed it was in some way their own fault, their own doing, their own responsibility. There was no need for scientific proof; observation and faith were enough to believe in anthropogenic climate change. How to combat or prevent or at least slow the decay of their ecosystem, that was the interesting question. In England the earliest answers have to do with the elastic and ever-evolving idea of "waste." And those answers arise in the poems I will study in this book, and in how those poems leverage and combine the nonpoetic discourses they draw from.

Those discourses are primarily biblical, legal, sermonic, and penitential. The poems are *Winner and Waster*, which centrally meditates on the problem of land shortage; *Piers Plowman*, which picks up where *Winner and Waster* left off but moves on to focus on food insecurity and famine; Chaucer's *Yeoman's Tale*, which tackles plague and pollution; *Sir Gawain and the Green Knight*, which meditates on climate change, climate revenge, and our susceptibility to a vast and ineluctable natural world that we can never possibly hope to control; and finally *Mum and the Sothsegger*, which experiments with a fantasy of a sustainable and just world, safe in its ecosystemic functionality.

CHAPTER TWO

THE LAWS OF WASTE

The Bible and the Common Law

ORIGINAL WASTE, OR DIVINE COLONIALISM

Medieval ideas about waste originate primarily in the Bible.[1] "Waste" (in Latin, *vast-*) arises in the Latin translation of the Hebrew Bible in specific contexts, not many of which resonate immediately with ideas of waste that are most readily available now. Part of the reason lies in the Latin etymology of "waste." In Latin, *vast-* denotes an emptying out, an evacuating that comes from taking away all the goods or resources of an area. When we in the twenty-first century say we "wasted" something, we do not generally mean we took away all the goods, emptying an area. We usually mean we "wasted" something in the passive sense of letting something go to waste, squandering something, frittering something away. We say, "I wasted my time," "I wasted my energy," and "I wasted my money." In fact, that Latinate sense of *vast-* as emptying out an area feels so archaic that we must resort to the verb phrase, "laid waste" to get across the Latin sense. But in the English early Middle Ages the most common use of "waste" as a verb was to mean laying waste, destroying, removing all value from lands and taking it for oneself.

When "waste" is used as a noun in the Bible, it describes a particular kind of place or landscape—a *vastitas*, or wasteland. In the Bible, *vastitas* means an empty place. But *vastitas* is distinct from other words used to describe empty places. Deserts are called *solitudines* or *deserta*; these two words denote places that are naturally empty, that had never been inhabited. Wastelands—*vastitates*—by contrast, denote places that have been emptied out by aggressors—usually the armies of God. Deserts, that is, are natural; wastelands are made.[2] A *vastitas* implies a history of violence, of military conflict, and of punishment.

Relatedly, when "waste" shows up as a verb in the Bible, as *vastare*, it denotes the emptying out of a settled, habitable place—a "laying waste." Revealing instances of this come in Ezekiel 33:21, "the city is wasted," in Jeremiah 4:20, "my tabernacles are wasted," and in Jeremiah 48, where Moab, Nabo, and Oronaim are all wasted.[3] Cities, buildings, tabernacles, and settlements can be wasted; they can be emptied. You never lay waste to a desert or an empty place, obviously, because there is nothing there to empty out. Waste converts a *place* into a *space*. It is how you make a wasteland from a city. But why would anyone want to do that? Why does waste come up so often in the Bible? The answer has to do with God's ecosystemic power and his agenda for his people.

In the tenth book of Exodus, God inflicts a plague of locusts upon the Egyptians. Describing the locusts, the Vulgate tells us they ranged over the whole surface of the earth, "wasting everything" so that the world's plants were "devoured" with nothing remaining (Exod. 10:15). Here "wasting" is a bestial act, a destruction by consumption, an emptying by eating. Wasting is a moment of crippling ecosystemic crisis for the people trying to inhabit the area. That the locusts waste *everything* emphasizes the totality of their destruction, so that they are said to eat the plants of the earth, the fruits that the Egyptians had cultivated, so that *nothing was left* of Egyptian agriculture. It is a scourge, and it is meant to be terrifying to readers, as it is to the Egyptians upon whom the locust plague falls. After all, *God* sends the locusts. And the idea that God throttles people by turning nature against them is horrifying.

Pressing on that idea, that God sent the locusts as his agents of punishment, and that he is therefore the real waster, has strange moral consequences. Since God is the ultimate waster—the waster who makes the locusts' wings flap and their jaws consume everything in sight—the wasting the locusts do on his behalf is just and fair, representing as it does his direct will. Though terrifying, and definitely not something you'd wish for your crops, wasting itself is not coded as a morally "bad" thing in the Bible. Quite the contrary, this wasting action of the insects is righteous by definition, because it is brought about by God's will. However frightening, this divinely willed waste is both purgative and punitive, designed to chasten the Egyptians. Wasting is a tactic God uses to place severe ecosystemic and therefore economic strain on an opponent.

The locusts' divinely willed wasting against the Egyptians points toward the more frequent type of wasting that arises in the Bible, when a human military force attacks enemies, "wasting" or emptying out their lands, houses, and people. Generally the wasting army is punishing someone for breaking God's laws or for being aggressive toward God's people. In the Bible this type of waste is also divinely sanctioned and, indeed, brought about by divine will. As Joshua explains to his army on the eve of their assault on the city of Ai, they will waste the city because God will deliver it into their hands (Josh. 8:7). Waste, again, is the divinely authorized, punitive purgation of a sinful people. It may not seem as overtly ecosystemic as wasting by locusts, but in fact it is: people, from God's vantage point, are part of the natural world that he created, and they are executing his divine will by emptying out an unhealthy settled ecosystem.

These ecosystemic acts of waste serve a political function: the wasting of the enemies of God's people by insects and armies purges the lands and empties them out so the chosen people can recolonize them. Wasting of the oppressors becomes the precondition for conquest by the chosen people—for land acquisition and for settlement itself. It is through waste that God's landless people become God's settled people. So, in biblical discourse *vastare* signals a destructive emptying of real property of all its value not simply as an end unto itself, but to make possible a resettlement of the lands.[4] It is only after the sequential wastings in the early books of the Old Testament that God's chosen people acquire and settle the Promised Land. In fact, biblically speaking, wasting is a precondition for colonization, for landedness, for securing property. Wasting is not just a punitive tactic of ecowarfare but an act of colonization.[5]

This may be a surprising claim, but it is important to remember that the Old Testament is in part a military and colonial narrative—it deals with the establishment and military challenges of the people of Israel as they come into possession of their land. And it is through a systematic and pervasive program of wasting that God assures his people that they will be dominant, that they will control resources and lands, and that there will be no one to contest their power. The formerly landless Israelites have waged military campaign upon military campaign, eventually to become the landed conquerors. This is the power of waste: to convert settled places into empty spaces, often precisely so that they can be converted back into settled places—although by new colonists. He against whom God wastes is cursed; he *for* whom God wastes is blessed, and the form of his blessing is property inheritance. Biblical wasting is about nation-building. In the first books of the Old Testament this is what wasting is, and it tends to work out well for the Israelites. But nothing good lasts forever.

In the prophetic books of the Bible, God's chosen people have become sinful; they have failed to adhere to God's law. This disobedience has prompted God to give prophetic powers to Isaiah, Jeremiah, Ezekiel, Daniel, and other "minor" prophets. With these powers, each of the prophets attempts to castigate the fallen people of God for their misdeeds and to warn them of their coming punishment. This punishment, the prophets warn, will come in the form of an army that will descend from the north and will devastate the settled people, purging them from their hard-won lands. So again biblical narration is, functionally, military and colonial narration.

Very early on in his prophecy, Isaiah tells of wasted cities and vineyards (Isa. 1:7–8), and he goes on to describe wasted homes (Isa. 23:1), wasted people and nations (Isa. 42:22–24), and wasted streets and destinations (Isa. 59:7, 60:18). All of these are physically wasted at the hands of enemy armies but, like all the other acts of wasting we have encountered so far in the Bible, they are willed and permitted by a wrathful God: as Isaiah emphasizes, "Lament, for the day of the Lord's wasting is coming" (Isa. 13:6). It is the *Lord*'s wasting—Isaiah is clear that God is the true waster here; the armies of man are merely his instruments. Isaiah understands and represents waste as an emptying, a destruction, a slaughter, and, perhaps most significantly, as a dispossession. As it has always been, the motivating force behind wasting is God's will to punish and purge bad people from his lands. The effect of all the violence that God will allow the northern armies to visit on his people is that the Israelites will again become a landless people. Here, too, wasting has to do with turning inhabited places—spaces where people live and work and have civilization—into *waste*lands, empty places, and forcing the inhabitants whose lands have been wasted to find a new place to dwell, a new ecosystem.

But the goal of wasting is not exclusively physical. The words associated with the wasting of cities point toward an affective goal of wasting as well. The forty-eighth chapter of Jeremiah makes that emotional goal quite plain, associating this wasting with "confusion," "fear," "clamoring," and, crucially, "contrition" (Jer. 48:1, 3). Wasting of this kind is supposed to inspire fear and confusion, and thereby to cause contrition. Fear triggers remorse. The affective terms associated with the wasting of cities remind us that, in the Bible, waste is meant not only as a demonstration of the power of God and a disinheriting of the wicked, but also as an invitation to being purged and made contrite, an invitation, implicitly, to ethical improvement.

This notion underpins perhaps the single most important medieval English context for "wasting" as a keyword of ecosystemic thought: the Common Law.[6] There, "to waste" will initially signal a punitive and purgative despoliation of lands, with the intention of eventually reincorporating the family of an offender into the community of law abiders. But from that initial meaning, legal "waste" will evolve in ways hugely consequential for medieval English ecosystemic thought.

THE COMMON LAW OF WASTE

From 1215 to 1400, "waste" (usually as the Latin *vast-* and sometimes as the French *wast-*) appears in the *Statutes of the Realm of England* more than a dozen times, sometimes more than once in a single statute, but almost never as the focal point. Responding to the recurrent attention to waste in the statutes, coupled with the scattershot brevity with which the subject is treated, legal historians have characterized the medieval law of waste as having developed "piecemeal, mainly on the basis of prohibitions, with unsystematic legislative assistance."[7] These legal historians are right, but, although the statutes never give an overview of the nature of waste or trace out the reasons for the prohibitions that arise over time, it is possible to retrieve the history of common law waste and to uncover why statutes sought to regulate it time and again.

The law's emphasis on waste connects with larger shifts taking place in fourteenth-century ecosystemic and economic thought, and in the way relationships among different social agents could be understood in terms of resource allocation, use, abuse, and squandering. The law of waste is where we see English lawmen try to map out a constellation of concepts about ownership, rights to use, rights to profit, and intersubjective legal obligations that play out in local ecosystems. As it seeks to coordinate these interrelated concepts, the law of waste articulates an idea of ecological accountability in which holders, owners, and users of land are accountable not only for their own property, but for the property of their broader community, whether held in common or held by other individuals.

But just what was waste, in the eyes of the Common Law? According to Old English law, the king is legally entitled to "waste" the lands of convicted felons for a year and a day.[8] This "waste" means that the king could legally take all the profitable goods from the lands in question—trees, fish, animals, harvests, water—so that the felon would be punished by the diminution of his and his heirs' assets in real property. Waste, in this context, is not a crime, but a *punishment* for a crime. It is an act of justice and of rectification. Wasting in this very early English law is a punitive and purgative act, committed by a lord against an offending servant. As such the king's wasting of felons' lands serves the same purpose as God's wasting of disobedient peoples' lands in the Bible. On the other hand, the wasting of a felon's property—the emptying out of its valuable contents and resources—also constitutes a revenue stream for the Crown and signals the Crown's symbolic taking possession of the lands in question. In the Bible, wasting was a form of punitive purgation; in human law, waste is a form of punitive purgation and also a form of profit.

Although this type of "waste," in which a king punitively and profitably lays waste to the lands of a felon, continues to be legal throughout the later Middle Ages, the Common Law statutes of the thirteenth century gradually engineer a new definition of waste, making some types of "waste" criminal offenses. This redefinition of the wasting of property as a crime—rather than as a punitive response to crime—constitutes one of the Common Law's two most significant contributions to the ideology of waste. The redefinition of waste from punishment to crime happens very slowly, as we will see, but also decisively, so that between 1215 and the middle of the fourteenth century the verb "to waste" shifts from signaling the morally neutral or even positive act of retribution undertaken by a lord to signaling a predatory, morally negative action committed by any one party against the goods or fortune of another.

The process of defining waste as a crime begins with Magna Carta (1215), which specifies the contexts in which waste is illegal and also specifies what actions will constitute criminal waste in the eyes of the law: "The guardian of the land of an heir who is thus under age, shall take from the land of the heir nothing but reasonable produce, reasonable customs, and reasonable services, and that without destruction or waste of men or goods."[9] So, first, Magna Carta sees waste as a crime that pertains only to situations of guardianship, where a landholder dies and a guardian holds that dead landholder's real property on behalf of the heir during his legal minority. As the statute goes on, it specifies that only *royal* wards—that is, wards who are theoretically under the protection of the king, and whose lands are held in guardianship (often by a sheriff or other appointed steward)—will be protected by this law.[10] This means that only the highest-ranking people in England are protected against waste; only when committed against them does wasting constitute a criminal act. Second, in defining what actions constitute waste, the statute specifies that a guardian can legally take only what is "reasonable" ("reasonable produce, reasonable customs, and reasonable services") as profits from his guardianship, and it names any excessive taking of profits "waste."[11] This opposition of "reasonable profits" to "waste" suggests that criminal waste denotes an overindulgence in a legally recognized privilege—taking profits from lands one holds temporarily in guardianship for a minor heir. Waste is an abuse of a privilege, an abuse that consists of overuse—felling too many trees, overfishing ponds, tearing down buildings for lumber, or otherwise stripping the land of its inherent value—of privileges to which guardians did indeed have partial legal rights. Thus waste is a crime of degree, not of kind: it is an overexercise of a legitimate right.

After having established the kinds of legal relationships in which illegal waste can occur and specifying the nature of that waste as an overuse of resources, Magna Carta names the punishment for waste as forfeiture of lands—the guardian's loss of the wardship. This forfeiture punishment indicates that Magna Carta construes waste as a proprietary offense, to be settled by a revocation of the privileges attendant upon property holding, as opposed to a personal offense, which could be settled by monetary compensation. The forfeit punishment reveals that the fundamental offense in waste is against the relationship between guardian and ward, by which the guardian enjoys temporary rights in the land, to be maintained only if he upholds his implicit contract to keep his ward's property safe. Waste, according to Magna Carta, is a crime against a proprietor by a temporary possessor. Magna Carta indicates the law's will to protect the rights of the upper classes to inherit real property at full value. The earliest laws against waste have to do with protecting the real estate assets of the wealthiest and most powerful people in the land.

A half century after Magna Carta, the Statute of Marlborough (1267) broadens the legal definition of waste so that more people are included in the legal protections against it. Now underage heirs in socage tenure will be protected from waste committed by their guardians.[12] Socage tenure is a type of landholding in which the tenant must perform services of husbandry to his landlord, as opposed to military service or the other services associated with a royal wardship. In specifying that a minor heir in socage shall be legally protected against waste, the statute expands the law's protection against waste to people other than high-ranking royal wards, thus suggesting that heritable property rights are not the exclusive privilege of the aristocracy, but instead that intergenerational inheritance should be protected for all freeholders.[13] Thus the statute gestures toward a theory of property rights that is not based on class status. The notion of criminal waste, then, is coming to encompass any destructive overuse of land committed by a guardian against his ward.

There is a secondary consequence to this expansion of waste law to protect people in socage tenure. Socage is a relationship in which guardians must render accounts of their usage of the lands during the ward's minority. Because of this rule, in trials of waste, the accused waster now must give full accounting of his stewardship to the notional proprietor of the property. This mandatory rendering of accounts recognizes the fiduciary basis for the legal relationship, and by extension for the act of waste. With the passage of Marlborough, criminal waste has acquired specific significance as an act in property that has consequences in cash—consequences that can and must be measured in currency as part of the court's evidentiary procedures.[14] Indeed, the statute's most important modification to the English Common Law is to nominate damages—monetary outlay—as the penalty for waste by a farmer. When farmers make waste, "they shall yield full damages."[15] "Damages" indicate that waste is now seen explicitly as a crime against the financial value of the lands in question, a crime against the money the lands could yield. Waste of lands, that is, isn't just about the actual, physical *land* anymore. In the law, "waste" is now officially being abstracted into monetary terms.

In addition to monetizing waste, Marlborough expands the law's definition of who can be the victim of waste. Until now statutory prohibitions against waste had been designed to protect minor heirs from their guardians—designed, ultimately, to protect the little guys from the big guys. Now the law moves to protect landlords against waste that might be made by tenant farmers—protecting the big guys from the little guys.[16] Here Marlborough specifies that farmers must not make waste in the lands they possess through their lords. This clause conceives of waste not just as a problem of top-down abuse (as Magna Carta had done), but of bottom-up abuse: waste is now recognized as a crime a farmer (as legal possessor) commits against his landlord (as legal proprietor), not just as a crime a guardian commits against a minor heir.

The dual expansion and monetization of the law's attempts to regulate waste continue in the 1278 Statute of Gloucester.[17] Through this statute, a writ of waste becomes available not only in guardianship relationships, but also in relationships of dowry, tenancy at courtesy, and tenancy for terms of years.[18] This means that nearly every kind of land-based relationship between a temporary possessor and a rightful proprietor is protected against waste. Thus, by 1278 the law constructs waste as a *generalized proxy abuse of land*.

In addition to its broadening of the legal definition of waste, Gloucester cements the role of money in settling disputes. Although

Marlborough awarded damages to the lord in cases of waste by a farmer, Gloucester is the first statute to award direct fiscal damages to any aggrieved party.[19] This award signifies that waste—whether committed in the context of a guardianship or a tenancy—is now fully recognized as a monetary offense as well as an offense in real property. Land and the waste of land are thinkable not just in terms of soil, trees, water, and buildings, but in terms of their cash equivalents. Wasters can be any temporary holders of land who damage the interests of that land's actual owner.

Aside from these overt consequences of Gloucester, there is a crucial procedural shift that the statute introduces into the law of waste. By specifying damages as a punishment for waste, Gloucester construes the crime of waste as a trespass. Trespassory offenses—analogous to modern torts—are settled by financial outlay. The significance, both practical and ideological, of waste's classification as a trespass inheres in two key facts about trespass procedure. First, a valid trespass claim must be expressed as a violation *contra pacem regis* (against the king's peace) and *vi et armis* (by force and arms).[20] Thus, although materially performed between two parties, trespass is rhetorically framed in this statute as a violent crime committed against the realm, and thus differs from standard suits in real property. Second, trespass suits can be brought by any free Englishman, irrespective of his class or wealth. Thus, now that waste is construed by the law as a trespassory offense, any free person can bring a suit of waste against anyone else. By classifying waste as a trespassory offense, the law implicitly claims a broad-based accountability between holders and owners of real property, an accountability that, when breached, constitutes a violation of the peace of the realm. Waste is being classified, that is, as a broader problem—an ecosystemic problem—rather than simply a problem between two parties. It is not just about what I do to you, but about how my treatment of your land affects you *and the realm.*

The next step in the thirteenth-century evolution of the law of waste comes in the so-called Statute of Waste of 1292.[21] I say so-called because this statute is in actuality a detailed summary of a lawsuit, the outcome of which was felt to be sufficiently precedent-setting to qualify as new legislation. In this suit an underage royal ward named William Butler claims that Walter de Hapeton committed waste in the Butler's family lands during the lifetime of Gavin Butler, William's older brother and the person from whom William's inheritance has now come to him in his minority. Walter (the alleged waster) held Gavin's lands during his life, and Gavin sued Walter for waste during Walter's tenancy. Unfortunately for Gavin—and for young William—Gavin died before he had obtained a judgment against Walter. After Gavin's death, William (the present litigant) sues Walter for waste, but Walter responds that he should not have to answer to a charge of waste made by someone who was not technically the proprietor of the lands in question at the time the waste was committed. That is, Walter claims he is not accountable to William for waste he may have committed during Gavin's lifetime, since the inheritance had not gone to William by that time but had still belonged to Gavin. The adjudicators of this case seem to have had a rather difficult time discerning who was right—William or Walter. Ultimately the king's justices decide that William (and all future heirs in his position) will be granted a writ of waste, which will recover not only damages, but also the property in question.[22] The law has invented a commutative property of waste: the farmer-waste committed against Gavin transfers into guardian-waste against William. This law makes waste committed in the past actionable in the present. This expansion indicates the law's willingness to recognize ownership or right as originating not just in one's own tenure and possession, but in the possession of one's ancestor. The law shows itself now willing to understand the heir's future interest in the land of his father or elder brother to reside concretely enough in the lands, even before he himself takes possession of them, so that an act of waste committed during his elder's tenure would be, essentially, an act of waste against the heir presumptive.[23] Put bluntly, waste becomes thinkable as a crime against the future.

The final step in the evolution of waste law centers on a kind of waste suit that becomes common in the late fourteenth century. This kind of suit happens when royal escheats are mismanaged. An escheat is an interest in land that arises anytime the normal channels of primogeniture are interrupted, as when a landholder dies with no heir. In cases of royal escheat, the lines of descent are interrupted in such a way that the Crown stands to inherit some or all of the property in question.[24] But the property and its wealth must be managed by someone en route to the king's coffers. That is when the escheator steps in. An escheator is, like a bailiff, a representative of the king's financial interests—a steward or manager. The escheator would collect escheats for the king and then certify those escheats into the royal exchequer. As a conduit of property and a reporter of its value, the escheator epitomizes proxy responsibility for lands or goods belonging to another. His possession of the property in question is of the briefest and most strictly administrative nature and is in no way based on his own "right"; therefore, naturally, any profits he might take from this managerial tenure would be construed as wasteful, and any abuses he might commit, or extortions against the people who owed goods to the king, would reflect badly on the will of the king himself. This type of waste seems to have been construed not just as a crime, but also as an affront against the majesty of the king: indeed, it was classified as "lèse-majesté" (diminution of majesty) by the fourteenth-century author of *The Mirror of Justices*.[25] This text is not the most legally authoritative of sources; it is known for its gnarled working together of fictional and actual law. Precisely for that reason, however, it is a good gauge of popular attitudes toward various criminal practices and laws, because it tries to harmonize actual law with moral ideals and cultural norms. In effect, it is pop cultural law.

Despite the restrictions on escheators' behaviors, the proliferation of statutory laws of the fourteenth century identifies escheatorial waste as a grave and recurrent problem. In 1340 a statute explains that, whereas the king is entitled to hold guardianships-in-chief during the minority of the heir, no escheator during that period is allowed to commit waste in those lands. The statute establishes that, upon the death of a tenant-in-chief whose heir is underage, escheators shall come into possession on behalf of the king without doing waste ("sanz wast faire") in houses, woods, parks, ponds, and such, because such takings might damage the interest of the underage heir.[26] Implying the inefficacy of this statute at curbing what seems to have been a deeply entrenched criminal practice among escheators, several more statutes were promulgated in the next thirty years. One statute specifies that escheators cannot waste clerically held lands.[27] Another specifies exactly what will be considered waste by an escheator, and it also awards triple damages for escheatorial waste, recalling the terms of Gloucester.[28] The Capitula Escaetrie concerns itself exclusively with outlining and specifying the duties and offices for which an escheator would be held accountable. Although framed positively, as it were, as a list of the actions an escheator *could* undertake—this document reverse engineers the boundaries of an escheator's power, making it apparent that his powers do not extend to committing waste.[29] Judging by the number of regulations seeking to curb it, waste by escheators seems to have been one of the most common modes of waste brought to court in the late Middle Ages.

What does this all mean? Why do fourteenth-century statutes go to such lengths to curb escheatorial waste in particular? What it seems to mean is that there is an emerging awareness that bureaucrats and representatives—that is, subjects who have in fact zero legal claim on the lands and resources in question—are nevertheless capable of committing waste and should be punished for it. Going back to what I said at the beginning of this chapter—that waste was at first a crime commissible only between legal intimates, like a guardian and ward—it seems that by the fourteenth century waste is a far more diffuse crime, not based on any direct link between criminal and victim, but instead generalized to apply to all instance of proxy abuse of real estate. Thus the later escheatorial statutes suggest that the Common Law of waste has come to recognize a distributed accountability for the future profitability of property, distributed among any who might ever—however briefly or transactionally—come into possession of that property.

To sum up, the English Common Law puts pressure on the idea of waste in a number of interconnected ways. First, it makes waste criminal rather than a right or privilege to be exerted by God or by the king. Second, it redefines waste from being something committed only between a guardian and heir to being committed between any holder of land and its notional proprietor. It makes waste, that is, a crime commissible between any two parties with a shared interest in a given piece of property. Third, waste shifts from being a crime in land, thinkable only in terms of land, to being a crime in *value*, thinkable in terms of monetary compensation and damages. Fourth, in escheatorial waste, we see waste take on a far more diffuse, attenuated meaning wherein a middleman can commit waste between two parties; waste, that is, starts to be a management problem.

One element in the notion of waste has remained consistent in the Bible, in the earliest English legal practices, in early statutes, in case law, and in escheatorial regulations: when you commit waste, you commit waste in real material property against the interest of someone else. You waste the land, the houses, the trees, the ponds, the animals, the real estate value belonging to *another person*. Waste is not a crime you can commit against your *own* interest. That's how things stand in the law, the realm of land, money, and interpersonal conflict.

But that's not how things stand in the realm of the spirit. In fact, if we then turn to devotional writings of the Middle Ages, "waste" is not so much a problem of material resources as a problem of how the energies of the soul are spent and whether that spending leads to the salvation or damnation of the individual soul. As we will see, there is an interplay between the legally derived meanings of waste and those that predominate in devotional writings. The legal evolution of waste *combines* with the devotional evolution of waste, so that waste can become the foundation for a sophisticated philosophy of ecosystemic entanglement in Middle English poetry.

CHAPTER THREE

WASTE IN SERMONS AND PENITENTIAL MANUALS

The Unjust Steward

In the Bible and in the Common Law of medieval England, "waste" denotes something one agent does to another's lands. It is a ripping out of all the valuable, usable resources of that land so as to create a "wasted" space where there was once a profitable, habitable place. Waste is always physical, material, and destructive. It can be licit and purgative (as in the Bible), but it also can be criminal (as in trespassory waste). But there is another usage of "waste" that becomes routine in late antiquity and is in broad circulation by the Middle Ages. This second usage is crucial to the evolution of the idea of waste as an ecosystemic misdeed in medieval England. It has to do with the wasting of *immaterial* goods, not just with the physical wasting of property and its resources.

This second usage appears in biblical commentaries. Late antique biblical commentators use *vastare* to comment on parts of the Vulgate that do not use *vastare* at all. In fact, in the actual text of the Bible *vastare* is a concept and term that is confined to the Old Testament—the part of the Bible most concerned with land and property. "Wasting" there is always a physical, material despoliation done to land and its appurtenances. There is no "waste"—no *vastare*—in the Gospels, presumably because Jesus's teachings have less to do with nation-building or the punishment of disobedience and more to do with the care of the soul and with social justice. But, despite its absence from the Vulgate Gospels, the word *vastare* comes up surprisingly often in late antique biblical commentaries on the Gospels, to talk about certain specific kinds of events. Commentators use the term *vastare* metaphorically, to describe how the soul—figured as a place—is depleted, destroyed, burned up, or emptied out by sin, often figured as a fire. In his ninth sermon on the Gospel of Luke, Augustine says "Peccatum cor vastat, interiora demolitur, animam suffocat, animam perdit" (Sin wastes the heart, demolishes the interior, suffocates the soul, ruins the spirit).[1] For Augustine the soul and its appurtenances are wastable; "waste" is in apposition to "demolition," indicating the destruction of a building or dwelling place. It makes sense here to use a verb often applied to dwelling places: the heart, the interior, and the soul are where you live, the human environments par excellence. From a spiritual standpoint, the soul is the only ecosystem that truly matters to our survival, and it is the one most worth protecting from waste.

By the Middle Ages this idea of the wastability of the soul is everywhere. The ninth-century commentator Rabanus Maurus notes that, in the book of Jeremiah, all the wasting directed at the city of Moab allegorically signals a wasting of people who trust too much in the philosophies of the secular world, entrusting themselves and their souls to that kind of knowledge rather than harkening to God's word.[2] In the twelfth century, Aelred of Rievaulx addresses the wasting that happens in the book of Isaiah by arguing that many of the various wasted cities should be understood as souls that are tortured by vices and need to be purged of them. Moab, for instance, figures the knowledge particular to the world of men, and when Moab is wasted that means the soul must be purged of that knowledge in the interest of salvation.[3] The walls of cities that are wasted by armies in the Bible become the walls of the obstinate and sinful mind, which must be destroyed to make room for virtue.[4] Aelred elsewhere says that the Waster (*vastator*) of the Bible should be understood as the ever-destructive spirit of fornication, or the demon of pride laying waste to the soul everywhere it turns.[5] Hugh of Saint Victor argued that the prophetic books of the Bible, when they described waste, were describing the actions God would take against heretics and false prophets—or any group of people whose schismatic beliefs threatened the church.[6] For better or for worse, whether purgative or destructive, wasting is happening *to people* in these interpretations, not to land. The scene of wasting is the soul itself, not someone's farmstead. Heretics, sinners, prevaricators, doubters, these are the people who will be wasted, and they will be wasted not in or because of what they own or where they live, but because of what they believe and how they behave. Waste isn't just about the material world or the world of property; it's about the soul. But even so, the underlying logic of waste remains the same: souls get wasted as a purgative and punitive action.

In the Middle Ages, however, another sense of *vastare* comes into play, one that resonates far more loudly with modern English usages of "waste." Medieval Latin commentators start to associate *vastare* with dissipation and squandering, to signal a kind of "dissipating waste" or a "scattering waste." We see this when the *Glossa ordinaria* draws the concepts of violent, bodily waste and diabolical, spiritual dissipation into parallel, glossing John 10 and its representation of wolves: "Lupus est vel violentus qui corporaliter vastat, vel diabolus qui spiritualiter dissipat"[7] (The wolf is either the violent man who wastes bodily, or the devil which dissipates spiritually). This opposition suggests that waste—violent and physical—takes place in the body, but carries with it a correlative dissipation that is spiritual. It suggests, in effect, that wasting and dissipation are parallel, comparable actions, but that one is more usually physical, the other more spiritual.

This shift—whereby "wasting" comes to signal a kind of dissipation, misuse, or squandering and not just a destructive emptying out—is widely attested by the late Middle Ages, in multiple vernacular languages. And during the Middle Ages it comes to be more squarely applicable to immaterial resources—what we might call the goods of the soul. By the fourteenth century the Middle English word "waste" regularly gets applied to the misuse of words, wits, will, breath, time, body, self, soul, and mind.[8] As we will see presently, this dissipating waste is central to later medieval explorations of waste as a particularly marked form of sin. And, as we will see thereafter, the increasing association of wasting with dissipation or misspending of the resources of the soul is central to medieval English ecosystemic poetry.

WASTING IN PENITENTIAL MANUALS

In fourteenth-century England, a genre of religious books draws together the biblical commentary tradition's notion of waste as a sin and the legal notion of waste as a crime, but it does so in a way that reflects the increasing tendency of waste to signal a misuse or misspending. These books understand waste as something that affects an individual soul (as do the biblical commentators) *and* as something that affects a larger community (as does the English Common Law), but they understand waste not as a purgative emptying out, but as a squandering. These religious books seek to define and to curb wasteful behavior, now by making it a sin against God rather than a crime against the king's peace, and thereby making it a sin committed first again oneself and second against one's fellow Christians.

These religious books are referred to as "penitential manuals" because their goal is to bring people to a penitent state of mind and thence to help them make an adequate, soul-saving confession. The way the manuals work is simple. They itemize each of the seven deadly sins, going into all imaginable subtypes of each sin, as well as the penitential acts most appropriate for absolving oneself. So, for instance, the sin of wrath would typically take up about a seventh of the book. The sin of wrath would be described, then its various manifestations would be detailed to enable a priest, cleric, or layperson to diagnose a sinner with that sin. The specific behaviors that characterize the particular form of wrath in question would be reviewed, then a remedy for the sin would be presented—usually a prayer or set of prayers, or a penitential ritual or behavior. Penitential manuals, then, are geared toward general diagnosis, then to specific sub-diagnosis, then to treatment. In fact, the closest modern analogue for these penitential manuals is the DSM series—the *Diagnostic and Statistical Manual of Mental Disorders.* I do not mean that glibly; for us as readers in the twenty-first century it is important to remember that to medieval Christians sin was a disorder—albeit a disorder of the will and not of the biological entity that is the brain—playing out in potentially destructive ways for the self, the family, and the community. Sin was a mental illness, priests were the doctors; they needed to be able to diagnose and treat, quickly and decisively, any sin that might crop up in a community.

Until the fourteenth century, these manuals were usually written in Latin or French and were read by priests and other clergy. But starting around 1300 they were increasingly composed in vernacular languages, giving more and more readers access to their ideas and schemes. The two Middle English penitential manuals I will focus on are called *The Ayenbite of Inwit* (1340) by Dan Michel and *Handlyng Synne* (1303) by Robert Mannyng. The first text is a translation of a French penitential manual called *La somme le roi*; the second translates the Anglo-Norman *Manuel des pechiés*. The *Ayenbite* was apparently not very popular, surviving in only one manuscript, but it was Michel's intention to present it broadly to unlearned people who could read neither French nor Latin. It was his intention, that is, to disseminate and democratize the principles of spiritual diagnosis contained in the original French work.[9] *Handlyng Synne* survives in nine manuscripts, indicating greater popularity and wider distribution, and Mannyng, like Michel, goes into detail about his imagined audience of uneducated readers, those who know only English and who are tempted into tales of moral depravity in part because that's all that really exists in English—in Mannyng's view. To distract readers from the temptations of sinful writings, then, he pens his translation, to give some edifying works to his less than totally literate fellow Englishmen.[10] For both texts, in fact, the purpose of translation is to educate people who have no access to formal religious learning, till then available only in French or Latin. These books' authors saw themselves as curators of a more moral, less sinful English society. They sought to empower people to diagnose and handle the sins of their parishioners, their own sins, and the sins of everyone else they knew. Although neither text takes "waste" as a central sin, both understand waste and wasteful behaviors as problems in the care of the soul and the management of sin.

"Waste" shows up about fifteen times in *Handlyng Synne*. When "waste" is used as a verb there, it means "squander." But, more often in *Handlyng Synne*, "waste" shows up as an adjective or adverbial construction, signaling that something is done in vain, is underused, is futile. Aside from good Christian mores, the text tells us, "all other belief is wicked and waste" (9666). We should try to speak "no wordys waste" (no words in waste) (3026). You should be aware that if you do not focus on virtue, "thou worchyst waste" (you act in vain) (1884). The things that are wasted in *Handlyng Synne* are immaterial, intangible: life, words, deeds, and beliefs. And they are things that belong directly and only to the individual sinner. "Waste" does not, in these texts, signal a misuse of concrete property that damages the material interest of another person. Instead, it signals a vain squandering of a spiritual resource of the individual soul.

If we turn to *The Ayenbite of Inwit*, composed a few decades later to translate the French *La somme le roi* (1279), we see a little more complexity in how "waste" matters in the diagnosis and saving of the soul. Following his French source, Dan Michel moves into his treatment of the seven deadly sins, beginning with pride. Characteristic sinful behavior by the prideful man is that he "wasteth and dispendeth in folyes and in outrages . . . the guodes that ne byeth naght his, ac byeth his lhordes guodes, hwer-of him behouveth straitliche yelde rekeninge" (wastes and misspends in follies and excesses . . . the goods that are not his own, but instead are his lord's goods, of which it behoves him strictly give reckoning) (18). Here the energetic, spiritual resources of our soul are shown not to be ours to use as we wish, but instead to be on loan from God. It is in that sense that "waste" has its greatest significance in the *Ayenbite*: we are not merely misspending our own things, we are wasting goods that should have been put to better use for another (in this case, divine) party. We are, in effect, bad managers of God's goods; we are wasteful escheators. Indeed, he says that a prideful man will waste the resources, or "guodes" "thet ne byeth naght his, ake byeth his lhordes guodes, huer-of him behoueth straitliche yelde rekeninge and scele. Thet is to wytene the guodes of suo grat pris and the timliche guodes thet he heth ine lokinge the uirtues of the bodie and the thoghtes and the consenteinens and the willes of the zaule" (that are not his, but are his lord's goods, whereof it behooves him to strictly yield accounting. That is to mean the goods of such great price and the timely goods that he has in keeping, the virtues of the body and the thoughts and the consentings and the wills of the soul).[11]

From Common Law, we should be familiar with the linking of waste with proxy misuse—the prideful waster wastes goods that are not his, belonging instead to his lord, much as our friend Walter in the Statute of Waste in 1292 wasted lands that were not his, belonging instead first to Gavin and then to William.

But the context from which Dan Michel draws this idea is *not* the

English Common Law; instead, he draws directly from his French source. *La somme le roi* reads,

> Donc est cil a droit fous et bestornez et bein die forsenez qui a sonescient et hardiement les biens qui ne sone pas sien—einz sone li bien son Seigneur, dont il li covandra estroitment render conte et reson, c'est a savoir les tens precious et les biens temporex que il a en garde, les vertuz du cors et les pensees et les consentemenz et les volentez de l'ame—gaste et despent en folies et en outraiges devant les ieus de son Seigneur, ne point ne se porvoit de son conte.

> [Therefore he is truly crazy and perverse and even insane, whoever knowingly and eagerly spends the goods that are not his own but are the goods of his Lord, of which he will have to render accounts strictly, that is, the precious time and temporal goods that he has in his charge, the virtues of the body and the thoughts and consentings and the desires of the soul—in folly and extravagance, before the eyes of his Lord, and doesn't think of his account.][12]

As does Michel's translation, this source singles out the prideful man for wasting and misspending goods that do not belong to him, but that he is instead keeping watch over for his lord—goods for which he must ultimately render accounts. The language *La somme* uses here—misspending the goods of the lord, needing to render strict accounting of those misexpenditures, wasting things he is meant to keep guard over and take care of—draws on a very famous and widely available cultural and textual authority: the parable of the unjust steward.

This parable details that a lord has had a steward—a manager—but the steward has mismanaged the lord's goods, treating them as if they were his own by overspending them. When the lord comes to demand an accounting of the steward's expenditures, the steward cannot make a satisfactory account, so the lord fires him (Luke 16:1–13). The goods the manager has wasted are material in the literal meaning of the story, but in the vast exegetical tradition surrounding this parable, the goods are understood to be spiritual, moral, devotional, and internal. The parable of the steward deals with the goods of the soul that God has lent man for the term of his life. It is up to man to use them wisely, to the Lord's glory and enrichment, rather than squander them, because man will be held strictly accountable for their misuse. Failing adequate management of those resources, the man wastes. So even when we *seem* to be misusing our own resources—our own time, our own words, our own wits, our own souls—we have to remember that those things are actually owned by God. The word the Vulgate uses to capture this wasting is *dissipasset*, dissipated. But Friar Laurent and the Middle English translators who work from his French text use versions of "waste."[13] This is because by the end of the thirteenth century in France, *gast-*, cognate with the English *wast-*, already signals dissipation and not just a purgative or punitive act of wasting. And *gast-* can already be applied to the immaterial resources of the soul, not just to the material resources of the world.

This meaning of "waste" as misspending comes up again and again in the *Ayenbite*, particularly in connection with the sins of gluttony and idleness, and it is always derived directly from Friar Laurent's text. A glutton, in the *Ayenbite*, is so focused on eating that he will eat too much, eat at the wrong times, and stay up late to eat. According to the *Ayenbite*, the sinner who eats too much and at the wrong times is violating the natural way that time should work: "Thus wasteth the wreche his time and his wyttes and his guodes and wretheth god and harmeth his bodi and more his zaule" (Thus the wretch wastes his time and his wits and his goods and enrages God and harms his body and, more, his soul) (52).[14] For the *Ayenbite*, wasting time, energy, words, beliefs, thoughts, consentings, and the other spiritual resources of the soul is a real and pervasive problem. But it is not yet clear that the problem is dangerous to anyone other than the waster himself, or damaging to anyone else's interest other than God's.

Later, however, again following Friar Laurent, when Dan Michel excoriates those sinners who overeat, his thinking gets more pointedly social. "The verthe bogh of thise zenne of than thet to nobleliche wylleth libbe. That despendeth and wasteth vor to velle hare glotonye hwer-of an hondred poure mighten libbe and ynoghliche by ueld" (The fourth branch of this sin is of those who wish to live too fancily. They who spend and waste to satisfy their gluttony whereof a hundred poor people might live and be filled enough) (55).[15] Suddenly the text conceives of the food economy as zero sum, so that if one person overeats, another person cannot get enough to eat. All the food I overeat is food I took from *you*. It is not just God who is injured by my sins of waste; now it's my fellow Christians. These penitential manuals thus construe every human soul and every human body as part of an extended ecosystem that includes every other soul and body in the realm. Because we live ecosystemically, our resources are never ours alone; they impinge on and indeed coincide with the resources of God and our fellow man. When we waste what seem to be our own spiritual resources, we actually waste everyone else with us.

SERMONS OF THE LATE FOURTEENTH CENTURY: THE RISE OF THE UNJUST STEWARD

In England the notion that wasteful sin has consequences not just for the individual sinner's soul, but also for other people becomes a focal point of ecological critique in sermons by the end of the fourteenth century. In fact, the socioeconomic and ecosystemic theory of sin that we see nascent in *The Ayenbite of Inwit* crystallizes in sermons. When the idea that *my* wasting could hamper *your* ability to thrive does crystallize in sermons, it does so, again, around the parable of the unjust steward.

As I mentioned, the Vulgate describes how this unjust steward *dissipasset* (had dissipated) the lord's goods. By contrast, the Middle English or "Wycliffite" Bible's (ca. 1382) version of the parable of the unjust steward uses "waste" as the English equivalent of the Latin *dissipasset*: "[Jesus] seide also to hise diciplis, Ther was a riche man, that hadde a baili; and this was defamed to him, as he hadde *wastid* his goodis" (Jesus said also to his disciples, There was a rich man, who had a manager; and the manager was defamed to him, since he had wasted the lord's goods).[16] The commentator here may have been inspired in his translation by reading some of the late antique commentaries that used vastare to talk about the wasting of the resources of the soul, or by vernacular (both French and English) penitential manuals that use "wasted" to talk precisely about bad stewardship. There is an emerging trend in devotional literature to see misspending and misuse of spiritual goods and material ones specifically as waste—and, often, to route that thinking through the parable of the unjust steward—and this translation is part of that trend.[17]

As the Wycliffite commentary goes on, the commentator goes further in his ecosystemic figuration of the parable of the steward than had either *La somme* or the *Ayenbite*. He does this by doubling down on the literal, material meaning of the parable. That is, the Wycliffite commentator will insist that we must think simultaneously about the wasted resources as immaterial or spiritual *and* as material and tangible. He gets at this duality by forcing us to think about the ending of the parable. The parable of the unjust steward has a famously weird ending. After being fired by the lord, the steward reduces the debts of two parties who owed debts to the lord—by half, in fact. When the lord finds out he has (again) been fleeced by his now ex-steward, he *praises* the man for reducing the debts: "And the lord preiside the fermour of wickidnesse, for he hadde don prudently" (Luke 16:8, Wycliffe Bible). Sermonists and commentators had to figure out how to make sense of why this second giving away of the Lord's goods somehow gets not only a pass, but an "atta boy" from the lord. About this strange narrative turn, a Wycliffite commentator says this:

> And sith Crist hath lent ech man here al that he hath and wole axe of this streite rekenynge, how he dispendith it, to each man of this world may this parable be applied; and whanne men dispenden not warly goddis goodis, thanne thei ben defamyd to him as thei hadden wasted hem, but dispending of alle goodis must sowne to Goddis worship. For alle men shulden knowe that alle thes ben Goddis goodis, and he wole that thei be spendid thus to profit of his Churche.

> [And since Christ has lent to each man here on earth all that he has, and will ask of these lendings strict reckoning, how he spends it, to each man of this world may this parable be applied; and when men spend not carefully God's goods, then they are defamed to him for having wasted them, but spending of all goods must resound to God's worship. For all men should know that all things are God's goods, and he wants them to be spent thus to profit his Church.][18]

According to this commentator, as according to Dan Michel, Christ, like the lord of the parable, lends to men all of their resources in life, to manage on his and his church's behalf. Humans have no inherent right to their own spiritual resources; Christ, like the lord, maintains a proprietary interest in all of man's goods. They remain, that is, "goddis goodis" and must be spent "to Goddis worship"—that is, for the benefit of the divine owner of the goods. All of man's possessions must be spent "to profit of [God's] church," just as a guardian, in the eyes of the law, should spend his profits to the benefit of an heir. Possession of property, the parable suggests, is legitimate only until it edges over into waste, where waste is defined as a spending of resources that fails to bring profit to the rightful beneficiaries, here conceived as the church. The misspent resources are not only the time, desire, and consent of the soul, but the actual physical and monetary resources that secular people have at their disposal.

But still: What do we do with the praising of the steward's second act of mismanagement? The reason for this praising, according to Wycliffite thinkers, lies in the steward's mercy toward those beneath him during his reckoning:

> Sum men thenken that this bailly that forgafe fifty barels of oile and therto twenty skippis of corn, dide wronge to his lord, and so the lord preiside him not wele; but we shal wite that this lord is God, and this bailly lord of this world, and so God approveth wele forgyvynge of mannes rente; and with graunte of the cheef lord, baillyes may forgyve ther dette, and discharge ther pore tenantis of many charges that thei ben inne.

> [Some men think that this steward that forgave fifty barrels of oil and twenty measures of corn did wrong to his lord, and so the lord praised him not wisely; but we must know that this lord is God, and this steward is lord of the world, and so God approves readily the forgiving of man's rents; and with the grant of the chief lord, stewards may forgive debts, and discharge their poor tenants of many debts that they are in.][19]

The steward is praised not for his dissimulation per se, but for its effect: he is praised for helping the poor. From this perspective it is natural that the lord (God) should forgive the steward (the king, or some other leader in charge of other people's well-being) for his false reckoning, because it was done to "discharge . . . pore tenantis" of their debts and obligations. It is good, that is, for secular people with fiscal power to make peace with material wealth, in order to take better care of their subjects and to foster a viable and equitable economic community "here in erthe."[20] The steward finds himself in a two-way system of obligation: he must not waste resources, lest he anger his lord, who owns them. But if he does waste resources through wasteful spending, he must not pass the responsibility or burden down to his subordinates. Instead, he must act as guardian and protector of the rest of the community, even when he himself is being called to account. The sermon recognizes, that is, a reciprocity or mutuality not only between the steward and God, but also between the steward and his subjects. This sermon conceives of worldly leadership not as debased, but rather as a pragmatic reality that mediates between God (the lord in the parable) and the people of the church (the debtors). The sermon suggests that the steward's fulfillment of his responsibility to his debtors—through his protection and mercy toward them—mitigates the severity of his punishment. Or rather, the steward's merciful act of debt forgiveness actually seems to *atone* for his waste against the lord. This atonement suggests a principle of redistribution at work: the refusal to allow personal improvidence to trickle down to the poor and injure them economically means that a ruler has not entirely failed in his dual stewardship.

To put things into a modern frame, the Wycliffite commentator suggests that a ruler can atone for fiscal misconduct by redistributing wealth. Implicit in this notion is that the initial "wasting" was somehow damaging to the people down the socioeconomic ladder, and that that wasting must be remedied by the redistribution. The manager wastes, the people suffer; that suffering is alleviated, the manager is rewarded. Wycliffite commentators, that is, see the steward's act of waste as an ecosystemic and socioeconomic problem, one that is remedied by taking resources from the lord and giving them to the debtors. The legal and penitential senses of "waste" are here being used to articulate a vision of economically based social justice. The waste of the steward is no longer just the abstract resources of the soul, but the real monetary resources of the shared secular world of medieval England. The steward's waste has become not just spiritual, but ecosystemic and economic.

In 1388 the clergyman Thomas Wimbledon writes and reads a public sermon that enters into this conversation with yet more socioeconomic and ecosystemic precision. Preached at Paul's Cross, the open-air pulpit at Saint Paul's Cathedral in London, the first part of the sermon begins simply enough: it analyzes the parable of the unjust steward to argue for the appropriate type of account keeping from each of the three estates—or classes—of human society. Traditionally, medieval England was understood to be divided into workers (*laboratores*), clergy (*oratores*), and aristocrats/warriors (*bellatores*). Each estate was understood to be in a symbiotic relationship with the other two: the workers provided food for the clergy and aristocrats; the clergy prayed for the workers' and aristocrats' souls; the aristocrats kept the workers and clergy protected. This idea of medieval social structure was pervasive, though often questioned, since it was increasingly obvious to people that the social world did not in fact break down all that neatly.[21] Wimbledon, though, seems rather invested in those three estates and eager to use the idea of the interdependent estates to mount a critique of excesses.

Focusing on those three estates, Wimbledon explains how clergy, aristocrats, and laborers should act to fulfill their status-determined roles in society in order to be good stewards.

> And o thyng y dar wel seye: that he that is neither traveylynge in this world on prayeris and prechynge for helpe of the puple, as it fallith to prestis; neither in fyghtinge agenis tyrauntis and enemyes, as it fallith to knyghtis; neither traveylynge on the erthe, as it fallith to laboreris— whanne the day of his rekenynge cometh that is the ende of this lif, right as he lyvede here withoutyn travayle, so he shal there lacke the reward of the peny, that is the endeless ioye of hevene.

> [And one thing I dare well say: that he who is neither working in this world on prayers and preaching for the benefit of the people, as befits

priests; nor fighting against tyrants and enemies, as befits knights; nor working in the earth, as befits laborers—when the day of his reckoning comes that is the end of this life, as if he had lived here without travail, so he shall there lack the reward of the penny, which is the endless joy of heaven.][22]

Different modes of stewardship are due from different people, but all people will be accountable according to their estate. No one can escape making an account to God at the end of his or her life; all shall be judged according to how well they fulfilled their social obligations. In an ideal socioeconomic ecosystem, the estates—preachers, warriors, and laborers—are interdependent, and each should recognize and respect the importance of the others. As Wimbledon puts it, "And certis this shulde be o cause why every staat shul love other and men of o craft shulde neither hate ne despise men of another craft sith they beth so needful everych to other" (And clearly this should be one reason why every estate should love the other, and men of one job should neither hate nor despise men of another job, since they be so necessary to one another).[23] Philosophically, so far this is unsurprising stuff; certainly, most literate and cultured late medieval English readers would find the estates model highly familiar. Probably, many less literate and less cultured people would have been aware of it too. And it is very clear that Wimbledon himself—preaching a sermon to the public in London—assumed they would be familiar with the idea, because he uses it without gloss or explanation.

But the mild platitudes about estates philosophy are a rhetorical ploy: Wimbledon's more heated argument lies just around the corner. Although integrated and interdependent, human society is not "equal" in its several levels of accountability, according to Wimbledon. Whereas all people (priests, rulers, and laborers) of all three estates (clerical, knightly, and laboring) shall be accountable to God for how they have lived their own lives, two social estates must "answere for himself and for other, that beth preostis that han cure of mennis soulis, and temperal lordis that haven governayle of peplis" (answer for themselves and for others, namely priests who have charge of men's souls, and temporal lords who have governance over people).[24] Secular rulers and priests, that is, are accountable to God not only for their own actions, but also for the ways those actions (and expenditures) affect the rest of society—again we see a two-way notion of accountability in the parable of the steward. Put otherwise, if you are a person of power—whether spiritual or secular—you are accountable not only up to God, but down to the laborers beneath you. Social justice again.

Wimbledon's sermon goes yet further in its indictment of bad stewards, to note that the priests and clergy—those responsible for the well-being of people's souls—are also responsible for the *material* goods of the people over whom they have pastoral charge. This is an expansion on the socioeconomic and ecosystemic thought we saw in the Wycliffite commentary, where it was the secular ruler who was materially accountable to those below him. Here it is even the *spiritual* elite who are accountable to those below them—precisely for their use of material things. Indeed, it is in his criticism of the clergy's material misuse of public goods that waste enters Wimbledon's diatribe as a central term.

> Yelde also the rekenynge how thou hast reulid and splendid the goodis of pore men . . . Dredeth, clerkis, dredith mynistris of the chirche . . . that they, noght holdynge hem apaied with swyche wagis that were sufficiaunt to hem, that overplus that nedy men sholde be susteyned by they beth not shamed to waste in the houses of here pride, and here lecherie, and withholdith to hemselve wickidly and cursedly the liflode of pore men. With dowble wickidnesse trewely they synneth; first for they reveth other mennes goodes, and sitthe for they misuse holy thyngis in here vanities and in here filthhedes.

> [Give accounts also of how you have ruled and spent the goods of poor men. . . . Fear, clerks, fear, ministers of the church . . . who don't consider themselves well enough paid by the wages that should have been sufficient for them; they are unashamed to waste in the house of their pride and lechery that surplus that needy people should be sustained by; and they withhold for themselves wickedly and accursedly the livelihood of poor men. With double wickedness truly they sin: first because they steal other men's goods, and then because they misuse holy things in their vanities and in their filthiness.][25]

Wimbledon becomes quite exercised about clerical wasting of poor people's material goods: he accuses the clergy of wickedness, accursedness, pride, and lechery. In fact, Wimbledon spends quite a bit more energy excoriating the clergy for their wasteful effect on the material well-being of the people in their curial charge than he does on other classes. Wimbledon sees clearly that the wasting of spiritual goods and the wasting of material goods are profoundly interconnected— especially when the clergy are the wasters. So the interpretive move made by *La somme* and *Ayenbite*—to abstract the material goods of the actual parable into the spiritual goods of the soul—is retained, but augmented by Wimbledon's overlaying of the more literal interpretations of the parable by the Wycliffite commentators. For Wimbledon, the material wastes are spiritual and the spiritual wastes are material.

The assertion of clerical responsibility for wasting public goods is new neither to the Wycliffite commentators nor to Wimbledon: the canon law maxim *bona ecclesiae sunt bona pauperum* (the goods of the church are the goods of the poor) was in wide circulation as a basic ethical principle throughout the Middle Ages. And in fact, for his characterization of priestly misuse of goods, Wimbledon more or less directly translates Bernard of Clairvaux's twenty-third sermon on the Song of Songs, composed in France in the early twelfth century.

> Timeant clerici, timeant ministri Ecclesiae, qui in terris sanctorum quas possident, tam iniqua gerunt, ut stipendiis, quae sufficere debeant, minime contenti, superflua quibus egeni sustentandi forent, impie sacrilegeque sibi retineant; et in usus suae superbiae atque luxuriae victum pauperum consumere non vereantur, duplici profecto iniquitate peccantes, quod et aliena diripiunt, et sacris in suis vanitatibus et turpitudinibus abutuntur.

> [Fear, clerics; fear, ministers of the church—who, in the place of saints, with such wickedness as they can, and who are minimally contented with stipends, which ought to suffice them—impiously and sacrilegiously retain for themselves the surplus meant to sustain the poor; and in their excessive and luxuriant uses they do not fear to consume the victuals of the poor. They are made sinners by a double iniquity: both that they

steal from others, and that they abuse sacred things in their vanities and turpitudes.][26]

Wimbledon's translation is fairly literal; but his divergences are telling. First he adds the line "they beth not shamed to *waste* in the houses of here pride, and here lecherie." He wants to get in the word waste (there is no *vastare* in the Latin); he wants to insists that it's not just abuse or stealing, but specifically *wasting* of the goods of the poor that is at issue. And second, and perhaps more important, Bernard is not talking about the unjust steward parable. He's talking about the Song of Songs, via a brief detour through Isaiah. So even though Wimbledon's translation is fairly strict, it is completely decontextualized from its original setting—he found Bernard's excoriations against unjust clergy and appropriated them for his own interpretation of the unjust steward parable. He took Bernard's language about "retaining" and "consuming" goods that were meant for the poor and made that language specifically about "wasting." Wimbledon knows that in fourteenth-century England waste has become a buzzword for theorizing the proxy misuse of goods, both material and spiritual, and he avails himself of it.

Specifically, he knows the Common Law connotations of the term waste, and he wants to leverage them. Wimbledon ramps up legal language about waste in his diatribe when he says that priests "haveth with fals title other fals and corrupt intencion . . . had pore mennes goodis to here mysysyng" (have with false title and other false and corrupt intentions . . . had poor men's goods for their misusing).[27] Wimbledon's emphasis here is indebted to legal discourse: according to him, the priests have "with false title"—false *legal* title—misused these other men's resources. Wasting of resources, which Wimbledon understands as reckless overuse without "title," no matter what exactly is being wasted or to whom it most immediately belongs, always has consequences for the poor, always harms the socioeconomic ecosystem of spiritual and material goods of those to whom the clergy are meant to minister lovingly and carefully.

Thus, by the end of the fourteenth century English religious writings have begun to insist not only that all resources—whether material or spiritual—are able be wasted, but also that waste always has an effect on others. There is no isolated, individual act of waste. And religious writers import the language and heft of biblical, exegetical, penitential, and even legal discourse into their manuals and sermons in order to emphasize the sociality of waste. Waste is *always* social; waste is *always* economic; waste is *always* ecosystemic. And the term waste, because it can apply equally to the sinful misuse of spiritual goods and to the criminal misuse of material goods, allows devotional writers to bring into cogent and socially powerful relation the legal logic of waste and the spiritual. It allows them to play up efficiently the interconnection between immaterial and material misuse, between misuses of what's mine and misuses of what's yours, or God's.

All of these accumulated biblical, legal, penitential, sermonic, and exegetical writings are swarming around "waste" by the middle of the fourteenth century. Together these writings have created a conceptual critical mass in "waste." Waste means physical emptying. It means overusing property. It means underusing the soul's resources. It means squandering material resources in a way that hurts other people. Physical, spiritual; overuse, underuse; personal, social: waste is a shifty, powerful term. And by the second half of the fourteenth century waste is ready to burst forth into poetry, where it will become the center of a full theory of ecosystemic connection and ecosystemic danger.

CHAPTER FOUR

WINNER AND WASTER

The Imperilment of the Land

HISTORICAL CONTEXT

Winner and Waster is an anonymous five-hundred-line poem, composed shortly after 1350, that appears in a single plain manuscript: British Library Additional MS 31042. Appearing only in that one manuscript and being directly referenced by no other surviving works of literature, the poem probably had very limited circulation even in the Middle Ages. Even so, it does seem to have influenced at least one major poem—*Piers Plowman*, to which I will turn in full force in the next chapter. So *Winner and Waster* is a short poem that exists in one copy and that influenced one other medieval poem. Rather unprepossessing. Yet this poem is one of the most daring ecosystemic writings of the English Middle Ages, focusing on the precarity of the land supply in England and on how the imperiled land could have catastrophic downstream consequences for rich and poor alike.

Winner and Waster was composed during a politically and economically turbulent period of English history—the middle of the fourteenth century—and it reflects on and dramatizes the sociopolitical and socioeconomic forces of the time. Since the poem was probably written in 1352, the Black Death of 1348 would have been very fresh in the mind of its author and its readers.[1] This cataclysmic loss of human life, and therefore of agricultural manpower, only compounded the gradual hemorrhaging of economic vitality that had long been under way because of the devastatingly costly and seemingly endless Hundred Years' War between England and France. In an effort to counteract the damage to the labor economy that both the plague and the war had caused, Edward III, already far from being a popular monarch for his fiscal profligacy and for his questionable political allegiances with merchant-financiers,[2] urged Parliament to enact two statutes.[3] The first was the 1351 Statute of Laborers, which sought to control and compel the labor of an increasingly restive working class.[4] The second was the Statute of Treasons, which sought to curb public resistance to the king by expanding and codifying the definition of treason against the throne.[5] These statutes met with considerable pushback, further testifying to the political unrest of the period.[6]

Perhaps urged by the collapse of agricultural labor markets, in the mid-fourteenth century the economy of England was already beginning to shift from being agricultural to being more concentrated in urban centers. With this shift the cash economy—along with mercantilism, trade, and the consumption and production of movable goods— became increasingly centralized, gradually beginning to compete with land-based agriculture as the engine of British economic productivity. With the shift of wealth into major cities like London, York, and Norwich, more and more rural workers migrated to urban spaces to take advantage of economic opportunities. This migration of laborers compounded the labor-market effects of the Black Plague and famines, creating serious shortfalls in the number of workers available to work farms.[7] So the poet of *Winner and Waster* had the dubious distinction of living in a time of profound upheaval: political unrest, economic turmoil, pestilence, and, above all, pressure on the agricultural labor market. And as we will see, the poem carefully deploys poetic, legal, and even penitential forms to make it clear that, when living in a time like this, you can't think economically without thinking about the ecosystem, nor can you think ecosystemically without thinking about the economy. It makes these claims through an exploration of waste and of how people are obligated to each other through their shared dependence on their most basic shared resource—the land.

POETIC FORM AND ECOSYSTEMIC CRITIQUE

Before getting into the action of the poem, I'll set the stage by addressing the three largest-scale poetic choices the poet makes. Each of these choices bolsters the trenchant ecosystemic critiques in the poem. First,

Winner and Waster is a dream vision narrative, recounting a dream its narrator supposedly had, a dream about a figure named Winner going head-to-head with a figure named Waster. The uneasy "truthiness" of this form—Did the dream really even happen? If so, what kind of truth value are we to assign to its contents?—helps the poet make some of his more uncomfortable observations about waste and about ecosystemic accountability. Since it is putatively just a dream, the poet cannot really be held accountable for what he learns in it. Setting up the poem's narrative as a dream classifies the poem comfortably as fiction, no matter how stern its critiques.

Working in conjunction with the dream vision genre, the second formal element that helps the poem think through waste is its topical allusiveness. It contains more than a few specific but nonobvious allusions to events of the mid-fourteenth century. Real historical people are named (the fourteenth-century Justice Shareshull); specific statutes are referred to (the 1352 Statute of Treasons); heraldic iconography is described in great detail, along with the clothing of various religious orders and figures. So on the one hand the poem decisively signals itself as a fiction—imaginary, merely a dream; on the other hand it insists on its own realness, its immediacy, its investment in current events. Together, the dream vision frame and the reliance on topical allusions allow the poem to toggle between overtly critical, overtly political commentary and an innocent narrative of a bizarre dream. The real and the fictive are woven together by these two forms.

Weaving the poem's fictiveness yet more tightly with its realism, the poem is a personification allegory—albeit a very strange one.[8] To highlight the poem's strangeness, it is useful to start with Morton Bloomfield's canonical three-part definition of medieval personification allegory. According to Bloomfield, medieval personifications are static, they do what their name states, and they are moralizing.[9] That is, they do not evolve the way characters do, they behave in predictable ways, and they impart concrete parcels of moral knowledge. So, for example, in a poem featuring a personification named Truth, we would expect that character to be truthful, to be unchanging in that truthfulness, and to have some readily apparent moral lesson for us. Probably something like "be truthful." Personification allegory, then, is a form that is obviously fictive—we don't actually *meet* characters like Truth in our daily lives—but it is also real, in that it gives shape, name, and voice to real forces in human life and human social experience, and it gives them real moral significance.

Bloomfield's three-part definition is useful in dealing with medieval personification allegory in general, but it fails conspicuously as a description of what happens in *Winner and Waster*. The two main personified figures in this poem, Winner and Waster, argue over their relative utility to the Prince and his people. Although Winner does "win" in some ways and Waster does "waste," the poem's ultimate goal is precisely to complicate the definitions of both "winning" and "wasting" as social, interpersonal, ecosystemic, and individual behaviors, though it will focus more of its energy on the nature of wasting than on the nature of winning. What this poem makes clear is that neither Winner nor Waster is static, or even straightforward. They both do what their names describe, but those deeds are multifaceted and variable. And they are not moralistic in any easily legible way. Rather than locking in moral certainties, as personification allegory is wont to do, the poem destabilizes our sense that we know exactly what winning and wasting mean.

LEGAL FORMS AND ECOSYSTEMIC CRITIQUE

The poem adds to these poetic devices a second set of mechanisms for understanding waste: the legal ideas and procedures that the Common Law had developed for theorizing and regulating waste in the previous century. Seeing the armies of Winner and Waster drawn up for battle, a royal emissary shows up to warn the two that neither army should step forward, lest either "disturb the peace" of the Prince (*Winner and Waster*, 130). This accusation, that two armies assembled for battle might threaten to disturb the peace, is comically obvious. But the poem takes this idea of "disturbing the peace" quite seriously, returning to it when the leader of one army is outraged at accusations that he "prikkede with powere his pese to destourbe" (321) (rode with power to disturb the peace). Scholars read this repetition as evidence that the poem is engaged with the fourteenth-century Statute of Treasons, which explicitly forbids aristocrats to raise armies.[10] That is true, but an additional element of English legal history is at play here, and it has to do with the mid-fourteenth-century coalescence of trespass law and its applicability to suits of waste.

"With powere his pese to destourbe" is a combined English rendering of the two Latin formulas required to initiate a trespass suit: *vi et armis* (with force and arms) and *contra pacem regis* (against the peace of the king).[11] If a fourteenth-century English litigant wants to bring a trespass suit, he has to claim that a crime was committed "with force and arms" and "against the king's peace." By using this technical legal phrasing—"with powere his pese to destourbe"—the poem casts itself as a trespass trial.[12] The trial format is sustained throughout the rest of the poem, and the unfolding action quickly fleshes out exactly what kind of trespass trial it is. When Winner accuses Waster of mismanaging his real estate, he says, "His londes liggen alle ley, his lomes aren solde, / Downn bene his dowfehowses, drye bene his poles" (His lands lie all fallow, his looms are sold, / his dovehouses have fallen, his pools are dry)(234–35). These accusations coincide with the definition of legal waste—allowing property to fall into disrepair, tearing down buildings, and ruining fishing holes by overfishing them. Winner deploys Common Law definitions of waste to implore the Prince to protect the resources of the land, resources that Waster threatens. Winner's initial charge against Waster is the opening move, then, in a dramatic trespassory trial of waste.[13]

Waster recognizes the nature of Winner's charge and mounts a response that is in keeping with medieval trespass procedure. Although in non-trespass trials a defendant can only admit or deny guilt, in trespass trials he can attempt a "special traverse."[14] A special traverse happens when an accused party does not deny that he or she committed the offense in question but asserts that he or she should not be punished for it. One type of special traverse is the demurrer, in which a defendant calls the law itself into question, saying, "Yes, I committed the act in question, but that act should not be seen as a crime."[15] In response to Winner's accusation, Waster deploys this legal device. He claims that *Winner* is the real criminal. He blames Winner for hoarding goods: "Thou . . . hase werpede thy wyde howses full of wolle sakes /

The bemys benden at the rofe, siche bakone there hinges / Stuffed are sterlynges undere stelen bowndes" (you . . . have packed your great houses full of sacks of wool / the beams bend at the roof, so much bacon hangs there / sterlings are locked under steel bonds) (250–52). Waster makes this accusation in order to set up his primary defense, which construes the "waste" that he himself commits not as a crime, but as a good deed: "What scholde worthe of that wele if no waste come?" (What would happen to that wealth if no waste should come to pass?) (253). Here Waster reengineers the definition of "waste," shifting it toward the penitential sense of "spending" but also adding a *positive* valence, so that "waste" now denotes a prosocial financial outlay, a beneficial spending of "wele," rather than the wasteful emptying out of lands that Winner decries. Indeed, in Waster's view spending "wele" is a social necessity, so much so that he reframes the idea of *not* spending wealth as a charge against Winner. His question, "What scholde worthe of that wele if no waste come" (What would become of that wealth if no waste came?) means, in effect, "Really, Winner, what should one do with wealth *other* than spend it?" The problem, Waster suggests, is with the law's definition of waste, not with Waster himself. Waster, who seems to understand waste simply as "spending," sees himself as someone doing his part to support a cash-based economy. He sees himself, really, as the redeemed unjust steward, who redistributes wealth down the socioeconomic ladder to those in greater need. Through his special traverse, Waster challenges the medieval English Common Law notion of what waste was, why it mattered, and whether the law should seek to curb it.

Winner's response to Waster resists Waster's reframing of "waste" by evoking the statutory developments in the law of waste during the thirteenth century. Winner says, "With thi sturte and thi stryffe thou stroyeste up my gudes" (With your agitating and your strife, you destroy my goods) (264–65). By asserting that Waster "destroys" Winner's goods, Winner achieves two rhetorical goals. First, "destroys" insists that a violent crime of despoliation has been committed, not one as innocent as "misspending"; that insistence is consistent with the Common Law definition of waste, going back to Magna Carta.[16] Second, by saying Waster's wastefulness destroys his (Winner's) goods, Winner makes it clear that Waster's management of his own lands impinges on Winner's economic well-being, reflecting the fundamental logic of the statutory laws of waste—that misuse of resources held by one person injures the long-term interest of another person. Waster may think he is simply spending his own goods, and maybe even for good reason, but his right to use those goods is compromised because their use impinges on other people. Winner wants the judging Prince to see, in effect, that Waster's wasting, however well-intentioned it might be and however much Waster might want to see himself as a good steward to the people who depend on him, actually does significant ecosystemic and economic harm to others. In Winner's argument, waste is an ecosystemic problem—a crime without boundaries—that highlights the connectedness among people.

Winner's critique of Waster grows more acutely reflective of thirteenth-century statutory law when he emphasizes that the crime of overspending money has consequences in real property. Winner indicts Waster for his expenditures on his wife, arguing that they damage the land:

> Lesse and ye wrethe your wifes, thaire willes to folowe,
> Ye sellyn wodd aftir wodde in a wale tyme,
> Bothe the oke and the assche and all that ther growes.
>
> [Lest you anger your wives, to follow their wills,
> You sell more and more wood in a great rush,
> Both the oak and the ash and all that grows there.] (395–97)

Winner's description of selling "wood after wood," not only oak, but also ash and "all that ther growes," depicts Waster clearing out not just the old and strong trees, but also the young trees and, indeed, everything that grows in the area. Waster is clear-cutting his land so that no profitable lumber remains.[17] Winner goes on to claim that Waster intends to sell off his lands eventually to pay the debts he has incurred (401). In keeping with the legal logic of waste, Winner insists that land is always the final concern when thinking about misuses of resources. Because of the land's vulnerability to being sold off, he suggests, Waster's assertion that spending money freely is good for the economy is bunk; for Winner, all modes of overspending are deleterious to society because they all impinge on and eventually imperil the one most basic shared resource: land. Wasting money may seem merely to harm the person who misspends his own lucre, but it is an *ecosystemic* misdeed, because it ultimately destroys the goods of the land, which all people share. Through his indictment of waste, Winner emphasizes that the health of the land and the cash economy are inextricably joined.

Winner urges us to notice that fiscal conduct can and does have ecosystemic fallout, whether or not that fallout is immediately visible. He urges us to notice that land is the ultimate referent—both economic and ecosystemic—of financial profligacy. He urges us to recognize that land is a finite resource, one we all depend on. Winner represents an aristocrat who looks around England and sees that other aristocrats—like Waster—are depleting and selling off their own lands and imping-ing negatively on the lands around them, to the overall diminution of available, arable, usable land in England. Winner's shrillness in his condemnations of Waster originates in his awareness of the fragility, the vulnerability, and the irreplaceability of the English agricultural ecosystem.

Winner and Waster uses the allegorical figuration of Waster, in com-bination with a carefully executed trespass trial that Winner brings against him, to engineer a vision of the interconnectedness of land and monetary wealth. It creates a fictive, vernacular meditation on the nature of the English economy as both a land market and a com-mercial market, a meditation born of the synergistic overlay—what I have been calling braiding or weaving but the poet calls "wrying over" or "overlaying" in the prologue—of legal ideas on poetic forms.[18]

PENITENTIAL FORMS AND ECOSYSTEMIC CRITIQUE

Eventually that "wrying over" extends to join penitential ideas with both legal ideas and poetic forms. To see this last layering in how and what "waste" can mean ecosystemically, we must turn our attention to Winner and his particular ontological status, both in the poem and as a force in late medieval English culture. In fourteenth-century English, "winning" means being victorious. Winning means earning. Winning is good. On the contrary, wasting in Middle English denotes "misspending." It means "destroying." It is wrongful consumption. Wasting is bad. Through Waster, the poet of *Winner and Waster* suggests that there *might* be something good and socially salvific about wasting, and that there *might* be something negative, selfish, and deleterious about winning. The poem, that is, uses the opposition and apposition of wasting and winning in part to force us first to register that the moral lines between them are blurrier than they may seem. This is a poem in which wasting might be necessary—in which we might need wasters to make the economy function, even if wasters are established as having negative effects on the interconnected system of land, trees, material resources, and money. Waste *might* be a good thing, at least in some contexts; it is worth thinking about. And winning—or at least winning too much, winning as it verges on hoarding—might be a bad thing.

If winning is bad, its badness ultimately has to do with the misexpenditure of energy. Now, the concept of energy may seem like a distinctly modern one. And to some degree it is: medieval poets were no more aware of petroleum than they were of bacteria. But they *were* aware of the ways misuse of land could affect the availability of firewood during the cold months.[19] Also, and more crucially for the emerging ideology of waste I am tracing, they were aware of how the misexpenditure of *personal energy*—one's time, one's thoughts, one's emotions—could affect a larger socioeconomic and ecosystemic whole.

Winner and Waster embodies this awareness. In his final rhetorical gambit against Winner, Waster aggressively redefines the concept of waste, saying, "Wynnere, with wronge thou wastes thi tyme" (Winner, wrongfully you waste your time) (439). In making this claim, Waster veers away from the legal sense of waste to draw on penitential ideas about wastefulness as misspent personal energy. Introducing this idea of waste as a problem of misused personal energy—calling Winner a waster because he wastes his own time—Waster makes the last move in his demurrer. Now he suggests that the common law of property should not be the final arbiter of what constitutes a dangerous kind of "waste." The only "waste" that truly deserves censure is the waste of his own time—the goods of his soul that are not truly his but are part of the liquid economy of energy that connects him to God. For Waster, his own use of material resources—land, money, wood, clothes, and such—can be thought of as good for the economy, good for the social world, and good for the self. Winner's vice of wasting his own time through hoarding, by contrast, cannot be defended as salutary. It is just plain wrong. And it is wrong not only for Winner himself, but for the broader social world.

Why? Because, in Waster's understanding, Winner's wasting of his own time enables his underuse of his material resources—that is, he wastes his time by sitting home and fixating all his thoughts on the keeping of his wealth rather than on its use. Wasting time, then, means refusing to distribute wealth equitably. It means hoarding food resources in a time of famine. And, as William Jordan has pointed out, there was almost no social crime more uniformly frowned on by medieval people than hoarding food in a time of famine.[20] Winner's time is not really his own, despite the poem's explicitly marking it that way by saying "thy time." Instead, Waster's ultimate point is that all the energy Waster spends worrying is intimately connected to his hoarding, to his refusal to spend or share, to his greed. The poem insists, through Waster's last move, that Winner suffers from false consciousness: he feels that his material resources are his alone, that his time is his alone, and that he can (and should) use all those things in entirely self-interested ways. Waster, by contrast, views all his resources as at least in part collectively held. He sees himself as the unjust steward: however wasteful he may be, he benefits others. His money is supposed to trickle down to the poor, as is his food. And presumably his time.

So the poem is actually "wrying over" a definition of waste drawn from the Common Law—Winner's definition of waste—and one drawn from penitential manuals and sermons—Waster's definition. Winner sees waste as a crime committed primarily in property, but with consequences also in other resources and in cash; he sees it as committed by one party (Waster) against the interest of another (Winner himself, as well as other people). Waster understands the waste of material goods as "spending" and sees it not as an evil, but as a type of use. He understands monetary spending as necessary to the functioning of the economy, and he understands the goods he spends—his money, his time, his energy, and his words—both as his own *and* as belonging in some way to other people, such that he is responsible for spending them to the benefit of those others. His primary accusation against Winner is that, by refusing to spend his own time well, Winner is committing a far worse type of infraction than Waster is. Winner is hoarding his time, not investing it in something good either for himself or for other people. Even if he is not wasting the real property of England, even if he is not spending money hand over fist, Winner's hoarding practices are deleterious for the populace as a whole. By hoarding his time and his resources, Winner is failing as a steward.

So the poem uses this allegorical, debate-framed dream vision to contemplate whether and how *any* resources—land, money, goods, time, words—ever belong exclusively to their user. Waster's claim is that he has not only a right but an obligation to spend his resources, for both his own benefit and that of others. Winner's claim is that he has a right and obligation not to overuse any of his resources, so that there will be resources for use in the future. For Winner, wasting is a crime committed against another; for Waster, wasting is a sin committed initially against oneself (and one's time), but ultimately against other people, by a refusal to participate in the redistribution of wealth. What the poem's overlaid meditations suggest is, first, that material and energetic resources are not truly distinct and, second, that no resources are the exclusive property of a single party. The poem sees that ecosystemic interimplication between people hinges on their economic interimplication, and that the foundation of the connection between economic and ecosystemic interimplication is always land.

AMBIGUITY AND ECOSYSTEMIC CRITIQUE

The poem's meditation on the nature of waste forces readers to recognize how muddy the conceptual terrain around waste is. It forces them, specifically, to recognize that the misdeed of "wasting" is truly a systemic infraction, with a plethora of possible objects. I can waste my own resources as well as the resources of other people; I can waste land, but also money, goods, words, and time. When I waste *any* of those things, I run the risk of wasting them *all*; when I waste any of my *own* things, I waste those of someone else. The sliding concept of waste allows the poem to think about land, money, goods, people, time, and energy all on a spectrum of usable goods, and it urges readers to think about where their personal accountability lies in the vast, sprawling, and significantly *economic* ecosystem of late medieval England. How are they accountable to others for how they spend their time? How are they accountable to themselves for how they spend their money? For how they use their land? For how they spend their time?

Or, finally, for how they use other people? This question arises covertly in the poem's initial frame, when Winner and Waster are drawn up for battle. I noted earlier that it seems ridiculous to observe aloud, as the Prince's emissary does, that two armies look as if they're about to do something violent. But that overdetermination of the scene serves a purpose—one I passed over earlier. There is a final, well-established discourse that the poem's definitions of "winning" and "wasting" leverage at the beginning and again slyly at the end. That discourse is military narrative. In war stories, there is inevitably one party who comes out on top—the "winner." That party, of necessity, as the winner, is also the one who lays waste to his vanquished enemies; he is therefore "the waster." The joke of the poem's beginning is that from a military standpoint a winner and a waster are by definition the same party. Only the winner can be a waster; a waster must necessarily have been the winner. It is patently ridiculous to stage a face-off between one army headed by Winner and another headed by Waster because you can't have two victors in a battle. So from the outset the poem is showing us something almost ridiculous about the idea of warfare: everyone *thinks* he will be the winner (and therefore also the waster) in a military conflict, but in fact there can only be one, and the other party will necessarily be the loser, and the wasted. The poem, that is, asks readers to consider the riskiness of engaging in battle at all when you know there is a good chance that you, and all the people fighting for you or with you, will be wasted.

With this not so lighthearted joke in mind, the poem's early decision to go to the Prince for a verdict seems much more markedly satirical, particularly given that, in the middle of the fourteenth century, England was engaged in war with France and was intermittently struggling with insurrections from Scotland as well. The chronic warfare that beset England (and much of Northern Europe) escalated and complicated the painfully entrenched ecosystemic disasters that were already going on: food distribution was complicated by war, labor availability was complicated by war, food rationing was complicated by war.[21] *Winner and Waster* is well aware of this dynamic, and it depicts that awareness in a proto-Shakespearean way: the trespass trial of Winner and Waster, set before a Prince, is a dramatic enactment of real-world economic problems, meant to catch the conscience of the Prince. And from there, I think, it is meant to make readers aware that their own real-life regent's constant warfare with France and with Scotland was laying waste to the people. Indeed, as William Jordan puts it, "The most deeply affected regions in rural society were those which suffered under the combined burdens of dense population, harvest shortfalls, murrains [animal die-offs], and war—especially war."[22] Put once again in the language of *Winner and Waster* itself, when many different ecosystemic pressures were "wryed over," or laid on top of each other, that was when life became untenable for people. And the staging of the trespass trial before the diegetic Prince on a field of battle makes that overlay uncomfortably clear.

This slyly "wryed over" subtext for the poem is given its fullest realization at the poem's end. The poem never comes to a clear verdict on waste, with the Prince deciding simply to send Winner to Rome and Waster to London, to continue to do their work unimpeded. As a result, the moral valence of "waste," either as an offense in real property or as an offense against one's own soul, and the efficacy of the Common Law and of penitential manuals in dealing with it, remains an open issue. Also wide open is the future of England's human labor force, since the Prince, presumably, remains on the battlefield with his own forces.

Open, that is, until William Langland composes *Piers Plowman*. *Piers* is keen to reexamine "waste" first by reenvisioning the poetics of waste that *Winner and Waster* devises through its allegorized trial scene and, second, by offering the explicit critique of the law that *Winner and Waster* stops just short of—a critique rooted in penitential treatments of waste.[23] Indeed, the first version of *Piers Plowman* picks up where *Winner and Waster* leaves off—both thematically and formally—by reimagining a trial scene of waste in far more ominous shades and by designing a personification allegory whose boundaries constantly shift and threaten to overwhelm any stable sense of what waste can mean, how it might be represented in a poem, or how human law or a fallible but well-meaning monarch might strive to curb it. And Langland, as we will see, confirms that any act of waste—be it material or energetic—hurts not only the waster's soul, but also the larger social world. And he doubles down on perhaps the most central theoretical insights that *Winner and Waster* contributes to the ecosystemic discourse of waste: showing waste to be a problem both economic and ecosystemic, and demonstrating that it is a problem of misspent time as well as of misspent material resources. For *Piers Plowman*, examining the connection between how we spend our time and how we use our land gives new insight into the second great ecosystemic cataclysm of the late English Middle Ages: famine.

CHAPTER FIVE

WASTERS AND WORKERS IN PIERS PLOWMAN

Famine and Food Insecurity

THE TRIAL OF WRONG

Like *Winner and Waster, Piers Plowman* begins its engagement with the problem of waste by staging a trespass trial of allegorical personifications.[1] Early in the poem a battered farmer named Peace appears before a King, demanding legal redress for injuries Wrong has done him. This scene revisits the opening scene of *Winner and Waster* but makes its status as a trespass suit much clearer: the "Peace" (the *pacem* of the trespass formula *contra pacem regis*) is violated and brings Wrong (an English translation of *transgressio*, the Latin term for trespass suits) to the King's court.[2] Peace accuses Wrong of nearly every type of trespass: he claims that Wrong has taken his wife, assaulted his maid, stolen his fowl and his horse, maintained a posse of men to attack Peace's men, broken down his barn, taken his wheat, and clobbered him over the head.[3] Barn breaking is a known form of waste in the Common Law. So, along with a host of other trespassory infractions, waste is onstage for us to contemplate.

Having established that Wrong is a wrongdoer qua trespasser, the poem urges readers to expect him to be punished: "Conscience and the King kneugh wel the sothe, / And wisten wel that Wrong was a shrewe euere" (Conscience and the King knew the truth well, / and they knew well that Wrong was always a shrew) (4, 153, 66–67). But at this point something shifts. Mede ("Payout") offers Peace "a presaunt al of pur golde" (a gift all of pure gold) (4, 155, 82), and Peace immediately drops the charges and prays the King to have mercy on Wrong: "[Pitousliche Pees thane] preyede to the Kinge / To haue mercy on that man that mysdede hym ofte" (Pitifully Peace then prayed to the King / to have mercy on that man that often did wrong by him) (4, 155, 85–86). Technically this exchange is appropriate: according to both the medieval English law of trespass and the practice of personification allegory, Mede does exactly what she should do, delivering payout, and Peace is correctly pacified by the act of paying damages.

But the poem registers a score that is not settled by this monetary compensation. As in *Winner and Waster*, so in *Piers Plowman*, the trial takes place before a royal judge. In *Winner and Waster* the Prince is ambivalent about how to assess waste. In *Piers* the royal judge isn't ambivalent at all; instead, he's furious at his lack of ability to inflict an outright punishment on Wrong—the waster in this scenario—for all his trespasses.

> "Nay," quath the King tho, "so God give me blisse,
> Wrong wendith not so awey er I wyte more.
> Lope he so lightly awey, laughen he wolde,
> And eft the boldere be to bete myn hewen.
> But Resoun haue reuthe on hym, he shal reste in my stokkis
> As longe as I lyue."

> ["No," said the King then, "as God gives me bliss,
> Wrong will not go hence thus before I know more.
> If he loped away so lightly, he would laugh
> And be ever the bolder to beat my servants.
> Unless Reason has pity on him, he shall remain in my stocks
> As long as I live."] (4, 155, 157, 91–96)

Apparently the King does not feel good about letting Wrong off the hook just because Mede offers a financial payout. Apparently trespass procedure does not seem adequate to the task of handling Wrong's misdeeds. As a result the King is of a mind to buck the law. But to no avail: despite this assertion that the King will put Wrong in the stocks, no further punishment ensues. Recognizing the limits of the King's power, Resoun laments that that "Mede hath maistrie to mote in this halle" (Payout has mastery to rule in this hall) (4, 161, 118), and Wrong gets away with it. Whereas the *Winner and Waster* poet deployed poetic devices for staging meditations on the nature of waste without decisively condemning either waste or the law that regulates it, Langland seems eager both to condemn waste—along with a host of other trespasses—and to show the impotence of human law to prevent or regulate it.[4] Waste happens, and when its legal remedy—payout—feels insufficient, no one can do anything further, not even the King. No one leaves the Mede scene satisfied—except maybe Wrong. The law is insufficient to handle waste—even when it follows its own protocols and procedures. Or perhaps *because* it follows its own protocols and procedures. *Piers Plowman* suggests in this scene that the emergence of trespass procedure has diluted the law's actual ability to crack down on trespassory behaviors, including waste.

The lack of satisfaction about the resolution of Wrong's trespass trial spills over into the next scene, when we find Conscience preaching to a field full of people. And in this scene the poem starts to focus its attention more squarely on waste—it starts to single out waste as a particularly troublesome behavior. Conscience decries a personification called "Wastour," who drains the shared economy of resources by his selfish consumption: "He bad Wastour go werche what he best couthe / And wynne that he wastide with sum maner crafte" (He bade Waster to go work at what he knew best / and win back what he spent through some kind of work) (4, 179, 24–25). He preaches against Waster's vice of self-indulgent consumption, but he associates that vice with a refusal to *work*, a refusal to produce: if one is going to consume or "waste," one must also earn that consumption by "wynning." Conscience picks up the logic and vocabulary of *Winner and Waster* and sides with Winner in suggesting that a person who only consumes is unequivocally a drain on the shared economy—a Wastour, deserving of censure. But Conscience goes further than Winner had gone, making it explicit that this shared economy hinges on the productivity and usage of the land as a fundamental shared resource belonging to all people. For Conscience, wasteful consumption is a symptom of a more sinister moral problem: the refusal to work the land for the collective good.[5] In his

86 : CHAPTER FIVE

emphasis on work, Conscience begins to draw together the worst of Waster's traits with the worst of Winner's: if we do not use our *time* well, as part of the agricultural labor force, we become wasters. He also expands the range of possible wasters to a much larger scale than we saw in *Winner and Waster*, to encompass essentially everyone. In *Winner and Waster* the primary focus was on how wealthy and powerful people—rich landholders like Winner and Waster—could affect the ecosystemic economy. In Conscience's speech—as in the Common Law of the thirteenth century—there is a recognition that waste can be committed by anyone, against anyone. Anyone who fails to work is a waster and is accountable to the rest of the community.[6]

TURNING TO SIN: GLUTTONY AND SLOTH

Soon thereafter the poem gives attention to wastefulness as a twin problem of consumption and hoarding—more fully integrating some of Waster's complaints against Winner into his poem. It now does so, however, in a decidedly nonlegal context. Once Conscience has condemned "Wastoure," the poem anchors its condemnation of wastefulness in penitential discourse. This shift into penitential discourse not only deepens the sense of what "waste" can mean in the poem, it also deepens the sense of how desperately inadequate the legal vocabulary of criminality is in accounting for or dealing with the socioeconomic and ecosystemic problems that waste poses. Waste, the poem recognizes, is not just a problem of land, money, or goods; it is a problem of misspent personal energy—just as Waster himself insisted it was at the end of *Winner and Waster*, and just as penitential manuals in medieval England insisted. How is trespass law supposed to wrangle that? How can the use of one's own time be criminalized?

Surely it cannot, so then waste seems to be more a problem for penitential discourse, or for sermons, than for the Common Law. A problem more for priests than for judges. Embodying that assumption, the poem presents a parade of personified sins—Pride, Envy, Lechery, Greed, Wrath, Gluttony, and Sloth—who march toward confession and try to show penitence. This passage figures waste as a sin rather than as a crime, and it focuses on two particular personified sins in that figuration: Glutton and Sloth. The poem shows a special interest in Glutton by depicting him, en route to confession, becoming distracted by the temptations of the tavern, relinquishing his resolve to repent, and succumbing to gluttony. In the scene that ensues, the reader witnesses Glutton gorging himself and drinking himself sick.

> Til Glotoun hadde ygulpid a galoun and a gille.
> He pisside a potel in a *Paternoster*-while . . .
> Whanne he drough to the dore, than dymmede hise eighen,
> He thrumblide on the thresshewold and threw to the erthe
>
> [Until Glutton has gulped a gallon and a sip.
> He pissed a puddle in the time it takes to say a Paternoster . . .
> When he drew to the door, his eyes dimmed,
> He stumbled on the threshold and puked on the ground.] (5, 227, 190–91 and 199–200)

By making this wasteful "Glutton" the only one of the seven sins we see "in action"—the other vices only describe their sinful behavior, while Glutton actually performs his own gluttony—Langland highlights Glutton as a particular source of ethical risk and trouble, representing him *in flagrante delicto*. This gruesomely performative representation of Glutton makes three contributions to *Piers*'s idea of wastefulness. First, it aligns gluttony with wastefulness explicitly through Glutton's overeating and excessive drinking—two kinds of consumption for which Conscience holds "Wastour" accountable in the previous scene of the poem. Glutton has not simply "wastide" or "consumed," he has disgustingly gorged himself—"gulping a gallon" at the local tavern. Gluttony, as a form of "wasting," is a practice of taking too much. This is something penitential writers well recognize; in fact, both *La somme* and the *Ayenbite* explicitly name the tavern as a location where waste is rife.[7]

Second, Langland represents the consequences of Glutton's overconsumption as horrifyingly effluvial—overflowing, shifting, uncontainable. After his binge drinking, Glutton "pisse[s] a pottel in a *Paternoster*-while"; that is, he pisses for the whole duration of a recitation of the Pater Noster prayer (5, 227, 191). He is introduced to us, then, as a figure whose excessive consumption results—immediately—in excessive by-product. Moreover, it is a by-product purged in a decidedly sacrilegious manner, being timed to the recitation of the Our Father. Glutton's excessiveness intensifies in his vomiting up what he has eaten: he has so grossly overeaten that his body rebels, creating waste matter from his wasteful consumption. In showing Glutton as an overeater and overdrinker who is also a generator of waste matter, Langland does something novel, recognizing that the inevitable and immediate side effects of overconsumption are dross, ordure, and effluvia. Wasters, by overconsumption, make waste—waste in the modern sense—though Langland does not call Glutton's dross "waste" by name.

The third key facet of Glutton's performance is how it paves the way for the appearance of the final sin—Sloth. In juxtaposing Glutton with Sloth, Langland suggests a relationship between excessive consuming and lazy, greedy hoarding. In his confession, Sloth vows he will "yelde ayen" (give back) what he has unfairly taken from other people, that he will give back "al that I wykkidly wan sithen I wyt hadde" (all that I wickedly won since I had sense) (5, 237, 229–30). In this phrase Langland casts Sloth much as Waster cast Winner: as someone whose greedy hoarding, which the poem refers to as winning ("al that I wikkidly wan"), has prevented equitable distribution of wealth. In this apposition of Glutton with Sloth, Langland's poem spatializes Waster's own paradoxical proclamation, toward the end of his demurrer: "whoso wele shal wynne / a wastour moste he finde" (whosoever wants to earn money, must find a spender). For *Winner and Waster*, there is no winning without wasting, and no wasting without winning. For *Piers Plowman*, "Sloth" is a dual concept, signifying not only the wicked "winning" that is invited into the poem by gluttonous bingeing (embodied in Glutton), but also by the refusal to work. This shimmering duality in Sloth's nature, that he is both a sinful hoarder *and* a lazy, underproducing slug, moves the poem toward its most crucial intervention into the discourse of waste. And toward its most horrifying rendering of contemporary fourteenth-century ecosystemic danger: famine.[8]

In the wake of Sloth's confession, *Piers* takes the unresolved socioeconomic paradox of *Winner and Waster*—that winning and wasting are two sides of the same antisocial coin—and resolves it in its investigation of a supervening ethical absolute: work. And specifically, agricultural work toward the production of food. Glutton consumes food and does not work to produce it; Sloth hoards and does not work. In *Piers* that refusal to labor is the archetypal and most dangerous form of waste. Overconsumption and hoarding are merely its surface manifestations, made possible, implicitly, by having too much time on one's hands and failing to recognize that that time belongs ultimately to a God who wants people to labor. And to the other people in one's community, whose lives depend on there being enough food to go around. Whose lives depend on the eradication of both gluttons—who overeat—and the slothful—who underproduce.

WASTE AND THE ARRIVAL OF HUNGER

But the poem comes around to its focus on famine slowly. Initially, in the cases of both Gluttony and Sloth, what is wasted by this refusal to work is time—echoing Waster's charges against Winner.[9] The stakes of time wasting, however, are felt not only in the fate of the soul—as they are in penitential discourse—but also, and perhaps more important, in the material world of production, consumption, and labor. For Langland as for Thomas Wimbledon, wasted time creates material shortage. The poem makes that dynamic plain when Piers the Plowman finally appears before the assembled "folk" and wishes to have his land worked by all present. This passage begins with Piers's articulation of the medieval social philosophy of the three estates, according to which medieval society is divided into workers, fighters, and clergy. He says to the Knight,

> I shal swynken and sweten and sowe for vs bothe
> And ek laboure for thi loue al my lif tyme,
> In couenaunt that thou kepe Holy Kirke and myselfe
> Fro wastours and fro wikkide men that wolde me destroye.

> [I shall work and sweat and sow grain for us both
> And also labor for your love all my life long,
> In covenant that you guard Holy Church and myself

From wasters and from wicked men that would destroy me.]
(7, 271 and 273, 27–30)

In this injunction to the Knight to fulfill his social obligation, Piers uses the term "wastours," a generalist plural noun, rather than the specific, singular personification "Wastour." This shift from singular proper noun to plural common noun indicates that now "wastours" encompasses a broad category of people. In Langland's view "waste" can be anyone's offense, and he underscores this by apposing "wastours" with "wikkede men," an amorphous category of evil people who would "destroye" him. Here Langland seems to understand "waste" as a catchall offense against a salvific and communal "work" that Piers wants his people to perform. Indeed, "working" the land is presented as the antidote to society's problems because it is incompatible with waste and its correlatives, gluttony and sloth.

This categorical description of "wastours" as people who refuse to work echoes back to the prologue of *Piers Plowman*, when Langland describes the fair field of folk:

> Summe putte hem to the plough, pleighede ful selde,
> In settyng and sowyng swonke ful harde,
> Wonne that thise wastours with glotonye destroiyeth.

> [Some men set themselves to the plow, played very seldom,
> In setting and sowing seed, they worked very hard,
> They earned what these wasters destroy with gluttony.] (Pr. 5, 20–23)

Thus the very beginning of the poem sets up a constellation of ideas that gains its fullest articulation only later:

> Ye ben wastours, I wot wel, and Treuthe wot the sothe;
> And I am his holde hyne and aughte hym to warne
> Whiche wastours in this world his werkmen distroyeth.
> Ye eten that hy shulde ete that eren for vs alle!

> [You are wasters, I know well, and Truth knows the truth;

And I am his dear servant and must warn him
Which wasters in this world destroy his workmen.
You eat what they should eat who work for us all!] (7, 285, 122–25)

A waster is not necessarily a devastater of land, nor is he necessarily
even a projectile-vomiting glutton. A waster is anyone who refuses to
labor for the good of the community. *Anyone.* Whereas Wimbledon
argued vociferously for the idea that the clergy's wasting of time and
material resources would have material consequences for their flocks,
and the Wycliffite translator insisted that waste by a secular ruler could
have consequences for the realm, both stopped short of saying outright
that *any* act of wastefulness—be it of spiritual or of material goods—
would have consequences for everyone else. For that assertion we need
Langland, building on the ecosystemic and legalistic thinking of the
Winner and Waster poet.

This idea that waste is committed when people refuse to work rather
than through any destructive act they might commit *vi et armis* or *contra pacem* is intimately linked to Langland's ongoing skepticism about
the power of the King's laws to successfully regulate waste, a skepticism
initially voiced during the trial of Wrong. Now Langland presents an
even more conspicuous failure of the law to regulate waste—embodied
in the Knight. As befits his station as keeper of laws and social order,
the Knight tells Wastour to "'abigge be the lawe, be the ordre that I
welde!'" ("obey the law, by the order that I wield!") (7, 289, 151). As
befits his wastefulness, Wastour replies slothfully, "'I was not wonid to
werche,' quath Wastour, 'now wile I not begynne!'" ("I am not accustomed to working," said Waster, "and I won't start now!") (7, 289, 152).[10]
Wastour's reply, both petulant and self-evident—naturally "Wastour"
would not be used to working and would no longer be "Wastour" if he
started now—signals, for the second time in the poem, that the King's
law is incapable of putting a stop to waste by compelling work.

There is a note of desperation here that resonates with contemporary ecosystemic anxiety: just as Langland wonders what is to be
done when the King fails or when the Knight fails or when the laws fail,
so twenty-first-century ecologically minded people wonder what we
can do when our own laws conspicuously fail. What do we do when

no regulatory power can stop the British Petroleum oil spill or when trash islands bigger than cities float anonymously in the sea? What do we do when giant clouds of methane spontaneously combust over the Siberian tundra? What do we do about the countless billions of plastic microbeads that circulate in the ocean, releasing chemicals and killing marine life? What do we do to urge people to consume less and thus cease to be "wasters"?

The first version of *Piers* has an answer, though a dark and paradoxical one: we embrace the ecosystemic disaster.[11] Specifically, we embrace famine. Once Piers realizes that no human law will move the "wastoures" to overcome their wicked ways and get to work producing food, he resorts to more desperate tactics. He invites Hunger to come to his aid: "'Awreke me of thise wastours,' quath Peris, 'that this world shendith!'" ("Avenge me on these wasters," said Piers, "that debase this world") (7, 291, 158–59). Hunger obliges Piers by eating everything in sight. Hunger's rapacious eating creates a famine, which makes all of Piers's people willing—even eager—to labor. This seems a good result, but of course there is a bizarre paradox. By inviting Hunger to create famine, Piers has fulfilled the logic of the act of waste—an overconsumption and underproduction that leads to shortage and privation. By inviting Hunger to aid him, Piers, the once and future hero of the poem, has brought about the consequences of waste itself: horrifyingly, he has realized the very situation he purported to fear, in which everyone would suffer through the act of one waster's overconsumption.

What is yet more horrifying than the idea that Piers would willingly and knowingly invite a waster like Hunger into his flock is what happens in the aftermath of that invitation. Seeing the suffering Hunger has wrought, "thanne hadde Piers pite, and preighede Hungir to wende / Hom into his owene erde and holde him there euere" (then Piers had pity, and prayed Hunger to go / home into his own yard and keep himself there forever) (7, 297, 186–87). But Hunger will not go home—he can't, because he is still, of course, hungry. Piers, a powerful figure throughout the poem, has no more power to stop Hunger's ravenous wasting than the Knight or the King had to stop the wastours. Finally, Piers's people are forced to give Hunger the best of their food and ale, until he falls asleep from gluttony: "Thanne was folk fayn, and fedde Hunger with the beste / With good ale and glotonye thei gart hym to slepe" (Then the people were eager, and fed Hunger with the best / with good ale and gluttony they sent him to sleep) (7, 311, 284– 85). Apparently and ironically, the wasteful Glutton itself becomes the cure for waste, by making Hunger sleep. But this cure is only temporary. As soon as Hunger is sated and asleep—and therefore as soon as, implicitly, the pressure of famine tapers off—Waster again refuses to work, and the cycle of wasteful consumption begins again: the people want only the best food, and they don't want to work for it. Seemingly *nothing* can enduringly keep earthly people from wasting: neither famine nor the laws of man. Langland's dire vision suggests that famine is inevitable—not even famine can prevent famine.[12]

In Langland's nightmarish vision, people can no more learn the lesson of moderate consumption than understand that productive labor is necessary and valuable. We are wasters to the core, unable to extricate ourselves from the cycle of overconsumption and underproduction and unable to find any authority—be it the law of man or the scourge of Hunger—strong enough to end that cycle. The hotly debated and irresoluble "crime" of *Winner and Waster* has become a particularly slippery and dangerous sin in *Piers Plowman*, by which mankind will destroy itself through a failure to recognize the continuum that exists between self and others, between energetic resources like time and material resources like land. If people consume with reckless abandon, refusing to work either for the good of the world or for the good of their souls, the world will be wasted—devastated, emptied out by Hunger and all that he signifies. This poem was written in the throes of an ongoing and crippling crisis of food insecurity; it bears the markings of that crisis, and it tries to make sense of that crisis by staging and exploring waste.

But here we have to pause, because Langland's "Hunger" is not an invention *de novo*. It is instead a provocative English rendering of a Latin word from the Vulgate: *Vastator*, the Waster. *Vastator* is the figure who appears as the agent of God's punitive and purgative wrath throughout the prophetic books of the Bible. *Vastator* is the one who wastes Moab, killing and consuming the people and lands (Isa. 16:4). *Vastator* will come like a lion, Jeremiah says, to devour false prophets and punish sinful peoples (Jer. 2:30). Later Jeremiah warns the daughters of his people to gird themselves and spread ashes over themselves because *Vastator* is coming against them (Jer. 6:26). Jeremiah also warns that God will bring devouring fury when wasters come (Jer. 12:12) and that he will bring the waster against the mothers of the youths even at midday (Jer. 15:8). There is no escaping *Vastator*; *Vastator* shows no leniency and no mercy, because *Vastator* comes at the behest of God to punish the wicked and take their people, goods, arms, and, especially, lands (Ezek. 39:10). Sounds a good bit like Langland's Hunger, especially if we take Piers Plowman himself, who invited Hunger to come, as a proxy for Jesus, as the poem itself urges us to do toward its apocalyptic end in later versions of the poem.

So the immediate question is this: Why, if Langland is fascinated by waste and obsessed with wasters, does he rename *Vastator* not Waster, but Hunger? One answer is that Langland wanted to focus his readers' attention not on the wasting itself that Hunger commits, but rather on its all too familiar ecosystemic result: shortage, famine, and starvation—hunger itself. The second is that Langland wanted to keep "waste" unambiguously negative in his poem. And Hunger, although arguably a bad guy, and very scary to boot, is still invited into the poem by Piers Plowman, the good guy par excellence of the entire poem. And Hunger, though a disaster ecosystemically and socially, serves the end of getting people to work, to participate in the economy of agricultural labor, at least for a time. In Langland's poem, then, Hunger cannot be collapsed or confused with Waster because wasters, for Langland, are associated with laziness, refusal to work, the wasting of time. Hunger is not lazy. Langland's Hunger is a workaholic taskmaster, constantly pressuring people to get into the fields and labor. Langland's Hunger is a new version of the Bible's *Vastator*, but Langland wants "waster" to have only and entirely a negative valence, so he renames his punitive, purgative figure in a way that would not have vitiated his message that waste and wasters are bad.

The last few parts of the first version of the poem (also called the A-text, and which I've focused on so far) entail the poetic narrator Will's quest to find "Do-well," a figure Will becomes interested in when Piers the Plowman seeks and receives a pardon for all the sins and wastefulnesses of mankind. The pardon reads, simply, "et qui bona egerunt, ibunt in vitam eternam; / qui vero mala, in ignem eternum" (he who does well, will go into eternal life; he who does ill, into eternal fire) (8, 344, 95–96). Following hard on the heels of Piers's earlier lessons about the importance of work in preventing famine, and then the importance of collaboration in ending famine, the lesson here strikes a reader as fairly simple: Do your work and you will find a place in heaven. Yet somehow Will, the poetic narrator, cannot or will not hear that message. So he ends the A-text of the poem in a desperate quest to find the figure Do-Well, turning what is obviously an action in the pardon ("bona egerunt") into a personified figure from whom one could potentially learn. In his quest, Will talks with Friars, who do not help him, and then with personified aspects of his own mind—Thought, Wit, and eventually Study. None of these interlocutors help him understand the message of Piers's pardon either. The A-text of the poem, then, ends in a kind of strange, epistemic paralysis: our protagonist, Will, cannot get himself to hear Piers's and the pardon's central message, which is simply that *work* is what saves us, both from eternal damnation and from earthly starvation. Work, a fairly straightforward, unmysterious, and mundane part of life, is what gets us eternal life and prolongs our earthly one. Work is the antidote to waste, which is the arch-sin and arch-crime of the A-text of the poem. But Will—whose name of course refers to William Langland *and*, in the allegorical framework of the poem, to readers' own willpower—doesn't get the memo. The A-text of the poem leaves us with the unsettling thought that we are all destined to be intractable wasters, precisely because of some failure in our will.

PIERS PLOWMAN, TAKES 2 AND 3

But that's not the end of the story. Langland wrote not only the A-text of his poem (1360s), which this chapter has focused on so far, but two additional versions—the B-text and C-text (1370s and ca. 1390). Both are approximately twice as long as A, and both aggressively revise earlier portions that do correspond with A. Despite Langland's apparent will to revise and re-revise his poem, his treatment of "waste" and his depiction of various "wastours" remain constant across all three versions. Both of the later versions include "wastours" as archvillains in their prologues; both include harsh excoriations of "Wastoure" by Piers himself during the plowing of the half acre. Both of the latter versions associate wastefulness with the sins of gluttony and sloth; both versions keep the representation of Glutton remarkably constant—even down to his pissing of the Pater Noster and his projectile vomiting. Both of the later versions include the ravagings of Hunger and Piers's inability to curb them. All three versions of Langland's poem, then, are dogged by fears of food insecurity, and all three understand that food insecurity to originate in "waste."

Despite this overall continuity of attention to waste across the three versions, Langland does make one important shift of emphasis. It is most obvious in how he amplifies the attention he gives to Sloth, whose description swells to larger proportions in B and gigantic proportions in C. This increased emphasis is symptomatic of a broader change in the later versions: as J. A. Burrow has shown, the later versions of the poem are increasingly obsessed with the ideas of wasting time and wasting words, perhaps indicating Langland's own increasing discomfort with the idea of spending his life as a poet rather than working more directly for the salvation of his own and others' souls.[13]

Langland's ratcheting up of his attention to the waste of time and words in the later versions is not limited to his concerns with the soul. As in the A-text, so in B and C, the poem focuses on the idea of misspent energetic resources (time, words) in conjunction with misspent material resources. This is made clearest in C, when Langland adds that one should "Ne spille speche ne tyme, ne myspende noyther / Meble ne vnmeble, mete nother drynke" (Waste neither speech nor time, nor misspend either / Nor movable nor unmovable wealth, neither meat nor drink) (C, 10, 381, 187–88). In this last version of his poem, then, Langland urges ever more decisively that energy and material goods are inextricable, and that wasting one must be thought of together with wasting the other. What happens in B and C, I suggest, is not limited to a greater anxiety about the soul, but extends to a greater awareness of how soul waste—embodied in the now overgrown Sloth—has negative consequences in the material resources by which a community sustains itself.

Although "waste" is not as prominent in the second half of the poem in B and C as it is in the first half (which corresponds with the A-text), this dynamic association between material waste and energetic waste, individual misconsumption and collective loss, returns to the fore at the very end of both B and C. Toward the end of both, Piers has returned to the plow but is blocked by Pride, along with an army bent on attacking Conscience and all the Christians with him. At this point Pride, who is accompanied by a "lord that lyueth after [lives according to] the lust of his body," announces that they will "wasten on welfare and on wikked kepynge / Al the world" (waste on their own happiness and on wicked hoarding / the whole world) (B, 19, 710, 355–57; cf. C, 22, 711, 354–56). Pride, the sin of inflated self-concept, threatens to annihilate the goods of the whole world in order to sate his and his lord's appetite to satisfy their "lust." Later, in the sins' ongoing assault on Piers and Conscience, Sloth appears with his army of corrupt priests. They pool their arrows, which take the form of sacrilegious oaths—paradigmatic instances of "wasteful speech"—and assault the Church of Unity, nearly bringing it down. At the very end of the siege, Pride and Sloth team up to make one final charge against Conscience and the Church of Unity. Seeing that he is powerless to defend the people against these sins, and seeing that the priests are unwilling to come to his aid, Conscience abdicates his position of rule and says he will become a pilgrim and go in search of Piers. At this point, with the Church of Unity abandoned by Conscience and left to the violent and predatory machinations of Pride and Sloth, Will wakes from his dream, and the poem ends. The B and C versions give more significance to Sloth early on in order to set up this final scene, in which Sloth joins with Pride—together embodying the wasteful refusal to work for the common good and the sense of the self as more important than the other—to destroy the Christian social world.

So by the end of a sprawling period of composition of the poem's three versions—a period that stretched from about 1362 to 1390—Langland has come to see the personal waste of one's own life, one's energy, one's attention, one's words, and one's actions as of great importance to the larger, more physical, more material socioeconomic problem of waste he had tackled in the first version of the poem. By the end of his career as a writer, then, Langland wants to emphasize that there is a continuum between material goods and immaterial ones, and between the self and the social world. For him waste becomes a kind of umbrella term, used to cover not just land and food resources, but also money, time, energy, and intention. *Winner and Waster* gestured toward this notion in Waster's condemnation of Winner as a time waster, but Langland goes further. He insists that refusing to work, laziness, overconsumption, and excess—though these may feel like personal actions that harm only oneself—are social misdeeds. The misuse of one's own life in sloth has consequences that reach far beyond the individual self.

Langland represents these continua between self and other and between energy and material goods through a crucial formal strategy that becomes more apparent in comparison with *Winner and Waster*. *Winner and Waster*, despite its constant "wryings over," remains a remarkably linear poem, a continuous scene of a single argument. By contrast, *Piers*'s vision of waste is episodic and fragmentary, distributed among several parts of the poem—and indeed among three different versions of the poem itself.[14] *Winner and Waster*'s narrative linearity tends to promote a gradual, steady accumulation of understandings of waste, so that each new nuance flows from the last one, via the poetic structure of Winner's legal and eventually penitential argument with Waster. By contrast, Langland's distribution of "waste" among separate parts of the poem creates a more disjointed mode of understanding: to grasp fully the socioethical import of the Hunger scene, one needs to recall the harsh condemnation of "wastours" earlier on. Then, to understand why Wastour gets so much attention from Conscience and Piers, one also needs to hold in mind the memory of Glutton and Sloth. The discontinuous logic of Langland's poem creates a different kind of meditation than exists in *Winner and Waster*, one far more unsettling. The poem enforces an interpretative unrest that keeps a reader in a state of heightened sensitivity to waste as a behavior that can come from any direction and be embodied by any character, be it Wastour, the wasters, Hunger, Glutton, Sloth, or Piers himself. This interpretive unrest, always eventually gratified by Langland's relentless looping back around to the inevitable truth that man destroys himself and his fellow man by overconsumption and underproduction, produces and constantly reaffirms the feeling of eerie futility that typifies Langland's poem and distinguishes it from *Winner and Waster*'s more exploratory and philosophical tone.

This feeling of futility suffuses the end of the later versions of the poem, as does the sense that waste triggers the coming collapse of the material and spiritual ecosystem in the poem. Toward the end of the B-text of the poem, Grace appears and makes Piers the Plowman steward of the lands and people. Grace gives Piers a team to till the earth with, a team consisting of the four Gospels. With these textual oxen, Piers is supposed to sow the seeds of virtue in the English earth. When Piers turns to the plow in earnest, with this mandate in mind, the poem reads, "Now is Piers to the plow" (B, 19, 708, 338). The deictic "now" reminds the reader that the present moment of the poem is contemporaneous with the moment of reading; "Piers" needs to get to the plow *now*, at all current present moments. The fields must be worked *now*, for the sake of everyone in England, or we will find ourselves back in a time of famine. But Pride will not abide that work; instead, Pride, again, urges his followers "to wasten on welfare and on wikkid kepynge / al the world in a while thorugh oure wit!" (to waste on their own happiness and on wicked hoarding / the whold world in a short time through our cleverness!) (B, 19, 710, 356–57). So toward the very end of the poem it is again wastefulness that threatens the delicate ecosystem of labor and moral virtue that Piers had tried to oversee and participate in. Piers fights back: "Right so Piers the Plowman peyneth hym to tilye / As wel for a wastour and wenches of the stewes / As for hymself and hise seruaunts, saue he is first yserued" (right so, Piers the Plowman pains himself to till / just as much for a waster and for brothel women / as for himself and his servants, though he will be served first) (B, 19, 714, 438–40). Piers's fundamental work, the work he does to stave off the coming ecosystemic apocalypse, in which all his people gather pathetically into the Barn of Unity, praying for spiritual and physical survival, is to work the land, even for the "wastours" themselves.

But in the end it becomes clear that Piers's compensatory labor will not suffice: Antichrist appears and chases everyone off the fields and into the Barn of Unity. Fascinatingly, the form Antichrist takes, as I mentioned earlier, is that of ecosystemic collapse. He, like Hunger, is a figure for famine. In particular, he's a soil spoiler. He overturns fields, he makes grains not grow, he sows rotten seed, he cuts back the branches of truth. He lays waste to the land, annihilating its current crops and reducing the odds that future crops will take hold. Individual human sloth—the wasting of time and energy—will bring the destruction of the land, the soil, the earth itself. There is no escaping ecosystemic collapse, it seems, if we are not willing to check our tendencies to let our own energies go to waste in sloth, moral turpitude, and selfishness. We cannot simply allow the Piers Plowmans of the world to labor for us; we must all show up, we must all fight against the coming of Antichrist, who is here an agricultural and ecosystemic force of destruction. He is an angry waster, come to punish a lazy, faithless, godless people by showing them that their bad faith will translate into bad harvests and mass starvation. Put otherwise, Antichrist is the famine that will not end, the Waster to end all wasting, the *vastator vastatorum*.

So the question is raised again: Why, if Langland is evoking a biblical *vastator*, does he not call that figure Waster? As with Hunger, so with Antichrist, Langland is not interested in calling a biblical destruction "wasting," because he is not interested in assigning the responsibility for the social ill he sees as "waste" to God or to the Antichrist. Hunger is its own entity, even though it does exactly what *Vastator* does in the Bible. By remaking *Vastator* now as Antichrist, Langland shows he is interested in how people initiate the cycle of punishment by their own wasting. He wants wasting to be something only people do, something they do primarily by refusing to work and by overconsuming resources. We are the wasters. Antichrist simply comes to punish us for our wastefulness.

And specifically, he wants waste to be something people commit by refusing to work *the land*. Langland is very sensitized—possibly due to his exposure to *Winner and Waster*—to the idea that the land is the ultimate referent of any act of waste, the ultimate end of wasteful behaviors, whether they take place in the land directly, in the tavern, in words, or in thoughts. The ecosystem he cares most about is the one that conjoins individual souls with community, through an ethos of labor, and that ecosystem is the agricultural land of late medieval England. Waste is agricultural for Langland because its result—famine—is agricultural.

For Langland, as for the poet of *Winner and Waster*, literary forms and poetic devices show several interrelated things about waste. First, they show how waste triggers ecosystemic crises. Second, they show

how those crises are, at their roots, economic. Third, they show that waste is a behavior that is always both material and spiritual, personal and social, overuse and underuse.[15] Waste is the arch-sin and the arch-crime of the interimplicated ecological world because it affects people, lands, resources, and labor markets. These ideas, taken together, are slightly beyond the reach of any single nonpoetic genre of writing— the common law of property, trespass litigation, penitential manuals, sermons. But in poetry they surge forth, availing themselves precisely of poetry's own capacity for nonlinear thought, for "wrying over," for overlay, for accretion.

So far in Middle English poetry of the fourteenth century, "waste" has become a keyword for articulating a broadly based ecosystemic and economic misdeed. By braiding together legal ideas of waste with penitential ones, late medieval poetry uses "waste" to understand the radical interimplication of people with each other, of land with money, of material resources with immaterial ones. "Waste" comes to signal a mismanagement of resources by one party that has far-reaching and potentially devastating consequences for another party, or sometimes for a whole society. Poetic "waste" highlights the ecosystemic entanglement of all people, their land, their goods, their bodies, and their souls. In *Winner and Waster* the ecosystemic imperilment of primary concern is the loss of land. In *Piers Plowman*, it is the lack of food. In both poems, being a Waster is primarily a problem in a rural, agricultural context.

The next chapter will explore how these ideas arise again in even starker and more horrifying terms in one of Chaucer's greatest and least-read poems from the *Canterbury Tales*—the tale of the Canon's Yeoman. But there, rather than being centered in an agricultural landscape, waste will become decisively urban.

CHAPTER SIX

CHAUCER'S YEOMAN'S WASTING BODY

Pollution and Contagion

By the end of the fourteenth century when Geoffrey Chaucer is stitching together the *Canterbury Tales*, this idea that waste is an ecosystemic behavior with consequences in both spiritual and material realms has gained a great deal of cultural traction, and Chaucer—ever a skilled interpreter of culture—sees that clearly. In *The Pardoner's Tale*, for instance, when the Pardoner warns against the sins of the tavern, he mentions how dangerous games of chance are, saying that they cause, "wast also / of catel and of tyme" (waste of both chattel and time) (594), as if that possibility of dually wasting material and immaterial resources is completely self-evident and unproblematic. Later, in *The Parson's Tale*, the Parson decries "wast of goodes, mysspendynge of tyme" (794) (waste of goods, misspending of time), again associating the loss of material goods with the misuse of time—just as had Thomas Wimbledon, the poet of *Winner and Waster,* and William Langland.

This emphasis on waste as something you can do to material as well as immaterial resources is given social consequences when Chaucer notes that one person's wasting of material goods inevitably has consequences for other people. *The Merchant's Tale* expresses fear about bad wives, including the fear that they might be "wastour[s] of thy good" (1535), where "thy" refers to fleeced husbands. In yet starker terms, *The Tale of Melibee* tells us that goods we acquire must be used in good measure, since people who "folily wasten and despenden the goodes that they han" (foolishly waste and misspend the goods they have) until they run clean out of such goods will ultimately steal the goods of another (1607). On the surface misusing one's *own* goods may not seem like a social problem, but it decisively is—just as it was for the poet of *Winner and Waster* and for Langland. For Chaucer waste is physical, monetary, temporal, and spiritual; its consequences are personal and social. Waste is ecosystemic misconduct par excellence, and, as for Langland and the *Winner and Waster* poet, that ecosystemic misconduct is also inescapably economic.

But Chaucer does something extraordinarily sophisticated with this conjunction of ideas. He embodies it not in an allegorical personification named "Waster," but in a human character—his strange pilgrimage gate crasher, the Canon's Yeoman.[1] In the Yeoman Chaucer devises a character who is cursed with a painfully and acutely ecosystemic body. A "wasting body," actually. By "wasting body" I mean an individual human body that is wasted by, and also wastes, the physical, material, and even chemical microclimates in which it lives and works. Conversely, by "wasting body" I also mean to invoke the idea of a body, a human body, as part of a larger ecosystem that in turn affects and determines the physical, spiritual, and economic well-being of other persons and creatures through its wasteful and wasting participation in the labor economy. The Yeoman, albeit in a very weird way, is Chaucer's ultimate worker and also his ultimate waster—a harrowing figure to someone like Langland, since for Chaucer the work is itself what becomes wasteful rather than what remedies the waste. Chaucer, then, uses the Yeoman to show a downside to work, or at least to remind us that wrong-headed labor is in fact worse than no labor at all for the ecosystems we live in and for our ability to live in them together, as a community.

The Yeoman is an alchemist, or rather an alchemist-in-training. He spends his days slaving away, working all the time, labor, labor, labor—ostensibly what Langland thinks everyone should be doing to save the ecosystem from waste, whether that waste is figured as Waster, or as Hunger, or as Antichrist. But there is a key difference between Langland's vision of assiduous labor and Chaucer's vision. The Yeoman is helping his boss, the Canon, try to transmute various base metals (mercury, lead) into purer, more valuable metals (silver, gold). So, part of what makes the Yeoman special is that his ecosystem is not agricultural but urban, industrial, and elemental. For him work is not about agriculture, as it is in *Piers Plowman* and *Winner and Waster*. Instead, his work is about rocks, metals, glass, sand, oxides, and salt; it is about cooling and heating processes, purgations and contaminants, distillations and filtrations. And, as we will see, his body will be constituted and compromised by these things. The Yeoman's wasting body will make literal and concrete all the ideas of late medieval English ecological thought—ideas about vulnerability, ideas about work, ideas about the penetration of the self by the environment and the damage a single person can do to a larger ecosystemic whole. Through his elemental, earthly, urban understanding of the ecosystem he belongs to, however, the Yeoman's character takes the idea and ecosystemic consequences of waste to a new and terrifying verge. For Chaucer, the Yeoman is the ultimate waster, not because he fails to work, but because he works wrongly.

In his depiction of his Yeoman-alchemist, Chaucer uses "waste" to draw together some ideas of ecosystemic and economic interimplication and precarity that I introduced in my first chapter but that haven't been worked over much in the intervening chapters. Namely, the Yeoman's body becomes a site at which to think about contagion and pollution and about how those two things work together, first within a single human body, and thence as a kind of creeping, oozing menace to society at large. The Yeoman is Chaucer's primary reckoning with the trauma of the plague years as well as with urban decay and pollution in the late fourteenth century. The Yeoman, as we will see, is a waster on a grand scale, though he never sets foot on a farm, on a field of battle, or in a forest. The kind of wasting processes he embodies are new, quick, and merciless, and they can be triggered by a single person acting badly. In that sense the Yeoman embodies the kind of worrying that the penitential works did about waste—the waste of his own body and mind well and truly has wasting effects on everyone around him. But he's a city boy, so everything works just a little differently.

THE YEOMAN'S WASTING BODY I: POLLUTION

When the Yeoman appears, he's riding full tilt with his boss—the Canon—to catch up with the other Canterbury pilgrims as they pass by a town. There is a distinct sense, as the Yeoman and the Canon race up, that they are running from something. And then, as the Canon becomes visible, it becomes clear something is physically wrong with him. He's sweating like a pig, so much that he's packed his hood with burdock leaves, though this absorbent packing doesn't come close to soaking up all the moisture he exudes. The narrating Chaucer pilgrim tells us that his forehead "dropped as a stillatorie" (580), or dripped like a distilling vessel. The simile Chaucer uses here—comparing the sweat to the moisture that drips from a still—hints not only that the Canon is an alchemist, but also that Chaucer will showcase the vulnerability of a body to its environment in a way that includes its technological and urban surroundings.

The Yeoman is also sweating profusely, as are his and the Canon's horses. The Host of the pilgrimage, Harry Bailly, notices, and he says to the Yeoman, "Why artow so discoloured of thy face?" (Why are you so discolored in your face?) The Yeoman replies, "I am so used in the fyr to blowe / That it hath chaunged my colour, I trowe" (I am so accustomed to blowing into the fire that is has changed my color, I think) (664, 666–67). The logic here seems straightforward: the Yeoman's participation in alchemy has transformed him physically; his constant blowing into the fire has altered his complexion. His work has wasted him.

But if the logic seems straightforward, the grammar does not: the phrase, "I am so used in the fyr," before it's filled out by "to blowe" makes the Yeoman both the subject and object of a passive construction governed by the verb "used." *He* is used in the fire—himself, his own body is used—for a brief second, before the syntax of the next line changes the sentence's meaning. For that glimmering second, the Yeoman's body turns into one of the raw materials of alchemy rather than the agent that does the alchemy. He is wasted by the work because he is implicated in it physically. He is a waster first because he wastes himself.

Then later, when he goes on to elaborate just *how* he has been changed, the Yeoman's vocabulary becomes more specific to the material nature of alchemy, his depiction of his body more grossly material. He says, "And wher my colour was bothe fressh and reed / Now is it wan and of a leden hewe" (And where my color was both fresh and red, now it is pale and of a leaden hue) (727–28). Now we find out that the Yeoman's complexion has been transformed from sanguine and ruddy to "leaden." That is, as he has steadily worked on lead to convert it into gold, the lead itself seems somehow to have infected him, to have polluted him, to have converted him from his pure, living natural state into an elemental, dehumanized, debased state. In his view, his constant working with base metals has made him baser in that it has shifted the balance of his bodily elements toward what's base. The stuff of his industry has used him, has become the stuff of his body. He is not just sweating like a still, he *is* the still, only the distillation seems to be working backward, converting his golden self to lead, rather than lead to gold.[2] He is an alchemical cyborg, wasted by his own labor.

Through the Yeoman, Chaucer asserts that the materials one surrounds oneself with penetrate and reconstitute one's physical body. He asserts that the human body is *not* a separate, independent, isolated island, immune and invulnerable to the world around it; it is instead utterly penetrable by, and even coterminous with, the material environment in which it is situated. It is not, that is, the sheer fact of the Yeoman's hard labor—his blowing into the fire—that changed his complexion. It's the nature of the materials he's working on polluting his body. There is no hard boundary between self and elements. Instead there is a porousness of the human body that Chaucer wants us to perceive through the Yeoman, a fundamental vulnerability to whatever we work with, whatever we touch. The Yeoman's tale offers, in part, a parable about the lack of integrity, the permeability, the radical vulnerability of the human body to infection by its environment—in this case, a proto-industrial environment. This conceptual parable poses a challenge to the complex proto-ecological philosophy that surrounds "waste" in other poems and discourses: there, wasting is always something a person does, whether to land and its resources or to the soul and its resources. Here wasting is something the environment does *to you.*

THE YEOMAN'S WASTING BODY II:
CONTAGION

And not just you individually, but you as a social being. In fact, as the Yeoman's narrative rolls on, he specifically associates alchemical participation with "infection." He says that alchemists can be recognized because their bodies have begun to smell like brimstone, one of their alchemical ingredients. In fact, he says, "For al the world they stynken as a goot; / Hir savour is so rammyssh and so hoot / That though a man from hem a mile be, / The savour wole infecte hym, trusteth me" (For all the world, they stink like goats; their scent is so rammish and so hot, that even if a man were a mile away, the scent would infect him, trust me) (886–89). The corruption of the human body by alchemical brimstone causes that body to stink; that stink then goes rogue, extending the corruptive powers of alchemy and its ingredients a full mile in every direction beyond the actual body of the alchemist, seeping into other people. This goatish, diabolical reek of brimstone not only will be smelled by other people as an annoyance, it will *infect* other people like an illness, like a plague. The Yeoman goes on to repeat that language of infection, saying that alchemists "wolde infecte al a toun" (will infect a whole town) (973) with their alchemical desires and ways. This assertion complicates the Yeoman's demonstration of his own physiological vulnerability to environmental contamination by insisting that that contamination is not just a form of pollution, but a form of pollution that morphs into contagion: once one person has become infected with alchemy, everyone else in the town becomes vulnerable, even though that town might be as great as Nineveh, Rome, Alexandria, or Troy (974–75). The Yeoman's understanding is that alchemy pollutes not only the individual body but also, by a kind of plaguelike contagion, the body politic. All it takes is one alchemist, one polluter, to bring a whole social world to a state of degradation and sickness. The alchemist's precarious susceptibility to his chemical environment creates a precarity for the polis.

This logic chimes with what medieval people knew about plague transmission. As historian Rosemary Horrox notes, medieval scientists believed that "the physical cause of plague was the corruption of the air—or, rather, since air was an element and could not change its substance—the mixing of air with corrupt or poisonous vapours, which when inhaled would have a detrimental effect on the human body. . . . Naturally enough, suspicion was extended to anything which smelt unpleasant—such as slaughter houses or the processes of the tanning industry."[3] Or, one imagines, the processes of alchemy, with its burning of sulfur and other odoriferous materials. Indeed, I'll argue that when Chaucer talks about the stink of alchemy infecting a town, he's processing the social trauma of the plague. And he leverages a cultural bias, one that Horrox gestures toward: medieval people associated urban, industrial work with plague. In the minds of medieval people it was the tanneries and slaughterhouses that helped transmit plague. And, according to Chaucer, it was also the alchemists' workshops. Your work is part of how you participate in your ecosystem; if your work is corrupt, you corrupt your body and the bodies of others. Work wastes the worker; work wastes resources; work wastes the social world it happens in.

But what kind of social world is it?

Whereas waste in poems like *Piers Plowman* and *Winner and Waster* primarily has its consequences in the countryside, waste in *The Yeoman's Tale* will be clearly marked out as an urban phenomenon—much like plague.[4] It spreads across a whole town, be it as large as the great cities of world history. *The Yeoman's Tale* makes us contemplate the possibility that waste—originally a local crime committed in real property—is now a far more diffuse thing. Land doesn't come into this poem at all except in the lists of ingredients the Yeoman spools out. There is no anxiety about a reduction of available farmland such as preoccupies *Winner and Waster*. There is no worry that Antichrist will come and overturn the soil, or that Hunger will come and waste the lands and their crops. Chaucer's Yeoman takes the earlier poetic worrying about waste and points out that the wasting of time, energy, and money doesn't even *need* to have consequences in the physical land to be a catastrophic social problem. All it has to do is trigger plague, the greatest *Vastator* of Chaucer's lifetime, or indeed ten lifetimes on either side of him. Waste, Chaucer seems to be warning us through the Yeoman, is no longer just a problem for plowmen. It isn't just a problem of real estate and its appurtenances. It's a problem of how the usage of one's own body and material resources can waste an entire city. Although he does not say it outright, Chaucer suggests that alchemy itself—or perhaps the greed that motivates its practice—has the potential to be the wasting plague par excellence of a modern, urban social world.

THE YEOMAN'S WASTING BODY III:
BAD MEDICINE

So where does "waste" per se come into the Yeoman's thinking? Having established that the dangers of alchemical pollution extend beyond individual bodies to encompass social bodies like cities, the Yeoman gets yet more precise about exactly how the material, physical, and environmental toxins of alchemy affect and infect the human body. He says, "For reednesse have I noon, right wel I knowe, / In my visage; for fumes diverse / Of metals, whiche ye han herd me reherce, / Consumed and wasted han my reednesse" (For ruddiness I have none of, I know perfectly well, / in my face, for the diverse fumes / of metals, which you have heard me before rehearse, / have consumed and wasted my ruddiness) (1097–1100). The Yeoman understands his physical decay and pollution as resulting from the fumes of alchemical chemistry entering into his lungs and *consuming and wasting* his redness. In Middle English the words "consuming" and "wasting" are very similar in meaning, and they're frequently used together in another discursive context— one intimately related to what's happening with the Yeoman, and that helps further ground the metaphoric yoking together of alchemy and plague. Or of contamination and contagion.

That other discursive context is medical. In medieval English medical manuals, "wasting" is frequently juxtaposed with other Middle English terms that signal consumption, terms like "boiling off"; the idea behind these passages is that fluid is boiled off and evaporated— literally consumed or eaten up by heat or fire. (This association of wasting with eating and consuming is present in Latin texts as well—*vastare* is often collocated with *consumere*.) In this sense wasting is often a desirable process, a process of purification, fortification, or distillation, in which a medicine or tonic is made stronger, more concentrated.

In John Arderne's *Treatise on Fistula in Ano*, he recommends the following recipe for an anti-itching ointment: "Agayn greuous ychyng and vnsuffrable in the lure take the iuyse of celydome, of moleyne, ana, hony scomyd als mych as of the iuysez, and boile tham togidre to the wastyng of the iuysez; after sette it downe fro the fyre and kepe to vse" (Against grievous and intolerable itching in the anus, take the juice of the celandine, of mullein, in the same amount, honey skimmed as much as of the juice, and boil them together to the *wasting of the juices*; afterward, take it off the fire and keep it for use).[5] Later Arderne notes that a mixture of honey and honeysuckle can be boiled together to "waste" the liquid. The resulting ointment can be used for various sores and ulcerations.[6] The wasting process in these instances is a process of strengthening, purification, and tonification.

But "wasting" in medical treatises can also be toxic. It can also mean that tissue or blood is consumed or rotted away by some disease. Arderne discusses how bodily tissues can be *wasted* by rotting processes, creating holes and abscesses in the flesh.[7] The Middle English translation of Lanfrank's *Science of Surgery* notes that tissues can be wasted so as to decrease their sensitivity and to weaken them. Lanfrank also insists that imbalances in the humors can result from excessive heat wasting the liquid elements of the blood, and that this wasting of blood can be highly detrimental to health. The *Science of Surgery* further specifies that when any humor is badly wasted, or diminished in liquid volume, as by a drying or overheating process, the wasted or evaporated humor should be replenished in some way, to restore balance to the body.[8] In this sense the wasting of blood or other humors is not a purification or fortification, but rather a degradation, a diminishment of life, a mortification of the flesh in a literal and not at all purgative or healing sense. Disease wastes us; plague wastes us.

And in *The Yeoman's Tale* alchemy—which ironically shares many of the processes and procedures of making medicine—wastes us. For the Yeoman's own body, alchemical pollution seems to work by this kind of wasting action; it is an acceleration of death rather than a turn toward healing, wholeness, and the preservation of life. The fumes of alchemy, designed of course to purify lead into gold, corrupt and mortify the body by evaporating its sanguine humors, wasting the Yeoman's vital energy and sapping his humanity. Moreover, in this context of detrimental bodily wasting, the Yeoman's, the Canon's, and even their horses' profuse sweating begin to appear in a far more sinister light: sure, they are sweating because they've all been running, but there also is a sense that this wasting or boiling off of water in the body by excessive sweating—rather than constituting some kind of beneficial purgation—signals rot, corruption, sickness, weakness, and the turn of the human body from the proverbial gold of health to something akin to mortified lead. Existing in an alchemical environment is anti-medicinal; alchemy itself is cast as a wasting sickness. As we will see, it is a wasting sickness that starts in social interaction, travels to the brain and then infects the whole person before moving on to contaminate new social groups. It's catching, like plague. The Canon had it, then exposed the Yeoman to its ingredients and procedures so that he then caught the bug. And, as readers, by our prurient interest in whether and how alchemy is going to work in the Yeoman's tale, we catch it too. Because it's *very* catching; alchemy is not just a plague on material resources, but also a plague on our attention, our minds, our words, our behaviors, and of course our bodies. It's so catching, it can even spread between species.

THE YEOMAN'S WASTING BODY IV: INTERSPECIES CONTACT

Returning for a moment to the frame of the tale, let's think a little more fully about what it means that the *horse* is sweating too. Obviously the immediate reason the horse is sweating is that it's been running. But the association that the tale makes between the Canon's and Yeoman's sweat and the horse's invites us to consider the possibility that the horse is somehow drawn into the wasting dynamics of alchemy as well. The association between human and animal sweating invites us to consider that the material toxins of alchemy might affect not only the individual bodies of humans and the human social world, but the animal world as well.[9] The tale, that is, invites us to consider that alchemical pollution might pose an ecosystemic danger that is not specific to humans, but instead embraces a larger slice of the natural world, affecting at a minimum those animals that come into physical contact with alchemically polluted humans. The wasting sickness that is alchemy is an interspecies sickness; thinking back to the plague-era materials that assert that plague could easily be passed to pigs, it's no surprise that Chaucer allows the Yeoman's alchemical plague to pass to horses. Thus the explicit "wasting" of the Yeoman's own humors becomes a lexical lightning rod for the tale's broader anxieties about how the ecosystemic precarity of a single human body has consequences for the social fabric and even the animal world. Just as I've argued it does in the discourse of property law, so in Chaucer's medically inflected discourse of alchemy, "wasting" conveys the capacity of one agent, through ecosystemic misconduct or misuse, to endanger or damage another agent—now, be it human or animal.

So what the Canon's Yeoman's performance contributes to an emergent discourse of ecosystemic precarity is, first, the material resources we work with can infiltrate, pollute, and infect our bodies, making us into de facto cyborgs who incorporate and are eventually remade by the materials of our industry. Second, this antimedicinal transformation of the sanguine, healthy body into a leaden, industrial one is socially contagious—alchemy can "infecte" a whole town. Thus "waste" is no longer just a problem for fields and souls. Third, the ruination of the body—its wasting away—spills over not only into the broader urban world, but also into the animal world. The alchemical subjects spread their wasting sickness even to their horses. The Canon's Yeoman's weird little tale shows us that there exists in the late Middle Ages a strain of thought in which individual bodies participate in a nexus of human subjects, animals, and material objects and chemicals. They participate in that nexus in part through their work—specifically, through industrial, urban labor. Wasting bodies are ecosystemic bodies not only in the sense that they are shaped and reshaped by their environments, but also in that they themselves are part of the environment that other people and animals are also constrained or condemned to participate in. Alchemy is cast as another plague, sparing no one who comes near it, corrupting their bodies, sending them into paroxysms of fever and destroying their blood, and triggering an infection among an entire urban populace—people and animals alike.

Of course, however, there are differences between the Black Death and the plague of alchemy. First, Black Death is a catastrophic biological scourge that kills millions of people, whereas alchemy is, initially, a mental scourge that, in Chaucer's telling, becomes a physical and social scourge that doesn't so much kill people as make them sick and poor. Second, and related, the plague of alchemy is largely economic in both its origins and its consequences. People would not mess with alchemy if they weren't interested in sudden, unearned economic gain. Alchemy is the protocapitalist venture par excellence: you take something nearly valueless (lead) and change it into the most valuable thing anyone could lay hands on (gold). That change happens in an instant, through the intellectual ingenuity and manual dexterity of the alchemist himself. Medieval alchemists were the aspiring tech startup wunderkinder of the fourteenth century. They were the ones who wanted to make it big through technology, arcane knowledge, and homespun brilliance. And Chaucer is saying that that kind of ambition, that kind of greed, that kind of gambling on the sudden creation of extreme wealth hurts *everyone*. It's waste, after all, so by the emergent definition of waste in this period, it's never just one person's problem.

THE YEOMAN'S WASTING WORDS

All of this thought about and staging of waste and wasting bespeaks Chaucer's profound and complex understanding of ecosystemic precarity and ecosystemic interimplication. But things get *really* interesting in how Chaucer registers his concerns about ecological subjectivity and environmental interimplication through his poetic form. Or rather through the poetic form and deformations that the Canon's Yeoman spools out, primarily in his notorious listing of alchemical ingredients and processes. The reason I find the poetry so interesting is that Chaucer's endgame in this tale is to see whether he really can export the wasting sickness of alchemy to his readers. How catching can he make it? The answer again, I think, is *very* catching, through the way the sounds of the poetry hit the ear, affect the eye, and drill their way into the brain as one reads.

Before I get into the metrics of the Yeoman's lists, however, a quick review of what we know (or think we know) about Middle English metrical practice, and about Chaucer's late-career rhymed-couplet lines in particular. Although they look very much like iambic pentameter, Chaucer's rhymed couplets in the *Canterbury Tales* are better understood simply as five-stress lines that conform to an accentual-syllabic pattern. In practice this means that a typical Chaucerian rhymed-couplet line should contain five stresses. It will very frequently also have five unstressed syllables, very closely resembling what will be the Early Modern iambic pentameter line. Chaucerians usually refer to this as the Chaucerian "hendecasyllabic line," and they treat that line form as the goal state for Chaucer's late-career couplets—so, for most of the *Canterbury Tales*.[10] But the five-stress Chaucerian line will also often have a less regular number of unstressed syllables; as a result, you can have lines of more or fewer than ten syllables so long as there are five stresses. So what counts as "normal" for a Chaucerian line, as Halle and Keyser demonstrated in the 1960s, is the number of stresses it contains, not the overall number of syllables or a precisely regular alternation between stressed and unstressed syllables.[11] As Jill Mann puts it, "The line may thus have nine syllables or eleven, instead of the more usual ten. But what it *cannot* dispense with is the five stresses that give it its shape and its dynamism."[12] Interestingly, *The Yeoman's Tale*, as we will see, often dispenses with the five-stress rule—far more often than any other tale from the *Canterbury Tales*. One could view this as evidence that the tale is not Chaucerian. I view it as evidence that it was in this late, weird tale that Chaucer bent his established five-stress form to the outer limits of its flexibility, and that he did so for a specific—and ecosystemic—reason.

To convey the sonic, rhythmic, and conceptual effects I believe each of the Yeoman's lists would have had to a medieval audience, I will include each in its entirety, then analyze it. From readers who might skip over a passage of fairly technical metrical analysis, I ask your indulgence, because this poetry is some of the most virtuosic of Chaucer's career, despite many Chaucer scholars' tendencies to dismiss the tale whole cloth as a scribal production.[13] So, first, the Yeoman is about to volunteer the names and quantities of ingredients—the tools of his industry—that go into an alchemical procedure. He begins with an expression of futility, "What sholde I tellen ech proporcion" (What should I tell of each proportion) (754), but then he proceeds with the obsessiveness of an addict:

Of silver, or som oother quantitee—
and bisye me to telle you the names

of orpyment, brent bones, iren squames
That into poudre grounden been ful smal;
and in an erthen pot how put is al,
and salt yput in, and also papeer,
Biforn thise poudres that I speke of heer;
And wel ycovered with a lampe of glas;
and of muche oother thyng which that ther was;
And of the pot and glasses enlutyng,
That of the eyr myghte passe out nothyng;
And of the esy fir, and smart also,
Which that was maad, and of the care and wo
that we hadde in oure matires sublymyng,
And in amalgamyng and calcenyng
of quyksilver, yclept mercurie crude?
For all oure sleightes we kan nat conclude.
Oure orpyment and sublimed mercurie,
Oure grounden litarge eek on the porfurie,
of ech of thise of ounces a certeyn—
Noght helpeth us, oure labour is in veyn.

[What should I tell of each proportion
of silver, or some other quantity
and busy myself to tell you all the names
of brimstone, burned bones, or iron filings
that are finely ground into powder
and how it's all put into an earthen pot
and salt is put in, and also paper,
before these powders I just spoke of;
and it's all covered up with a glass bell;
and of the many other things that were in there
and of the pot and the sealing of the glasses,
so that none of the air could pass through,
and of the gentle fire, and the sharp as well,
which was made, and of the care and woe
that we had in the cooking of our materials,
and in amalgamating and calcifying

quicksilver, called raw mercury?
For all our tricks, we can't conclude [i.e., we can't perform alchemy]
Our brimstone and sublimed mercury,
Our ground litharge, and on the porphyry,
Of each of these things, a certain number of ounces—
Nothing helps us; our labor is in vain.] (756–77)

Several elements, so to speak, are of note here. First, the specific ingredients and tools of alchemy listed are derived directly from the earth: iron, earth itself, mercury, brimstone, salt, glass, litharge, porphyry, and orpiment. In making this list the Yeoman demonstrates the perhaps counterintuitive reality that the materials of alchemy are not otherworldly or magical. Instead, they are of the earth; they are what we would now call "natural." Alchemy isn't so much a mystical or magical discipline as an acutely earthly one. Second, all of these natural ingredients, slapped together in a rather haphazard order syntactically (in that it's often hard, in this passage, to figure out grammatical relations between words), and heaped up to abundance sonically and lexically, work to create a feeling, a sonic impression, of excess, of a certain linguistic burden, or overuse. Third, as though struggling to contain the lexical profusion of the passage, the rhythm and meter of this passage is likewise overworked, overused, overburdened. Fourth, this surplus of earthly ingredients and procedures, combined with this aesthetic of overuse that comes through in the rhythm, is capped off by the Yeoman's defeated claim "oure laboure is in veyn." Their alchemical labor, that is, is *wasted*—it goes to waste, it is underproductive, underused, used in vain—even as the verse form itself produces a kind of wasteful excess, an overuse of terminology, a wasting of syntax.

The Yeoman's second list of alchemical ingredients and procedures strains not just his syntax and lexicon, but also and more urgently his meter and rhythm. To see how, it's important to remember that Chaucer's preferred verse form at the *Canterbury Tales* phase of his writerly career is the five-stress line, in rhymed couplets. The number of hypo- and hypermetrical lines in his late rhymed-couplet corpus is very, very small—there are a few here and there in the entire *Canterbury Tales*.

But as we'll see, many of them cluster in the Canon's Yeoman's performance. So here's that second list.

> As boole armonyak, verdegrees, boras,
> And sondry vessels maad of erthe and glas,
> Oure urynales and oure descensories,
> Violes, crosletz, and sublymatories,
> Cucurbites and alambikes eek,
> And othere swiche, deere ynough a leek.
> Nat nedeth it for to reherce hem alle.

> [(Such) as red ammonia, copper rust, borax,
> and sundry vessels made of earth and glass,
> Our chamber pots and our distilling chambers,
> Vials, crucibles, and subliming vessels,
> Gourds as well as alambic stills,
> And other such, expensive at any price,
> there's no need to go through it all.] (790–96)

Rhythmically, these lines are difficult to say the least. Maybe even defective. "VIoles, CROSletz, and subLYMatorIES," doesn't work in terms of stresses, having only four; the way to get this line a standard Chaucerian five-stress line is to pronounce "sublymatories," as "SUBlymAtorIES," which significantly distorts how we would normally stress the word, or, perhaps, to place stress upon the "and," though that word rarely takes stress in Chaucerian meter, and, when it does (as I will suggest below), it usually happens through a kind of additive cascade. The next line, to arrive at a five-stress pattern, must be read as "cuCURbitES and AlamBIKes EKE," even though to do so requires—within a single line—two different going theories of whether an *-es* ending should be stressed when following a long vowel and a consonant. A far more reasonable reading, honoring standard stress patterns on each word, would put stress only on "cuCURbites and aLAMbikes EKE," resulting in a three-stress line—which is *extremely* unusual for Chaucer. From the vantage point of stress, metrics, scansion, and rhythm, it's tempting to call the Yeoman's poetry bad, doggerel, or lazy; but I think, from the vantage point of the tale's larger concern with waste and wasting, it is truer to the ecological philosophy of the Yeoman to call it *wasting verse*. It's verse that's rhythmically underused, with emptiness instead of stresses.

The Yeoman's third and final list takes these dynamics even further and outfits the poetry yet more fully with wasteful metrics and wasteful rhythms.

> Watres rubifyng, and boles galle,
> Arsenyk, sal armonyak and brymstoon;
> And herbes koude I telle eek many oon,
> As egremoyne, valerian, and lunarie,
> And othere swiche, if that me liste tarie;
> Oure lampes brennyng bothe nyght and day,
> To brynge aboute oure purpos, if we may;
> Oure fourneys eek of calcinacioun,
> And of watres albificacioun;
> Unslekked lym, chalk, and gleyre of an ey,
> Poudres diverse, asshes, donge, pisse, and cley,
> Cered pokkets, sal peter, vitriole,
> And diverse fires maad of wode and cole;
> Sal tartre, alkaly, and sal preparat,
> And combust materes and coagulat;
> Cley maad with hors of mannes heer, and oille
> Of tartre, alum glas, berme, wort, and argoille,
> Resalgar, and oure materes enbibyng,
> And eek of oure materes encorporyng,
> And of oure silver citrinacioun,
> Oure cementyng and fermentacioun,
> Oure yngottes, testes, and many mo.
>
> [Rubifying water and bull's bladder,
> Arsenic, ammonia salt, and sulfur,
> And I could tell of many herbs,
> Such as agrimony, valerian, and moonwort,

And other such, if I wanted to tarry,
Our lamps burning both night and day
To bring about our purpose, if we may.
Also our calcifying furnace,
And bleaching waters,
Dehydrated lime, chalk, and eye's glare,
Diverse powders, ash, dung, piss, clay,
Withered sacks, saltpeter, metal sulfate,
And diverse fires made from wood and coal,
Potassium carbonate, alkaline, and refined salt,
And burning matters and coagulating ones,
Clay made with horse hair and oil,
Of tartar, potash alum, fermenting scum, wort, and potassium bitartrate,
Arsenic disulfide and evaporating materials,
And of our compounding materials,
And of the yellowing of our silver,
Our sealing up and our fermentation.
Our metal molds, crucibles, and many more.] (797–818)

Of these lines, at least "ARsenYK, SAL arMONyak and BRYMSTOON," "As EgreMOYNE, vaLERiAN, and LUNarIE," "Of TARtre, ALum GLAS, BERME, WORT, and ARgoille," and "POUdres diVERSE, ASSHes, DONGE, PISSE, and CLEY" are hypermetrical, containing six or seven stresses rather than Chaucer's usual five.[14] This verse, now with too many stresses, is used to try to convey something real and concrete about the nature of alchemy: it wastes, it is wasting, it over-consumes.

And here, adding to the hypermetricality, we've got a pattern of intermittent "And" anaphoras: "And diverse fires . . ." "And combust materes . . ." "And eke of oure materes . . ." "And of oure silver. . . ." This hiccuping list of additive anaphoras reinforces the same logic of surplus, of excess, of effluviality, rendered metrically and rhythmically, that Chaucer elicits from his poem thematically with all the sweating at the outset. The Yeoman's breathlessness, his lurchiness, the sheer excess of his verbal habits reinforces our sense that his obsession with alchemy has wasted him. *And* it must be noted that if you repeat an "and" anaphora enough times, it creates an additive cascade, where the "and" starts to take stress, which would make three or perhaps four additional lines in this passage hypermetrical. It's easy to see why Chaucer scholars have historically tended to question the Chauceri-anness of this tale.

Even Mann's wonderful analysis of metrical practice in Chaucerian verse largely ignores *The Yeoman's Tale*. It doesn't fit into Mann's argument because it simply doesn't conform to the die-hard five-stress rule.[15] To me, part of the point of establishing an almost totally regular meter is to be able to break it, from time to time, to great effect. Virtuosity is not about a slavish adherence to an established rule so much as about the willingness, when content or context demands it for effect, to break that rule. *The Yeoman's Tale* is Chaucer's ecstatic breaking of his own cardinal metrical rule—for a reason.

This metrical infidelity to the five-stress rule, I think, is where and how the tale's sense of ecosystemic interimplication and eco-systemic bodies gets most acute, and most perceptible to a reader's senses. Becomes most contagious. Most pollutes our ears and thence our minds. As we, the readers of this bizarre tale, try to make our way through these massive lists of ingredients and procedures, none with a clear or directional relationship with any others, we are drawn, sensorily, into the disorderly, wasted mind and habits of thought of the Yeoman himself.

To my mind there are two reading strategies for responding to these lists. The first is to speed up—to skim the lines. In this strategy the lines go to waste, in that passive sense of being underutilized, fruitless, evacuated of meaning. In this strategy the Yeoman's poetic lists are reduced to static. The second is to slow down—to try to make the poem actually *scan* and maybe even make sense. In this strategy a reader wastes the lines, in that active sense of overconsuming them, trying to dig all the value out of them until they again, I think, dwindle into noise. But this time it's more like the noise that occurs in the mind when a word is repeated until it stops making sense, a noise that results from an overinvestment in sound and meaning. As the Yeoman himself puts it about an alchemist's effect on his audience: "For in his termes he wol hym so wynde, / and speke his words in so sly a kynde, / Whanne he commune shal with any wight, / That he wol make hym doten anonright" (For in his terms he will so wind himself, and speak his words in such a sly manner, when he communicates with any person, that he will make that person dote immediately) (980–83). "Doten" is an interesting verb for the Yeoman to use here, since it can mean both "behave foolishly" or "become deranged" *and* "rotten" or "disintegrated."[16] Wasted, we might say.

The Yeoman himself does more or less say just that, in a passage toward the end of his performance.

> For though ye looken never so brode and stare,
> Ye shul nothyng wynne on that chaffare,
> But wasten al that ye may rape and renne.
> Withdraweth the fir, lest it to faste brenne;
> Medleth namoore with that art, I mene,
> For if ye doon, youre thrift is goon ful clene.
>
> [For even though you might look so wide and stare,
> you will earn nothing in that labor,
> but waste all that you might seize or make off with.
> Withdraw the fire, lest it burn too fast;
> Meddle no more with that art (of alchemy), I mean,
> For if you do, your thrift is entirely gone.] (1420–25)

Given that these lines come less than sixty lines from the very end and that the Yeoman refers to his craft here as his "art," it is tempting to read this passage metapoetically, and even to see it, as some have, as the beginning of Chaucer's "dismantling" of his poetic project, which then dominates the rest of the *Tales*: *The Manciple's Tale, The Parson's Tale*, and of course the *Retractions* all seeming to body forth skepticism about the value of poetry.[17] But I am more inclined to read this passage as the culmination not in the poem's musing about poetry itself as wasteful, but, rather, in its musing about poetry's power to *think* about waste, and to make readers think about it as well. When the Yeoman urges us to abandon *that art* of alchemy, it seems to me there is a quiet, implicit validation of *this art* of poetry as a more desirable activity. In its poetic apposition with *wynne, wasten* signals loss and spending, specifically of money. It signals, that is, the kind of wasting that poems like *Piers Plowman* and *Winner and Waster* are more concerned with. But by immediately following that sense of waste with the injunction to "withdraw the fire, lest it burn too fast," the Yeoman also reminds us of the kind of wasting at work in an individual body, the kind of evaporative wasting that arises in medical and surgical manuals, the kind of wasting the Yeoman's own body is so sadly subject to. The poem blends these different registers and discourses of waste seamlessly, allowing readers simply to dwell in the wonderful semantic—and metrical—haze that results.

And I say "wonderful" deliberately. Chaucer flags the affective response of the other characters to the Yeoman's appearance specifically as wonder. The Yeoman "so swatte that it wonder was to see" (sweated so much that it was a wonder to see) (560); the Host refers to the Yeoman's situation as "wonder marveillous" (wonderfully marvelous) (629). The pilgrims are fascinated by the wasting, sweating, overflowing bodies of the alchemists, just as readers, I think, are meant to be captivated by the sounds and rhythms of the Yeoman's wasting verse. The wonder, the marvel, that the tale so conspicuously marks as responses to the Yeoman's and Canon's wasting bodies, that is, should cue readers to the wonder and marvel they will feel at navigating the wasteful and wasted verse of the Yeoman's poetry. But by the end of the Yeoman's performance, we should learn that the wonder and marvel we might feel at the alchemist and his processes is dangerous and deceptive.[18] And that if we get sucked too far into the dynamics of waste, the world may become wasted with us. Because that wonder and marvel should clue us into the reality that our own bodies, minds, and communities are subject to wasting. Something about the wasteful dynamics of alchemy is compelling, seductive, contagious.

Part of what interests me in this tale's meditation on how alchemical wasting becomes an ecosystemic, social, and interspecies problem is precisely the tale's weirdness, its littleness, its marginality, and how they function as part of Chaucer's attempt to shake his readers into attentiveness about the problem of waste broadly. I think Chaucer deliberately includes the Yeoman's disruptive cameo late in the *Can-*

terbury Tales narrative so as to urge readers to consider that it is not always from known, expected places that pollution and corruption might come. Ecosystemic imperilment has a way of sneaking up on us, catching us off guard. As the Yeoman's prologue states, the alchemists who join the pilgrimage come out of nowhere to overtake the other pilgrims suddenly, with no warning (556). That lurchy suddenness is part of the nature of the tale's musings on ecological precarity: we do not recognize a threat as a threat until well past the moment it is upon us. The other pilgrims are captivated by the polluted and polluting bodies—what we might call the wasting bodies—of the alchemists, just as we readers are captivated by their wasting verse.

This last point I take to be the high-water mark of Chaucer's ethical poetics in this tale. The Yeoman's wasting and wasted verse creeps up, sneaks around the corners of lines of verse, much the way the Yeoman describes where he and his Canon dwell: "Lurkynge in hernes and in lanes blynde" (lurking in corners and in blind alleys) (658). Suddenly we find ourselves in a cascading list of hyper- and hypometrical alchemical ingredients, having no real idea how we got there or when or how we'll get back out. And it would have been the same for medieval readers: the vocabulary in these passages is so alienating, the verse so lurching, that it's not just modern readers who would be disoriented by it. Part of the Yeoman's true poetic alchemy is to draw us readers into his wasted and wasting verse and thereby to get us to *feel* our way into the larger ecological and environmental issues surrounding waste, without our even fully realizing it's happening. We are made not only to read about but actually to experience a sensory-driven meditation on waste and wasting, a meditation on overuse that is somehow also underuse, a meditation on how individual bodies are not in fact individual but are instead stitched into the larger fabric of society in ecological and economic ways *and* are suffused with the earth and its elements. Wasting is not just—or in this poem even *primarily*—a problem of land use. It's a problem of the use of the *self* with a flagrant disregard for how one's own overflowing, dysregulated, wasted body, energy, tools, and even *words* can spread wastefulness like a plague. The Yeoman is a corrupt escheator, a corrupt steward, and a corrupt tale teller—and his corruption is contagious.

To get back to this book's initial claim—that unearthing medieval ecological thought could shed light on contemporary ecological thought—let me point out that even the most liberal among us, those most totally committed to the idea of anthropogenic climate change, could stand to be reminded, first, that words and ideas are ecosystemic entities too. The resources of the soul and mind are part of the environment. It's not just blowing into the brimstone that makes the Yeoman sweat; it's clearly also his obsession with the ideas and words of his art. Second, we could all, I think, take a lesson from the Yeoman in remembering that industrial contamination of an individual body *is* a kind of contagion. We are all composed in part from plastic, esters, estrogens, pharmaceuticals, lab-filtered nitrogens, heavy metals, and electromagnetic waves that our machines generate. We tend, I think, to consider the waste we put into our bodies as our individual problem, not posing much risk to other people. But those extrahuman elements are not as sequestered in our individual bodies as we might like to think; they pass through the placenta to fetal tissue and are transmitted through blood donation, organ donation, fecal transplant, and many other medical procedures as well as through social actions like sharing water bottles, a meal, or clothes and jewelry. And our ideas and words can cause others to take wasteful elements into their bodies too, just as they do in the Yeoman's tale.

We are all, in some terrifyingly real sense, blowing too hard into the fire. Chaucer's tale reminds us that the Yeoman's wasted body is the wasted body of us all. His wasteful words are the wasteful words of us all. And his verse is designed to make that wastedness truly resonate with us. Chaucer in that sense goes one poetic step further than Langland or the poet of *Winner and Waster*. In those works the concrete properties of the writing—personification, debate format, legal forms—were designed, I think, to make us understand and think differently about waste. In *The Yeoman's Tale*, the metrical wasting seems to me designed to make us actually *feel* sensually the oscillations between privation and excess that typify waste and that make it such an intractable and dangerous social, economic, and ecosystemic problem.

By the end of the fourteenth century, when Chaucer wrote *The Yeoman's Tale*, climate change, contagion, pollution, land contraction, food scarcity, and worries about the fate of human souls all ignited the English literary imagination to new heights of ecosystemic awareness and critique. Much of that awareness and critique was fundamentally worried, pessimistic, even desperate. That desperation reaches a fever pitch in perhaps the single most famous romance of late medieval England: *Sir Gawain and the Green Knight*. And there the desperation is shot through by an awareness that the natural world is mercurial, changeful, vengeful, and very, very cold. *Sir Gawain and the Green Knight*, as we will see, insists on showcasing the terrors and traumas of climate change, the inescapability of ecosystemic collapse, the ongoing aftermath of long, frigid winters, and the seemingly endless cycle in which a sadistic, vengeful, trickster natural world tries to break mankind down.

CHAPTER SEVEN

THE WASTED LANDS OF THE GREEN KNIGHT, AND THE WASTING OF CAMELOT

Climate Change, Climate Revenge

Sir Gawain and the Green Knight appears in a single manuscript, often called the *Pearl*-manuscript, but which I will refer to as the *Gawain*-manuscript. The four poems of manuscript, *Pearl, Cleanness, Patience*, and *Sir Gawain and the Green Knight*, seem to have been written by the same poet, despite their differences in tone and subject.[1] Testifying to the unity of the manuscript, a strong sense of ecosystemic peril runs through each poem. As I mentioned in chapter 1, *Pearl* works through the death of the narrator's young daughter, possibly from plague. *Cleanness* obsessively describes landscapes that are destroyed and wasted by an angry God, who can't seem to stop himself from using weather to punish people. *Patience* is a dramatic retelling of the story of Jonah from the Bible, which involves a vast quantity of water, flooding, fear of drowning, and a general sense that the sea and the sky are not to be trusted. I will return to these three earlier poems toward the end of this chapter, but the poem I will focus on, the poem whose theoretical sophistication and resonance about ecosystemic collapse are the most pervasive and powerful, and most centered on an idea of the natural climate as something cold, old, changeful, and vengeful, is *Sir Gawain and the Green Knight*.

Now, to say that this particular poem is ecosystemically minded is far from news and far from shocking: when a bright green man on a huge green horse shows up at your court and invites you to a grudge match at a "green chapel" a year later, something funky is clearly going on with the natural world.[2] But looking at the poem through the lens of waste and wastefulness helps to illuminate the poem's particular ecosystemic genius. So to begin with, there is a type of "waste," a lexical instantiation of waste, really, that I have not yet dealt with head on since we were deep in the Bible: waste as the noun that means "wastelands."

As I discussed in chapter 2, *vastitas* in Latin signals not just an empty place, but specifically an *emptied* place, a formerly occupied and settled place that has been devastated and purged. Wastes in the Bible are places that have been emptied out because of sinful misconduct against the law or the Lord. *Sir Gawain and the Green Knight,* although it relies only limitedly on the term "waste" itself, is profoundly concerned with this dynamic: it is concerned with how sin, and especially the profligate wasting of resources and words, can trigger an occupied, settled place to become a desolate, empty wasteland. More particularly, the poem is concerned to remind its readers that we are living in a fantasy if we believe, even for a second, that the natural world is kind, beneficent, or predictable. *Gawain* envisions a world in which nature is constantly threatening to encroach on the world of civilization, the world of culture, the world dominated by the illusion of human control. *Gawain* shows a nature that has left its notional bounds and is hell-bent on dragging the ordered world of civilization to rack and ruin. *Gawain* shows, in effect, climate run amok.

THE TROJAN BACKSTORY

The beginning of the poem sets up this narrative of wasting and the wastability of cultured human society by opening with the Trojan backstory of England.

Sithen the sege and the assaut was sesed at Troye,
The borgh brittened and brent to brondes and askes,
The tulk that the trammes of tresoun ther wroght
Was tried for his tricherie, the trewest on erthe.
His was Ennias the athel and his highe kynde

That sithen depreced provinces, and patrounes bicome
Welneghe of al the wele in the West isles . . .
And fer over the French flod Felix Brutus
On mony bonkkes ful brode Bretayn he settes
        With wynne
    Where were and wrake and wonder
    Bi sythes has wont therinne,
    And oft bothe blysse and blunder
    Ful skete has skyfted synne.

[Once the siege and assault of Troy had ceased,
The borough smashed and burned to brands and ashes,
The soldier who had there wrought the stratagems of treason
Was tried for his treachery. And truest on earth,
It was Aeneas the prince and his noble army
Who afterward beat down provinces, and became patrons
Nearly of all the wealth in the Western Isles. . . .
And far over the French sea, Felix Brutus
On many very wide banks of Britain he sets
        With winning.
    Where war and rack and wonder
    For ages has dwelt therein,
    And often both bliss and blunder
    Immediately have moved ever since.] (1–19)[3]

As we have seen at other points in this book, the semimythical Trojan
prehistory of England comes into play here. Trojan escapees from the
Trojan War were said to have decamped to Europe; Aeneas set up camp
in Italy, and Brutus went on to found England. Nothing surprising or
even unusual. But there are some emphases in this version of the Trojan prehistory that are worth pausing over. First, the overemphasis on
burning Troy to a crisp. This is a poem that wants to foreground not
just the fact of the Trojan defeat, but the totality of the city's destruction. Troy gets burned up entirely, obliterated, emptied out, wasted.
Troy gets converted from a settled, urban place to a desolate, uninhabited space.

The passage goes on to specify that Aeneas, on escaping from wasted Troy, colonizes many lands, but that it is ultimately Brutus who settles upon Britain's many wide banks "with wynne." *Wynne* as a noun can simply mean "joy" or "luck" or "happiness." A felicitous conquering, as it were, of Britain by Brutus. But this is a moment when the poet of *Gawain* puts his verse form to good use: by carving off the short phrase "with wynne" from the longer lines around it, he highlights that phrase and puts pressure on what we think he means when he says "with wynne." Because of course, "wynne" does not just mean joy or luck, it also means "win," as in to win a battle or a war. The poet hives off this line, I think, to highlight the semantic multiplicity of the term and thence to call to mind the association between "winning" and "wasting" that we have seen in both *Winner and Waster* and *Piers Plowman,* an association widely available by the end of the fourteenth century when *Gawain* was written. That sense of military winning and its necessary complement wasting is brought out more strongly by the carrying over of the *w*-alliteration into the next line, with its description of "werre" and "wrake." The Trojan backstory in this poem is a story of wasting and winning, a story of ruination and colonization.

In this emphasis on England's prehistory as a history of winning and wasting, *Gawain* is exploring a dynamic from a poem not usually taken to have any relation to the *Gawain*-manuscript: *Winner and Waster.*[4] And maybe there is no direct relation between them; there definitely are, however, some strong consonances. Like *Gawain, Winner and Waster* begins with a brief overview of the settling of Britain by Brutus, but *Winner and Waster* avoids talking about the violence of that settlement, instead opening with, "Sythen that Bretayne was biggede and Bruyttus it aughte" (When Britain was settled and Brutus held it) (1). But like *Gawain, Winner and Waster* specifically describes the "tresone" (2) that wasted Troy. And from there *Winner* goes on to describe the "selcouthes" (wonders) (3) that have been seen in England, and how those wonders are lately getting out of control. People have become afraid, the poem says, to send their boys to the south of England, which likely alludes to major cities like London or centers of learning like Oxford and Cambridge, because those boys may never return. As I discussed in chapter 1, this fear of losing one's sons and one's security with them has something to do with ecosystemic collapse:

> When wawes waxen schall wilde and walles bene doun,
> And hares appon herthe-stones schall hurcle in hire fourme,
> And eke boyes of blode with boste and with pryde,
> Schall wedde ladyes in londe and lede hem at will,
> Thene dredfull Domesdaye it draweth neghe aftir.

> [When waves shall grow wild and walls be down
> And hares upon hearth-stones shall hunker down in groups
> And also well-born boys with boast and pride
> Will wed ladies and lead them at their will,
> Then dreadful Doomsday approaches after.] (12–16)

Winner and Waster envisions a world in which formerly inhabited human spaces—hearths—are overrun with hares. It envisions a world of maritime floods. A world of ruined walls. It envisions a world racked by climate change. But, crucially, it imagines that kind of detail not in *Troy*, but instead in *England. Winner and Waster* urges readers to remember the fundamental vulnerability of all human culture, of all human dwellings. You don't have to go to Troy to find a toppled city or town—you can just look around the landscape of England. You don't have to go into the distant classical past. You can just watch the rabbits overrun the ruins all around you. Because even though the poem casts its imagining of ruined, wasted places in the future, the landscape of England was already famously littered with ancient ruins.[5] And, as I described in chapter 1, the English landscape was increasingly dotted with sodden ghost towns, made uninhabitable by the brutal climate change of the late Middle Ages. *Gawain* bodies forth the same kind of apocalyptic ecosystemic imagination, though it goes much, much further than *Winner and Waster* in thinking through what the gradual but catastrophic reclamation of civilization by the natural climate would look like.

COURTLY CLIMATES I: CAMELOT

Before staging what a catastrophic climactic reclamation of civilization might look like, the poem lays out the conditions under which it might happen in the first place. After the poem's introduction, the first proper scene in *Gawain* is a feast at the court of King Arthur. Indeed, it is a scene of "rych revel oryght and rechles merthes" (rich revels aright and reckless mirths) (40). It is a scene of merriment, to be sure, but it is also a scene of waste, in the sense of overconsumption. It is a scene of surfeit. A scene of excess. It is exactly the kind of scene Winner takes Waster to task for when he makes his case against waste, though the poet of *Gawain* does not tip his hand quite so early that he condemns the revelry of the court. There is a moment when we readers are invited into the revelry uncritically, to enjoy it, to partake imaginatively in the mirth and the feasting. The main narrative of the poem starts in party mode; it starts as *fun*.

The earliest moment at which we see the poem seem to condemn or at least question the party atmosphere of Arthur's court is in its initial description of Arthur himself as "sumquat childgered," which can be rendered benignly as "somewhat childlike" or "almost boyish," as Simon Armitage renders it.[6] But it seems more consistent with the negativity of *Winner and Waster*'s lamentation that "a childe appon chere, withowttyn chyn-wedys" (a child in a chair, without a beard) (24) is a poor substitute for "lords in londe that loved in thaire hertis / to here makers of myrthes that matirs couthe fynde" (lords in land that loved in their hearts to hear storytellers who could find substance) (19–20).[7] *Winner and Waster* worries about a situation where there's a child at the helm, partly because a proper lord must be mature enough to appreciate "myrthes" with real "matir." The implicit association between childishness and insubstantial merriment in *Winner and Waster* seems very much to obtain in *Gawain*: it is ultimately Arthur's childish eagerness for a good story that gets Gawain into trouble (94–95). As the poem characterizes Arthur, "so bisied him his yonge blod and his brayn wylde" (so roiled his young blood and wild brain) (89). *Gawain*, in fact, seems to be enacting in Arthur's court the kind of social endangerment that the poet of *Winner and Waster* rails against, where the whims of the young replace the measure of those who should properly rule. Indeed, when the Green Knight eventually appears before Arthur, he specifically notes that "Hit arn aboute this bench bot berdles chylder" (there are but beardless children around this table) (280). I will put this deliberately provocatively: *Sir Gawain and the Green Knight* fantasizes about what would happen if we played out the kinds of ecosystemic and social crises limned in the prologue to *Winner and Waster* and carried through in Winner's critiques of Waster. What does happen when a child really is in charge, a petulant child who wants fun and parties more than anything else? What happens when pleasure counts more than "matir"? The answer is that the natural climate of the outside world comes charging into the civilized court, seeking to correct and perhaps eventually reclaim it.

GAWAIN VERSUS THE GREEN KNIGHT I

Indeed, the Green Knight himself famously barges into Arthur's court and challenges anyone there to strike off his head; after that person strikes, the deal is that the Green Knight will get a chance to strike back a year later. Everyone sees the lunacy of the offer—anyone who decapitates the Green Knight, presumably, will be protected from the Knight's vengeance by the simple fact of his having been decapitated. But there's something spooky in the challenge—maybe it's that the challenge comes from the mouth of a massive, armed green man riding a massive, fancy green horse. So no one steps up until Arthur offers himself and Gawain—the unwilling hero who immediately sees the inappropriateness of the childless and childish king's putting himself forward like this—volunteers to take his place. Gawain strikes off the Knight's head. Awkwardly, the Knight doesn't die: instead he picks up his own head, hoists it aloft, and carries it off on his green horse, to await his chance for revenge on Gawain a year thence. As a figure of the natural world, the Green Knight is terrifying, mysterious, and vengeful.

GAWAIN VERSUS THE COLD, WET WIRRAL WILDERNESS

Once the year has passed, Gawain sets out to meet his destiny. En route to his date with the Green Knight at the Green Chapel, Gawain must first experience his own vulnerability to nature. Specifically, he has to encounter cold, wet weather and the lack of shelter and succor in the "wyldrenesse of Wyrale" (wilderness of Wirral) (701).[8] This specification of locale is important: Wirral is a spit of land just inside England, adjacent to Wales.[9] This part of Britain was politically volatile, though sparsely populated, and the *Gawain* poet capitalizes on both of those traits. As Lynn Arner points out, "the frontier in *SGGK* is vastly underpopulated—at least by humans"; Arner further notes, rightly, that the battles Gawain endures in the Wirral wilderness are with beasts, not people.[10] On his journey in the wilds he encounters fierce animals that he must battle—snakes, wolves, bears, boars, and bulls, and even giants. This Wirral wilderness is empty of people—*terra vastata*—a wasteland. But significantly, the poem withholds that exact term until later, when we will encounter a far more terrifying kind of wasted place.

For now this Wirral wasteland proves challenging to Gawain despite all his training and martial might. And for good reason: the pinnacle of his ecosystemic challenge on this journey, of course, is not another knight, or even the beasts he fought, but the cold: "For were wrathed hym not so much, that wynter was wors" (For battle grieved him not so much, that winter was worse) (726). The poem goes into great detail about the sheets of frozen water that came down from the skies, how Gawain slept cold in his sleety chain mail, huddled in cracks of rocks with icicles as his chandelier (728 ff.). This poem is haunted by the prospect of frost, sleet, cold water, and of freezing alone, out in the weather, exposed and vulnerable. This is a poem whose great hero, the unequaled Gawain, is shown to suffer not only the dints of animal aggression, but also the dints of weather and a hostile natural environment. All the care that has been taken to arm Gawain against the Green Knight—he has his chain mail, his specially fashioned and decorated shield, his sword—will amount to nothing if he freezes to death in his war gear before he gets to the Green Chapel. No matter how much we may want to believe that our greatest acts of heroism are about chivalry and courtliness, the poem suggests, our *actual* heroism often entails simply staying alive when besieged by our ecosystem. Gawain's first and perhaps most dangerous enemy is nature itself—a changing nature, a cruel nature, a cold and wet nature. His most dangerous enemy, that is,

134 : CHAPTER SEVEN

is the actual climate experienced by fourteenth-century English read-ers.[11] He is a hero of the Little Ice Age.

COURTLY CLIMATES II: HAUTDESERT

Gawain gets a temporary reprieve from the dangers of the wasted, wet, and freezing ecosystem around him when he stumbles upon a myste-rious castle. This castle is more ornate than anything Gawain has ever seen; and indeed, it seems to be more ornate than anything *anyone* has ever seen. Everywhere it bears the signs of its artistry, its constructed-ness, its status as a highly achieved cultural object. Everything about the castle is accomplished, elegant, and curated: towers are balanced, carvings are exquisite, the contours of the building are perfect, the chimneys are chalk white. In fact, so beautiful and perfectly wrought does the castle seem "that pared out of papure purely hit semed" (it seemed cut purely from paper) (802). The castle is, in a word, *art*. It is a work of culture. Or, somewhat more insidiously, maybe it *is* a paper castle, a castle made as a toy. Whether understood as art or plaything, this castle in all its ornamentation is the antithesis of the cold, fierce, slushy weather Gawain has slogged through, the antithesis of the chaos of nature, of a climate gone wild. In its papery elegance, it is the civ-ilized space that marks the adjacent Wirral wilderness as *so* painfully and unmitigatedly waste and wild. The luminous castle is the perfect structure to seduce Gawain with, because he is so desperate to escape the brutality of the wilderness. But once he is inside the white castle, we find (before he discerns it himself) that he is only going to become less chivalrous, because he becomes yet more prone to his own base desires, his own mortality, and his own beastly wish to survive.

In the castle, Gawain enters into an agreement with its lord, namely, that the lord will go out hunting every day and give Gawain what he catches, while Gawain stays home and gives the lord whatever he earns in his domestic roamings. During the three days of this deal, the lord captures a deer, a boar, and a fox; Gawain captures one, then two, then three kisses and a girdle from the lord's wife. Though we can't really say Gawain captures them so much as that the lady captures him: she is the aggressor all the while, hunting him sexually, just as her husband hunts game outside. Indeed, the pun that mutely underlies this two-tiered sequence in the poem is on *venerye*, a Middle English word familiar to all readers of Chaucer, which means both "hunting" and "sexual behavior." Gawain, in being the lady's sex toy, parallels the deer, the boar, and the fox; without realizing it, he is the prey, the hunted creature—just as he was outside the castle, fighting animals, fighting frost. The paper castle offers no true shelter but instead just seems to shield him while actually exposing him all the more to his own mortal (and moral) vulnerability. If the castle's papery appearance is meant to evoke the idea that the castle is a toy, Gawain is the paper doll being played with inside.

On that third and last day of the game of the exchange of winnings, the lady gives Gawain a green girdle to bind around his waist; she tells him it will protect him from being "slayn" (1854). He takes it, loops it around his waist, and keeps it secret from the lord. The kisses the lady also gives him that day, those he returns to the lord. But the girdle he keeps, because he is afraid. He is mortal. He believes he is going to be slaughtered by the Green Knight, just as the deer, boar, and fox have been slaughtered by the lord, unless he takes steps to safeguard his life. The exchange of winnings and Gawain's welshing on the part where he should have returned the girdle expose Gawain's delusion that he, as the paragon of courtliness, is in control of his situation. And if we are playing close attention, we should worry just a little because the lady's girdle is so conspicuously *green*; what does it mean to encircle your waist with green en route to a fight with the Green Knight?[12]

GAWAIN VERSUS THE GREEN KNIGHT II

Once he leaves the castle in quest of the Green Chapel and what he believes may be his final contest, Gawain is warned about the Green Knight one final time—this time by his manservant. The warning comes in language that has consequences for how we read the entire poem. Part of the danger of the Green Knight lies in his dwelling, a place held to be "ful perelous" (2097). Gawain's "burne" (man, servant) (2089) warns further that the place is a "waste" (2098). A waste. An emptied-out, destroyed place. A wasteland. A *vastitas*. A place formerly occupied but now ruined. The Green Knight's place, this "waste," is "perelous" to anyone who ventures there. Gawain is walking away from a perhaps too perfect, curated, ornamented castle and into a deep and devastated wilderness—a landscape, it seems, emptier and more wasted than the Wirral wilderness he wandered through earlier.

The poem uses the term "waste" advisedly here, and did not use it earlier, as an anchor for some of the biggest revelations of the end of the poem. As Gawain approaches this "waste" chapel, he wanders through a "wylde" place, seeing no sign of habitability anywhere. He sees high craggy rocks, but no Green Chapel—at first. He sees instead a green mound, or hill (2171). He examines the hill; it's a bit weird. It seems to have a kind of entrance at one side and at either side; but everything is overgrown with grass and greenery. Gawain is staring right at the Green Chapel without at first realizing it, because it has been reclaimed by the earth. It *is* earth. It is grass. It is a place of worship that is a natural space, or maybe a natural space that was once a dwelling place—it's difficult to tell. And that difficulty is acutely poignant; as Jeffrey Jerome Cohen phrases it, "the Green Chapel is an architecture of unremembered origin."[13] When Gawain finally realizes he has arrived there, he goes into great detail to describe his horror at the place.

> This oritore is ugly, with erbes overgrowen;
> Wel bisemes the wyye wruxled in grene
> Dele here his devocioun on the develes wyse.

> [This chapel is ugly, overgrown with grasses;
> It befits the Green clad man
> To dole out here his devotion in the devil's way.] (2190–92)

The Green Chapel horrifies Gawain because it is an "ugly" ancient place, overgrown by nature.[14] He calls it a chapel of bad luck, a cursed place. He is horrified and disgusted by this "waste" place because he sees in it the annihilation of a former place of worship that has now been reclaimed by grass and moss. In Cohen's words, "Who built or inhabited the place and why it fell into decay are unrecounted. It is enough that the space is heavy with forgotten history, a threat of oblivion."[15] Nature, in this poem, is not kind or friendly. This is instead the freezing, hostile, overgrown, wild nature of the beginning of *Winner and Waster*. It is the deeper waste within the wasted wilderness of the Wirral. It is the nature that is imagined by a poet living through the Little Ice Age.

This wasteland is a landscape that subsumes culture. No Camelot could take root here. The force of the wilderness is too powerful, too vengeful, too cold, and too green. This is a vision of an ecosystem as something hostile, something eradicating, something indifferent or even opposed to the works and cultures and the wishes of men.[16] The mound of the Green Chapel serves as the ultimate *memento mori* for Gawain and for readers, reminding them not just of their own inevitable individual deaths, but of the inevitable death of culture, the impending death of Camelot, the end of the age of chivalry, its subsumption under the cold loam.[17] Gawain's seeming respite in the paper castle was, of course, a tease; what really awaits him, and all of us, is a wasted place that is so ruined it has become illegible as a place of human culture.[18]

But surprise: Gawain ultimately gets a reprieve from the Green Knight; this is not the hour of his death. Instead Gawain returns to Camelot a sadder and wiser man, chastened by his knowledge that he cravenly kept the green girdle in hopes of preserving his life from the Green Knight's blade. In solidarity with Gawain and his love for his own life, the rest of the knights of the round table take on the girdle too, as a sign of their allegiance and fellowship. But Gawain himself is broken by his experience, made aware that his love of his own life outweighed his courtliness, his chivalry, his honor. The beast in Gawain, that is, got the best of the knight in him. But in getting wasted by the Green Knight, Gawain also gets purged—he is cleansed when he is wasted, in the biblical sense of waste. I will address Gawain's purgation further in a moment, but first I want to loop back and think about the beginning of the poem in the context both of *Gawain* overall and of its cultural and manuscript context.

Returning to the beginning of the poem, the Trojan backstory becomes all the more devastating. Britain, in the *imaginaire* of this poem, is a landscape shot through with the signs of loss: lost civilizations, ruins, wastes. The British peoples who held Britain before the Anglo-Saxons are gone. The Anglo-Saxons who held Britain before the Normans are also gone. Perhaps this Green Chapel is a relic of the times of the first Christian Britons, a monument to an early Christian way of life that leaves almost no trace on the social ecosystem of Arthurian England. Or perhaps it is a relic of the notionally Trojan settlers who came to England via Rome. Gawain's revulsion—his aestheticized moral reaction that the "waste" chapel is "ugly"—signals his inability to fully accept the fundamental reality of ecosystemic existence, which is that we all eventually become earth. Troy is burned to ashes and absorbed into the ground. Whatever the Green Chapel once was is now a green spot of earth. Camelot will be overgrown with weeds, so overgrown that it too looks like a mound. This notion that Camelot would melt into the ecosystem, never again to be fully legible, was highly available in later medieval literary culture: there was a superabundance of literature about this marvelous place, Camelot, *but where was it?* In theory it was lost in some vast field, a large green mound testifying mutely to a glorious chivalric past.[19] But in reality it was nowhere. It was nowhere to be found. *Gawain and the Green Knight* brings that audience awareness about the evanescence of Camelot to Gawain himself.[20] The changing, vengeful, cold, wet climate of England will bury and erase Camelot and any courtly culture that seeks to replace it.

This radical ecosystemic fatalism in *Gawain* is not the only literary monument of its kind to the inescapability of our reconversion to earth.[21] In fact it reminds me of the gorgeous and enigmatic much earlier fourteenth-century medieval lyric "Erthe toc of erthe," except that the lyric seems more fundamentally at peace than *Gawain* does:

Erthe toc of erthe erthe wyth woh;
Erthe other erthe to the erthe droh;
Erthe leyde erthe in erthene throh;
Tho hevede erthe of erthe erthe ynoh.

[Earth took of earth, earth with woe;
Earth drew other earth to the earth;
Earth laid earth in an earthen trough;
Then had earth of earth, earth enough.][22]

In this lyric "earth" itself is subject, object of verbs, object of prepositions, and adjective. Earth takes everything, including other earth, and makes everything, well, earth. Earth is an inevitability. Earth is a sign, a signifier, and a referent. Earth is a word repeated so often that it both colonizes the poem and loses all specific meaning. This lyric poem speaks from the same impulse that moves Gawain to speak in horror of the green "chapel": an impulse to recognize the ineluctability of earth itself, to recognize how the land itself will overtake everything. The lyric poem seems to have a certain balanced calm about it; "Erthe toc of erthe" is enigmatic, even somewhat epistemologically flirtatious. Gawain, on the other hand, raised in a culture that values agency and self-determination, resists with all his might the notion of the earth as an overwhelming power, until he realizes that, when he bound the green girdle around himself in a desperate effort to preserve his mortal life, he was binding himself to base, physical nature. He unwittingly bound himself to the Green Knight, to greenness itself, to the grass, the ground, the earth, the wastes. Gawain realizes this and flings his green girdle to the earth (2377), seeking—too late—to disavow his own earthiness, his vulnerability, his beastly love of his own life. Chivalric life, the life of the court, is predicated upon the notion that people and their culture can somehow indeed have mastery and dominion over their fates, over land, over nature. But as Gawain's tale proves, time and again nature is calling a disproportionate number of the shots. Gawain wants to be above the fray of nature, to live in castles, but the poem insists that those castles are flimsy, made of paper, and that Gawain is the prey, the plaything, and ultimately the pupil of the greenness. He cannot escape it: even though the Green Knight spares his physical life for now, greenness will claim him (and all of us) in the end. His life is determined by the natural climate—literally, bound by green.

CLIMATE CATASTROPHE IN *CLEANNESS* AND *PATIENCE*

The *Gawain* poet is quite broadly interested in the idea of purging the earth by wasting. The earlier poems of the *Gawain*-manuscript are if anything more forthcoming with this fatalistic sense that the human world of culture, civilization, ambition, and courtliness is poised to be wasted, leveled, and turned to mere earth by fickle and vengeful weather. And in the earlier poems of the manuscript it is clear that purgation is not a *bad* thing, however terrifying. In *Cleanness*'s passage about the Noah story, God warns that he will "waken up a water to wasch all the worlde, / And quelle alle that is quik with quavende flodez. / Alle that glydez and gotz and gost of lyf habbez, / I schal wast with my wrath, that wons upon urthe" (rouse a water to cleanse all the world / and extinguish all that is alive with trembling flood / All that flies and moves and has the spirit of life / I shall waste with my wrath, all that dwells on the earth) (323–27).

In *Cleanness*, God is terrifying but also purifying; this is the God of Noah, the God of the prophetic books like Ezekiel, Isaiah, and Jeremiah. He will waste the world for the world's own good. Later in the same story we read that after many months God began to allow the waters to abate, after "al watz wasted that ther wonyed the worlde wythinne" (all was wasted that dwelt there within the world) (431). God is the *vastator* who wastes the world of all its inhabitants, but as such he is also the one who makes room for a new people, for new cities and dwelling places, in the wreckage of those who had come before.

The underlying affective dynamic of *Cleanness* is one of horror—and often a horror produced by climate.[23] Throughout the poem we see a dynamic where human rule violation triggers a punitive, purgative action from the Divine. Throughout the poem readers are encouraged to feel fear and awe and to muse upon the unfathomable power of the Lord, as well as upon how that power manifests through the land and the weather. This dual cultivating of fear and cognitive overload is central to how *Cleanness* understands, depicts, and seeks to export its moral purgations to its readers. Climatic horror, in *Cleanness*, is meant to heal. Specifically, it is supposed to heal individual people and their cities of sin, of the wasteful misuse of religious vessels, of gluttony, of pride.[24] And the horror that the poem wants both to narrate and, in part, to inflict on readers is a horror of waste, of the wastability of our cities and our selves by a divinely enraged natural world. It is the horrified sense that the natural world could at any moment be smashed flat or sunk into darkness by the ultimate waster, who is of course God.

The poem *Patience*, too, is built on a narrative foundation of divine purgation-by-nature. Early in the poem God complains to the prophet Jonah about the wickedness and moral dissipation of the people of the city of Nineveh. God enjoins Jonah to warn the Ninevites, to tell them to mend their ways. But Jonah flees God, not wishing to be persecuted as a doom-and-gloom prophet. Crucially, Jonah believes he can escape the infinite knowledge and awareness of the Lord—he underestimates the Lord's long reach and specifically underestimates his ability to find Jonah on the open sea. Using nature and climate as his agents yet again, God rouses the winds, which tear across the surface of the water so roughly that the fish are terrified and cling to the bottom. The massive sea storm—perhaps less cold but surely at least as dangerous as Gawain's winter weather—tears at Jonah's boat, wrecking masts and breaking ropes. The other passengers panic, first throwing their goods and wealth overboard to lighten the load, then concluding that there is someone on the boat who has angered his own God, someone for whose recklessness the weather is making them suffer. They swiftly discern that it's Jonah, decrying him for what must be his deadly crimes and evil deeds. Jonah confesses and volunteers to be pitched overboard. Once in the sea, Jonah is quickly swallowed by a whale. Just like Gawain, Jonah suffers a combination of bad weather and animal assault for his sins. He suffers the vicissitudes of a climate run wild, though this time the sea rather than the waste and wild Wirral.

In the belly of the whale Jonah repents, and God orders the whale to spit him out; Jonah lands on a "spare drye" (empty, dry land) (338). But that dry bit of land is adjacent to Nineveh, where Jonah goes to pay his debt to God and preach his warning. Here's what he says:

> Yet schal forty dayez fully fare to an ende,
> And thenne schal Niniue be nomen and to noght worthe;
> Truly this ilk toun schal tylte to grounde;
> Vp-so-doun schal ye dumpe depe to the abyme,
> To be swolyed swiftly with the swart erthe,
> And all that lyuyes hereinne lost the swete.
>
> [Yet shall forty days fully pass to their end,
> And then Nineveh shall be taken and turned to nought;

Truly this very town shall fall to the ground;
Upside-down shall you plunge deep into the abyss,
To be swallowed swiftly by the dark earth,
And all that live here lose their life blood.] (359–64)

Having dragged himself from an empty beach to a city, Jonah warns the Ninevites about waste—specifically, about the kind of waste God is going to inflict on these people for their sinfulness. He warns the Ninevites about what the *Winner and Waster* poet tries to warn us about at the beginning of his poem. Jonah warns the Ninevites about the taking of a city and the absolute wasting of it, turning it "to noght." He warns of people plunging headlong into a black chasm and being swallowed by the earth itself. Earth taking earth again. *Patience*, like *Gawain*, is fixated on the fundamental vulnerability of human beings and their dwelling places to being subsumed by the earth itself. Turning back to *Cleanness*, the scene where God destroys Sodom and Gomorrah resonates. We read that Sodom and Gomorrah, for their sins of impurity, are "plunged" into "a pit" filled with "pich" (pitch) (1008) and that God committed a "uengeaunce uiolent" (violent vengeance) there that "voyded this places" (emptied these places) so that the people and the cities sank into the earth (1013, 1014). If you sin against God, you and your cities will be wasted, erased, voided, reabsorbed into the "folde" of earth (1014).

As in *Cleanness* and *Patience*, so in *Gawain*, what is really at issue is the terrifying prospect that our civilized places—our privileged places of art and culture and learning, but also our places of overconsumption, overindulgence, juvenility, frivolity, and disrespect for the long, long reach of the Divine—are profoundly vulnerable to total annihilation. Our places can be wasted into mere spaces, abysses, nothingness. In *Gawain*, the Green Knight functions as God's wasting agent—the *vastator*—who empties Gawain of his pride and readers of their confidence in the shelter that can be afforded by courtliness in the first place. Put otherwise, the Green Knight is the waster of courtliness, the waster of the fantasy that we can take refuge from the wildness and wilderness of nature in civilized, collective life. That his castle at Hautdesert is so conspicuously compared to "papure" only highlights its transitoriness, its unreality. And even though Gawain is invited back to the castle for conviviality after the test at the Green Chapel is over, he declines because he now knows the castle is a space of magic and trickery. In *Sir Gawain and the Green Knight*, a wasting "wodwyse" figure obliterates the fantasy that there is any way to escape the encroachments, punishments, and humiliations that the natural world has in store for us. We can party in paper castles, but loamy silence awaits us all at the end— even when we seem to be spared, for a time, from the deadly blows of nature. Indeed, I read *Gawain*'s vision of a wasted and wasting nature as committedly critical of the fantasy that civilization and courtliness have any real power in the world. It is in that sense an antiromance.[25]

In how it wastes the conventions of romance, *Gawain* is the third in a series of poems that enact an Old Testament–style meditation on the imbrication of the human world and the natural world, directly in line with the less-loved poems *Cleanness* and *Patience*.[26] And it enacts the *fourth* in a series of poems that are obsessed with the reality that, possibly someday soon, we will all merge with the earth. Indeed, the most painful variation on the terrifying theological embodiment of the "erthe toc of erthe" theme in the *Gawain*-manuscript is *Pearl*, in which the body of the speaker's beloved little girl is buried in the dirt; her spirit is with Christ, as we are supposed to learn to believe over the course of the poem, but the speaker remains fixated on her body, which lies "withouten spot" in the earth.[27] Even after all he learns about her new life with Christ, at the end of the poem he attempts to leap into the river that separates them and swim to her. God flings him back, which makes the speaker very unhappy—it "payed [him] ful ille to be outfleme / so sodeynly of that fayre region" (made him very unhappy to be banished / so suddenly from that beautiful place) (1177–78). It is only in the last few stanzas that the speaker seems to come to terms with the idea that his pearl is in a better place now, with Jesus. The *Gawain*-manuscript is preoccupied throughout with a fear of human beings lost, erased, wasted by the earth. Three of the four poems locate that preoccupation squarely in climate, in nature, and in the weather.

144 : CHAPTER SEVEN

GAWAIN'S VENGEFUL CLIMATE AND THE ECOTHEOLOGY OF THE WASTES

For a long time the conventional problem scholars had in trying to identify the logic of the poet's inclusion of *Gawain* in this manuscript was how to account for *Gawain*'s apparent secularism, its courtliness, its seeming lack of devotional energy—at least, relative to *Pearl*, *Patience*, and *Cleanness*.[28] Larry Benson asserted that "the subject of this romance is romance itself."[29] John Bowers noted that "The plotline of *Gawain* provides a perfect example of the quest romance."[30] Even though the pentangle painted on Gawain's shield associates him closely with the Virgin Mary and with Christ, and even though the poem starts with a Christmas feast, it was long classed unproblematically as a quest-romance.[31] To be sure, romance and Christianity were known by scholars to be compatible categories,[32] the former often being built around a quest in the service of the latter, but it seems awkward that a manuscript that is otherwise so obviously devotional and religious should end with what is widely considered one of the highest achievements of English, secular, courtly romance—even if that romance does seem animated by a moral message.[33]

But in recent years a great deal of scholarship has insisted that *Gawain* is in fact a highly theological piece of writing, with devotional energies and insights on par with the other poems in the manuscript. Nicholas Watson has been the voice that has most loudly championed that perspective, to say that he sees in *Gawain* deliberate and structural "vernacular theology" and that all four poems of the *Gawain*-manuscript "advance a common set of theological propositions." Moreover, Watson argues that, even compared with other specifically English, specifically vernacular theology in the period, the poems of this manuscript are aimed squarely at a lay readership, and one local to the scenes described in the poem—Wirral, the north of Wales.[34] Watson sees the poems as manifesting "indifference to interiority," privileging "word and deed over thought and feeling."[35] Watson sees the earlier poems in the manuscript as in part setting up the embedded theological and devotional meanings of *Gawain*, but his argument stops short of arguing that *Gawain* itself is *primarily* theological and devotional in its bent.[36]

Pushing further to articulate *Gawain*'s theology, J. Stephen Russell has demonstrated the poem's systematic reliance on Marian devotional tropes and has suggested that such reliance originates in—or at least resonates with—Cistercian writings.[37] Karen Cherewatuk has argued for the centrality of incarnational devotion to the poem's plot and narrative logic.[38] Cecilia Hatt has suggested that Thomistic theology is the primary organizing principle of the entire manuscript and that *Sir Gawain and the Green Knight* is no exception.[39] Piotr Spyra sees *Gawain* instead as the culmination of the manuscript's sustained engagement with Augustinian theology.[40] The gradually emerging consensus on the poem, then, is that it is profoundly theological in its concerns—more the apex of the rest of the manuscript's theological sophistication than a divergence from it.

In my view the poem's theology is best understood specifically as an *eco*theology—one that challenges us to rethink what we believe about participation in courtly, civilized life. *Gawain and the Green Knight* deploys the full arsenal of its literary and theological sophistication to perfectly embody the courtly tradition—to embody it as perfectly yet as falsely as the paper castle embodies castleness—precisely in order to tear down that tradition, to show its contingency, its frailty, and its creeping perforation by a divinely underwritten natural law that is far older and more untraduceable than that courtly world. And that natural law is the Old Law of God, just as it was in *Cleanness*, just as it was in *Patience*. Along with Gawain, we readers are supposed to feel, deeply and creepily, every heartbeat of that old, green law throughout the poem. The law that swallowed up Sodom and Gomorrah. The law that swallowed up Jonah. The law that swallowed up Pearl. And the law that will someday swallow up Gawain and everyone he knows. *Gawain* is pervasively and profoundly a work of ecotheology, rooted in Old Testament theology, where the divine hand blasts the human and natural world at will, through an agent called *vastator*. An agent that we might now call climate change.

The ostensible goal of the Green Knight's dressing-down of Gawain and of the world he inhabits and embodies is to diminish their pride. When Gawain finds out the Green Knight is Bertilak, and that Bertilak knows Gawain kept the lady's girdle in order to save his own life, he is mortified: "So agreved for greme he gryed withinne. / Alle the blode of his brest blende in his face, / That al he schrank for schome that the Schalk talked" (So aggrieved for shame, he roiled within. / All the blood from his breast surged to his face, / So that he shrank for shame at what the knight said) (2370–72).

Gawain sees his love of his life, as the Green Knight magnanimously calls it, as a terrible failure, a sign that he is not as noble and brave as he should be. To Gawain's self-remonstrations the Green Knight replies laughingly, "I halde the polysed of that plight and pured as clene / as thou hades never forfeted sythen thou was fyrst borne" (I hold you polished of that danger and purified as clean as if you had never misbehaved since the day you were born) (2393–94). Gawain, it seems, has been purified by his trial-by-wastelands and trial-by-waster. Gawain himself recognizes the sins he had to be purged of as pride and excess, saying that he will forever wear the green girdle as a "syngne of my surfet" (a sign of my excess) (2433), so that "quen pryde schal me pryk for prowes of armes, / the loke to this luf-lace schal lethe my hert" (when pride shall goad me for martial prowess / a glance at this love-girdle shall loosen my heart) (2437–38). Gawain's pride and his tendency to excess have been curbed by his encounters with the freezing winter, the icy chandelier, his own susceptibility to being hunted (both by the lady and by the Green Knight), and by the Green Knight himself, also formally known as Sir Bertilak de Hautdesert (2445).

Hautdesert, of course, means "high desert."[41] I noted in chapter 2 that in the Vulgate *vastitas* means something different from *deserta*: *vastitas* means a formerly inhabited land, now wasted. *Deserta* means a land natively barren, an actual desert. But the Old English term *westen* means any kind of uninhabited place—a desert, a wasteland, a wilderness[42]—whether it's that way dispositionally, like a desert, or incidentally, like a city flattened by martial action or divine wrath.[43] There's a confluent etymology in the Middle English word "waste," where the word takes its root on the one hand from the Latin *vast-* and on the other from its Old English *westen*. That confluent etymology papers over a dissection of meaning such that waste in Middle English can mean a place blasted flat *or* a place naturally uninhabited. Picking up on that older English sense that wasteland, wilderness, and desert were all the same kind of land, the *Gawain* poet knows that in Middle English "desert" can be used almost synonymously with either "wasteland" or "wilderness." It can mean either an emptied place or an empty place.[44] The *Middle English Dictionary* notes that it can refer to an uninhabited land that is either arid or wooded.[45] Bertilak, as lord of the "high desert," is the lord of the wastes; he is literally the lord *of the wastelands*.

Thus, by wearing his green insignia, the girdle he got from Bertilak's wife, Gawain shall forever be bound by waste. Gawain, that is, shall forever wear around his belly the sign of the waste's power over him—of his subjection to a climate that can at any time subsume human culture. He can never forget his mortality, his vulnerability, and his susceptibility to being wasted, to being undone by the wasted and wasting climate around him. With Gawain's chastening, Camelot, with all its revelry, its song, its feasting, its "surfet," has been chastened too—it has been purified. The ecosystem of the wastelands has taken the bodily form of Bertilak to put paid to the idea that the court of Camelot is truly at the top of what we would now call the food chain.[46] The Green Knight, also known as the Lord of the Wastes, is God's moral ambassador to Camelot, who seeks to better the knights by mortifying their pride and curbing their excesses. The Green Knight is not just another romance challenger-figure.[47] He is the waster. *Viridis vastator*.

A potential problem with this reading is that in the end we find out that none other than Morgan le Fay, the often not very Christian sister of Arthur, has been behind the tests Gawain has been subjected to.[48] It was her magic, it seems, that transformed Sir Bertilak into the Green Knight. She apparently lives in his castle (2446). So the force that drives the green *vastator* through the tale is not God but a sorceress, an enchantress, and one whose precise moral character is notoriously difficult to discern in Arthurian literature.[49] Surprising, but there is a warrant for reading Morgan in a more theologically positive light. In 2008 an Anglo-Norman Arthurian text was discovered, quite a bit older than *Gawain*, that identifies Morgan le Fay as "empress of the wilderness."[50] Moreover, it identifies her as being made empress of the wilderness "by the grace of God." There is some precedent for construing Morgan le Fay *not* as a maleficent witch, but as God's designated ruler of the wilderness. To be clear, there is no reason to adduce a direct relationship between the manuscript that called Morgan, in essence, Divinely Appointed Ruler of the Wastes; the newly rediscovered text is much earlier than *Gawain*, written in a different language and from a different region. But the fact that there is some cultural attestation to this notion helps us puzzle through the overarching Christian logic of the *Gawain*-manuscript overall. And in point of fact Bertilak, the lord of the wastes himself, calls Morgan

> Morgne the goddess
> Therfore hit is hir name;
> Weldes non so hyghe hawtesse
> That ho ne con make ful tame.

> [Morgan the goddess
> Is thus her name;
> There exists no haughtiness so high
> That she can't make it entirely tame.] (2452–55)

In my view Morgan serves in the poem in precisely the role adumbrated in the Anglo-Norman work. She is a divine agent, a goddess-empress who is also a healer of moral failures.[51] She comes to Camelot to cleanse it of its moral impurities by dragging its highest haughty man—Gawain—through the wilderness, through the wastes, and exposing him to the wasting wild man par excellence, Lord Hautdesert, the lord of the wastes.[52]

The *Gawain* poet, then, uses the romance frame as a feint for a strange and haunting ecotheological meditation. We are not meant to read this poem and to end by venerating courts and courtliness; the poem is not an encomium to romance, or to chivalry itself. If anything it is the opposite: *Gawain* stands as a reminder that, behind the *ostensibly* Christian and *ostensibly* orderly world of chivalric virtue lies another world, one that is older, more anciently Christian even, and definitely greener. Indeed, I would say that the poem is *primarily* an ecosystemically motivated work of theology and only instrumentally a work of romance—a work of romance, again, that critiques the positivist fantasies of romance culture.[53] The poem offers us an opportunity to connect with the idea that all civilized places are, as it were, castles of paper, soon to be overtaken by the encroaching green of a climate that is everywhere underwritten by God: the weather, wild animals, the desert, the wastes, Bertilak, and Morgan le Fay herself.[54]

The Yeoman's Tale asks readers to imagine a city and its denizens in relation to the natural world and its material resources; in Chaucer's poem that relation is toxic, poisonous, plaguey, and unsustainable. The *Yeoman* asks us to imagine a city in danger of being overcome by disease and by industry—or even by disease *as* industry. In *Gawain*, in the relationship between the natural ecosystem outside Camelot and Camelot itself, that outside ecosystem is clearly in charge. Camelot and its residents are allowed to maintain their illusion of importance, their illusion of control, only at the pleasure of ecosystemic conduits like Morgan le Fay. Where the Yeoman asks us to imagine a city overcome by the plague of greed, *Gawain* asks us to imagine a city in danger of being overcome by nature itself, a city overwhelmed by an all-consuming, encroaching, vengeful, and cold climate. *Gawain* asks us to imagine a city that will soon be erased, made into a green mound that only vaguely recalls a built structure, when the Old Law of nature gathers itself up and overflows its bounds, wasting everything in its path. *Gawain* asks us to imagine the wastelands themselves as our once and future dwelling places. It asks us to realize our own radical vulnerability to the outlying ecosystems, just beyond the reach of city, of culture. It asks us to acknowledge our own hubris in thinking we can somehow game the system, avoid the eventual conversion of our dwelling places into wastes. It asks us to register that all the pomp and finery of Arthur's court is at best a distraction from our eventual fate and at worst an acceleration of it.

CHAPTER EIGHT

GARDENS, BEES, AND WASTOURS

Political Waste and the Fantasy of Sustainability

Winner and Waster, Piers Plowman, The Yeoman's Tale, and *Gawain and the Green Knight* represent and explore the ecosystemic interimplication and ecosystemic peril of fourteenth-century England. To do so they deploy the full arsenal of poetic form and literary language: variously they rely on dream visions, dramatic debates, personification allegories, poetic meter, alliteration, allusion, semantic plasticity, and of course the capacity of literary language to weave together—or "wry over"—numerous other discourses, including biblical, legal, sermonic, penitential, surgical, military, and romance. All these poems understand "waste" as a keyword for unpacking and analyzing the ecosystemic perils facing their worlds, and all use that term to convey the connectedness of people with the land, people with each other, soul with body, money with land, and body with land. "Waste" for these poems captures the radical interdependence of individual selves, society, and the natural world. And for all these poems "waste" is a dangerous force, something that destabilizes the sustainable functioning of that household system that binds together self, other, and nature. All these poems are profoundly skeptical about humanity's capacity to regulate or prevent waste—or to respond to it at all. All of them ask us to dwell in some degree of fear about our own precarity, our own subjection to waste, to wastefulness, or to the wastes.

But in the fifteenth century, probably in its first decade, a poem is written that, while focused on waste as an evil of the English ecosystem, offers a more sanguine vision of how to combat it. Or at least it seems to. This poem recognizes that righteous social and ecosystemic action is urgently needed, and not just because of the climate crises, pestilence, famines, the loss of arable land, and the pressures those factors bring to bear on the labor market. As we will see, the Middle English poem *Mum and the Sothsegger* understands the political world to be an integral part of the broader social ecosystem, and it uses nature metaphors and allegory to articulate a sophisticated vision of what a functional, just, and sustainable political world might look like.[1]

Over the course of the Middle Ages, one particular figure for how nature and governance meet gains more and more popularity. That figure is the garden.[2] Gardens have a long history in the Western imagination—though not a straightforward one. The paradigmatic garden in Judaism, Christianity, and Islam alike is obviously Eden, a place of plenitude, beauty, and ease that requires from its occupants only obedience. But Adam and Eve do not obey, so they are cast out, punished by being far from God's love and enduring hard and painful labor on unyielding ground. Gardens are sites of privilege, but also sites of punishment. To be in a garden is to be in the Lord's good graces; to be cast out is to be alone, bound to a lifetime of hard work and suffering. If we self-govern well, we thrive in the garden; if we self-govern ill, we are cast out. The desire to get back to some version of Eden, some closeness with God, to an easy life of abundant food and physical pleasure is an enduring fantasy in subsequent Western literature.

The garden poem I'm going to focus on is a little-read fifteenth-century work, *Mum and the Sothsegger. Mum* is political in tenor, staging a face-off between Mum (as in "mum's the word"), who says nothing in the face of political corruption and misconduct, and Sothsegger (literally, soothsayer, or truth speaker), who speaks the truth with limited regard for how it will affect his own fate. But this philosophical assay of truth telling is not the most interesting part of the poem. Deep in the poem, the narrator somewhat abruptly finds himself wandering in a natural landscape. And unlike most of the other landscapes, whether fictive or historical, that we have been thinking about so far, the landscape he wanders into is beautiful, well-ordered, and replete with good things. It's a garden.

Mum and the Sothsegger revisits and revises the duality of privilege and prohibition that animates the Eden story in light of the eco-systemic thought of fourteenth-century England and the ecosystemic realities of living in an imperiled world. But at the same time, *Mum* dares to imagine a new Eden—a saved and secure one. In *Mum*'s glorious landscape, the hedges and woods are "so grene" (so green) (885), the meadows freshly mown (887), and the trees "ytraylid fro toppe to th'erthe / Coriously ycovrid with curtelle of grene" (trailed down their curiously covered skirts of green from their tops to the ground) (892–93). It is a landscape at once well tended (the mown meadows) and let run wild with bountiful natural energy (the trees' flowing leaves). Moreover, it is a landscape of extraordinary agricultural fecundity: the grain yields abundantly, fish of countless varieties swim in the running river, branches of briars bend down from the weight of their delectable charge, chestnuts and cherries "that children desiren" are everywhere, pears and plums hang from the trees, and grapes fill the gardens (895–904). The hunting is excellent there, the land full of rabbits and obedient dogs (913–16). The sheep and their lambs relax in the shade. A herd of four hundred deer run into the woods (923–30). On top of all that, the place is full of sweet music because of the cheery babbling of birds "in every bussh" (938), and the air smells of wonderful spices (941). This is a fantasy landscape, an antidote to the food scarcity, the assarting, the climate change, the bad crops, and the general chaos of the fourteenth century. It's a new Eden.

Impossible as it is to enter fully into the imagination of the average medieval reader, whoever exactly that might have been, *Mum* gives us a reason to try to get as close as we can. Regardless of gender, class, age, or occupation, medieval English readers of this poem, I think, would have found it painfully, maybe even excruciatingly, beautiful. To imagine sweet-smelling air rather than the stench-filled, smoky air of their city. To imagine berry-laden branches, chestnuts and cherries all around to fill the mouths of children—children who were not starving, children who were not dead from plague, who were just *children*, searching for delicious treats. To imagine well-tended and well-mown grounds to which one had seemingly unrestricted access. Loads of grain and fish everywhere, and the sound of birdsong rather than the din of the city. This is a landscape of plenty, freely accessible to all, clean, pure, and fresh. It is a landscape where adverse climate change—freezing, wet, endless winters—is unimaginable. It is a landscape where urban pollution and plague have no place. Where loss of arable land is unthinkable and famine unimaginable. Although this description must have been agonizing for many medieval readers to read, it must also have been inspiring and encouraging: this garden offers itself as an antidote to the ecosystemic ills of the fourteenth century.

The precise nature of that antidote becomes clear only a bit later. The narrator finds himself at a lovely, well-kept house, with "the gladdest gardyn that gome ever had" (the gladdest garden a guy ever had), where the "noble" ground was loaded with grafted trees and herbs of various kinds (947, 961). How does a garden so beautiful come to be? It has an ideal gardener: a white-haired old man with a fresh face and earnest eyes, who is serious of appearance, gentle of speech, strong of body despite his hundred winters (955–62). This gardener gives the narrator the most important lesson of the entire poem: to save the world from waste, we should follow the example of bees. And he should know, since he's a beekeeper.

The beneficent beekeeper tells the narrator that the garden is his own, and that he works hard to tear out weeds and kill worms that might threaten to waste herbs (980). But the prize exhibit is his beehive. Bees, according to this hoary beekeeper, are the best workers in all nature, the best, as he puts it, "ygouvernd / Yn lowlynes and in labour and in lawes, eke" (governed in humility and work and in laws, too) (907–8). Bees have a king, whom they devoutly serve and obey. (Medieval people thought the queen bee was male; hence, "king bee.") All the worker bees bring the king honey, they build intricate and beautiful honeycombs, and they are aware of the dangers of "wastours" (1017) who might take their product from them. The bees divide their labors among themselves, then they take all their meals together—no one eats alone—to prevent any "waste" of resources (1028). The king is meek and mild, not even armed with a stinger. The only trouble in the idyllic and beautiful, well-governed beehive is the drones. They eat more honey than twenty worker bees, yet they contribute nothing to the nectar-gathering labor: evil and sneaky, the drones "haunten the hyve for hony that is ynne" (haunt the hive for the honey inside)

(993–94). The poor worker bees do not always see the drones entering, and that, the beekeeper tells us, is where a beekeeper comes in. A beekeeper must find the drones and crush them before they can get into the hive, so that the honey will not be all wasted and eaten before it can be eaten by the workers and king or harvested by the beekeeper.

What I find most striking about this passage is its commitment to the idea that the drones' "waste" is the arch-crime that threatens the hive. The poem has many affiliations with *Piers Plowman* that have long been noted by scholars, but to my mind the treatment of waste is where those affiliations are clearest and most powerful.[3] As in *Piers* so in *Mum*, wasters are the biggest threat to a functional, well-governed, and just society. In fact *Mum* amplifies Langland's worry: for Langland, although wasters are a huge threat, they are not the *only* threat to a functioning society. Sin is also a threat. Juridical corruption is a threat. Windstorms and plagues are a threat. In *Mum* it is really *only* wasters—the drones—who threaten the safety and security of the beehive. There is no mention of bee pestilence, pollution, bad weather, flower shortages—nothing like that seems to threaten the hive. Nothing at *all* seems to threaten the bees except the wasters, whom the poem defines as those who overconsume and underproduce. *Mum's* wasters are Langland's wasters, though here they are understood as a political threat as well as an agricultural one.

But at least *Mum* imagines a beekeeper who can swoop down and smash the wasters. No need to call on Hunger to punish the wasters (and everyone else, indiscriminately); here we have a kind-eyed, white-haired man at the helm. A man who crushes drones but spares and indeed protects the worker bees and the king. As long as the worker bees work, the beekeeper will keep the climate steady, the fields heavy with crops. This is certainly a far more comforting ecosystemic vision than we get in *Piers Plowman*. Or for that matter in *Gawain*, where it is precisely Arthur's insouciant desire for adventure that invites ecosystemic catastrophe into Camelot in the form of the Green Knight. Instead, *Mum's* is an inspiring vision of a highly functional society, predicated on shared labor and shared devotion to a two-tiered system of kind and beneficent monarchs: the king bee and, above him, the old hoary man himself.

But it is also cautionary, because of the drones. The drones and the threat they represent to the functioning of this equitable and just society are elements of the political allegory in which the poet was clearly very invested: the source from which he derives this bee passage does not give anywhere near as much attention to the problem of the drones as the *Mum* author puts in.[4] Evidently the *Mum* author wants to convey some warning about the drones to his contemporary readers. He wants to convey that we absolutely must all labor, and that we must be vigilant against the wasteful "drones" of the human world, those who consume grossly but never produce.

But there is a real problem in applying the lesson of the bees to the world of people. Sure, listening to the beekeeper, we should understand that, ideally, we must work all the time for what the poem calls the "comune profit" (common profit) (1078), so as to avoid waste and destruction. But it's deeply disquieting to learn that the bees are not themselves always able to recognize drones for what they are. And it is in part *because* the bees are so busy working for the common profit that they don't notice the drones—they've got their sights set on more important things, so they miss the wasters that buzz around them and threaten the whole project of a just and sustainable society. The bees *need* the beekeeper to keep them safe from the wasteful drones. But the beekeeper is outside the beehive; he is not himself a bee. Who, then, is his analogue in human society? Who will play the role of the beekeeper for a corrupt humanity, beset always by wasteful drones who threaten the workers' productivity? Who will stand outside the hive and wait to crush the human drones? It can't be the king, because his analogue is the king bee, who, like all the other bees, is inside the hive and needs the beekeeper's protection as much as they do.

Surely it's God. The white-haired, kind-faced old man must be a figuration of God, with the king bee representing the divinely anointed worldly king below him. As Helen Barr has noted about the poem and its relationship to medieval culture more broadly, there's a long-standing tradition of portraying Christ as a gardener.[5] So maybe the message is that we must have faith that the divine hand will crush the drones to nothingness before they commit damaging waste against the "common profit" of the rest of us? Maybe the message is that in a well-governed society, full of workers and with a mild-mannered, righteous king, God will show up to help punish and indeed destroy all wasters, rather than just arbitrarily scourging the good worker bees? Maybe the *Mum* poet wants to suggest that the divine hand will intervene into the lives of men (and bees) to punish the wicked wasters. Maybe we are seeing another ecotheology here, in which we have a God who would never harm his people, figured as the bees; his only real focus is keeping the wasters away.

Putting *Mum* into the larger context of medieval English ecosystemic crises, it's not hard to see why the poet would want to reimagine the divine hand in this way: no longer punitive, scourging, angry, and seemingly sometimes arbitrary—such as medieval people could see in the biblical Noah or Job, in three of the poems of the *Gawain*-manuscript, as well as in the weather, the plague, and the famines of England—but rather nurturing, loving, tender, and supportive. *Mum and the Sothsegger* asks its readers a poignant "what if" question: What if we try to understand our world not as one that God uniformly punishes for the sins of a few wasters, but instead as one that God desperately wants to protect and nurture, a world where the true wasters can be discerned and crushed by a dexterous, selective, and otherwise tender hand? What if we did not live in peril of being ejected from the promised land? What if there were no possibility that God would scourge us for our sins by destroying our families and our fortunes or laying waste to our lands? What if we instead lived in the beehive?

If we could relax into the certainty of a benign divine hand, protecting us from wasters, what would living in that well-kept hive require of us? How would we hold up our end of the deal? The *Mum* poet is clear on that score: we would work. We would labor. We would do our part to support the functioning of the economy, to avoid food scarcity. We would not overconsume. We would treat our labor as truly collective, recognizing that we all work to support a single hive and a single monarch. We would obey our earthly leaders, and that obedience would take the exclusive form of putting in our hours at work and producing food. In exchange, we could trust our leaders to take good care of us, to treat us with meekness and love, because the king and his people would be in an ecosystemic relation to each other, a relation of mutuality and trust. Every bee must do its work to keep the hive in honey, and in good order. If we can live that way, if we can gather honey every day for the collective good, maybe we will live in a garden perfectly tended by a perfect gardener.[6]

Mum and the Sothsegger offers a fantasy of prosocial political behavior—collective labor—as a way of guaranteeing the beneficence of God as the guardian of the climate. It imagines a world in which devoted work and a refusal to waste ensure humanity a place of honor in a garden that is perfectly tended, a place of plenitude, a place of abundance and beauty. This is a garden that the climate change and climate revenge of *Gawain* will never touch. A garden free from the plague and pollution Chaucer imagines in his tale. A garden immune to Langlandian famine. With no floods, no soil erosion, no clear-cutting, no assarting—nothing that *Winner and Waster* teaches us to fear. For the *Mum* poet, the solution to ecosystemic crisis is to recognize that we must work collaboratively and assiduously, in exchange for which we can rely on the abundance of natural—which is to say, of course, divinely providential—grace. Work is offered as the only possible safeguard against ecosystemic disarray, the only possible way to remain in the garden, close to the gardener.

Pressing on these ideas a little harder, the mandate on work seems not only to chime with *Piers Plowman* but also, and rather loudly, to anticipate the so-called Protestant work ethic. So on the one hand, what's surprising about this poem and its ethos is that it anticipates the rise of that Protestant work ethic by about two hundred years, suggesting that a work ethic may originate as an ecosystemic response to all the pressures brought to bear on the climate—geophysical, social, and political—of late medieval England. But what I find more striking than the idea that something like a "work ethic" already exists in late medieval England is that, traditionally, the rise of the work ethic is held to be part and parcel of the development of capitalism. And here in *Mum*, but also in the other labor-oriented works we've encountered in this book, like *Piers Plowman* and Chaucer's *Yeoman's Tale*, we see a notion of work as salvific and beneficial not when it supports protocapitalist systems of *personal profit*, but instead when it supports something like socialist or collectivist systems of *distribution*.

It is significant, of course, that the natural analogue *Mum* imagines for a laborer is a bee. Bees all perform the same function below the "king" bee, with no hierarchy, no class distinction, no difference in compensation. Bees all deal in honey and wax, and they all earn the same wages: honey and protection from the king. In the bees' world there is no profiteering aristocracy that skims off the best honey. Instead, there is the king, and then there is everyone else, working equally, thriving equally. In the unhealthy hive, the ecosystemic and economic malefactors are the drones: they sneak in and eat the honey that others produce, contributing nothing themselves. And this is why they must be extirpated. For the *Mum* poet, then, ecosystemic survival is about equitable economic distribution, such that the workers—equally—get all the benefit from what they produce, and those who fail to produce are prohibited from consuming anything. Bees are the antithesis of wasters: bees work all the time, and they understand that their survival entirely depends on their constant, zealous work. Bees are also the antithesis of alchemists: bees take pollen and convert it to honey not for their own individual gain, but for the collective good of all the bees.

Sharpening that focus on collectivity, bees live in a kind of hybrid landscape that is both urban and rural: the hive is a densely populated, implicitly urban society, ensconced in a beautiful natural landscape. The hive is safe from the horrors of ecosystemic collapse, both by its communitarian urban functionality and by the rich interchange of labor and goods with the plants of the natural garden outside. In the healthy hive there is a mutuality between dense, collective urban living and a thriving agricultural richness outside that city. You can't fix nature without fixing the labor market; you can't live in an Edenic city within an Edenic landscape if you're surrounded by wasters. It is the equal distribution of labor and goods that enables and ensures ecosystemic stability. Ecosystemic health, and our access to it, hinges on economic justice. And it hinges on humanity's ability to create sustainable cities—hives—devoid of wasters and in perfect synergy with the natural landscape around them.

How we, as human beings reading this poem, could possibly *achieve* this sustainable, just, apian socioeconomic and socioecosystemic cityscape, however, is left hauntingly unclear. As fifteenth-century readers knew every bit as well as twenty-first-century readers, there is no kind-eyed, white-haired man hovering outside our hive to slap down all the wasters. Instead, we are decisively left on the outside of the beautiful garden, peering in with wonder, but also with a fundamental sense of exclusion and inaccessibility.

CHAPTER NINE

AFTERMATH

From Wasting to Waste Matter

So medieval English poets of the fourteenth and fifteenth centuries thought ecosystemically. They understood their bodies, their property, their trees and waterways, their money, their goods, their time, their words, their beasts, their neighbors, their labor, their material resources, and their culture to be constituent parts of a shared, precious, precarious household system. The ecosystem was not something apart from them, or something for them to contemplate from afar, but something they participated in and helped to constitute, and in ways that could and did have deleterious or salubrious effects for themselves and for other people. The poet of *Winner and Waster* believed that profligate spending could result in shortages of land and fuel, and he also believed that the greedy hoarding of resources could impede the circulation of wealth in ways that would harm the entire social landscape. William Langland passionately condemned overconsumption and underproduction as the twin plagues of mankind; for him, active and assiduous participation in labor was the only way to forestall things like plague, famine, and bad weather. Geoffrey Chaucer considered pollution and contagion analogous and recognized the dangers of focusing overly on money, rather than on the common good, in keeping the urban ecosystem of humans, animals, metals, and air functioning sustainably and heathily. Using changing, freezing, vengeful, and personified climates as a lens for its ecosystemic meditations, *Gawain* reminds us that, no matter *what* we do, earth will take of earth—we are not in control of the natural world, no matter how fancy our castles, no matter how courtly our words. Like *Piers*, *Mum and the Sothsegger* construes overconsumption and underproduction as the twin evils of a blighted natural and socio-economic ecosystem. But *Mum* envisions a solution that is relatively straightforward and seems to guarantee a joyful outcome. It imagines a reboot of the Edenic ecosystem, a garden of perfect balance, overseen by a beneficent caretaker who keeps us safe. *Mum* sees collective labor as the ecosystemic participation that offers the possibility of a tractable and nurturing world—though it does not, in the end, make any recommendations for how to achieve perfect, collective labor other than, implicitly, to pray for the kind-eyed, white-haired figure to come and smash all the wasters.

In medieval England this ecopoetic thought was built around the term "waste" and the overlapping discourses—biblical, legal, penitential, sermonic, surgical, and ultimately poetic—that undergird "waste." The original, biblical sense of waste as a colonial act of punishment and purgation that God used as a way of determining the fate and landedness of his people gives way in the Common Law to a meaning of waste not as punitive, but as criminal. Between 1215 and the end of the thirteenth century, English statutes redefine waste as a generalized act of proxy overuse, where the temporary possessor of a resource damages the proprietor's interest. In that redefinition, the law becomes more comfortable assigning monetary value to land damage, so that fungibles (like money) become interchangeable with usables (like land). In the fourteenth century, penitential discourse adopts waste as a key term as well, using it to define any misuse of the goods of one's own soul or of material resources like food or money. Typically, in this discourse, the passive sense of waste—the sense of squandering, letting something go to waste—predominates. But it's not until fourteenth- and fifteenth-century poets start thinking critically about waste that all its senses are simultaneously activated, making waste a catchall term that encompasses misuse of any resource in a way that has negative consequences for the whole ecosystem, including not only land, plants, and animals, but also and perhaps most urgently other people.

So "waste" in the late Middle Ages provides a way for English poets to conceptualize ecosystemic crisis in relation to work, money, intention, individual selfhood, and social justice. "Waste" in the twenty-first century tends to mean either the squandering of an intangible resource like time or the unwanted by-products of bodies and industries. But it rarely seems to mean both things at once, or even to suggest how intimately connected *my* wasting of time might be with *your* wasted goods. So there has been some kind of shift—atrophy, really—in the meaning and range of the word "waste." When do we start seeing the term lose the full reach and scope it had in the late fourteenth century? What happens to the term and the ecosystemic thought it enabled? Where did English culture lose its clarity of thought on the dangers of waste as an ecosystemic problem—a problem at once personal and social, at once economic and psychological, at once rooted in the land and reaching far, far beyond it?

WASTE FROM 1500 TO THE INDUSTRIAL REVOLUTION

The atrophy in what and how "waste" could mean began in the Renaissance and lasted until the middle of the eighteenth century. In the Tudor period, the broadest trends are these: as a verb, "waste" more and more often refers to squandering the resources of the individual self and soul. People waste their breath, their lives, their sighs, their thoughts, their work, their time, and their words.[1] These acts of waste almost exclusively affect the wasters themselves; there is no real sense of social danger involved in wasting the goods of the soul. Waste has become less ecosystemic and more personal. If we turn from the verb "to waste" to the noun "waster," there is still a limited ecosystemic reach, since "waster" primarily means a domestic misuser of goods—a misspender.[2] Those misuses usually affect one household. Being a "waster" in this period, moreover, has primarily to do with misusing money, not with the destruction of material resources like land or of immaterial resources that belong to the soul. These "wasters" of money, like those who simply "waste" their breath and wits, have far less impact on the social ecosystems around them than wasters did for Langland, the *Winner and Waster* poet, or the *Mum* author. Being a waster is mostly harmful to the wasters themselves, or to those tied to the wasters by immediate financial obligations. It is still bad to be a waster in later periods, but "waste" does not have quite the conceptual and ethical complexity that it has in late medieval England. It has lost its ecosystemic range.

Continuing the trends from the Tudor period, seventeenth- and eighteenth-century English poetry associates wasting with misspending, and almost always with misspending that only really hurts oneself. "Waste," as a verb, is very common, and it signals the wasting (misusing) of mostly intangible resources: time, words, thoughts, breath, tears, years, strength, sighs, conscience, sights, smells, selves, spirits, age, and reason. "Waster" does occasionally occur too, most often as a description of a riotous overspender or an uneconomical wife who misuses material resources in a household.[3] The rich polysemy of the verb "waste" that we saw in the late English Middle Ages is gone.

At the same time, the term "wastelands" is gaining sociocultural heft. Vittoria Di Palma shows that in the sixteenth, seventeenth, and eighteenth centuries there was a dramatic increase in cultural awareness of and reactivity to the wastelands, specifically as a disgusting, dangerous, hostile place in need of "improvement" by human industry. Over the course of this period, as she shows, three types of "wasteland" were cleaned up and, in essence, modernized: swamps, mountains, and forests. No more would the wastelands terrify people with their illegible emptiness; instead, they would be in some way integrated and incorporated into the world of economy, industry, and sociality—even though some residual wildness would always remain. There is, in general, a wish in postmedieval English culture to sanitize, regulate, and control the wastes—to make them productive instead of, as Di Palma emphasizes, "useless," as the wastelands came to be seen during the Early Modern period and into the Enlightenment.[4] The sense of "wastelands" that *Gawain* so plangently meditates on, where the wastelands will, inevitably, eventually consume all civilization, is actively being combated in later periods.

WASTE IN THE INDUSTRIAL REVOLUTION AND BEYOND

According to the citations in the *Oxford English Dictionary*, in the nineteenth century "waste" as a verb can take many objects. It is something you can do to your money, your time, your sorrows, your joys, your mind, your thoughts, your breath, your life, your days and nights, your words, your talents, your books, and your opportunities—the intangibles—but also sometimes your muscles, your blood and body, your material goods, and your estates.[5] The Industrial and Postindustrial usage of the verb "waste" also seems to conserve the Renaissance's decoupling of the waste of self from the waste of others. There is not much evidence from the late eighteenth and nineteenth centuries that wasting one's own time or one's own money was perceived as contagious, as it was for Chaucer's Yeoman, or as deleterious to the agricultural economy itself as in *Piers, Winner and Waster*, and *Mum and the Sothsegger*. The verb "waste" does not have that kind of denotative or connotative elasticity; instead, it is mostly used to describe individuals' self-harming behavior rather than their dangerous tendency to waste a broader community.

The *nominal* meaning of "waste" in the Industrial and Postindustrial era, however, changes dramatically. "Waste," when used as a noun in the English Middle Ages, as well as through the Enlightenment, most frequently meant "wasteland" or "emptied place," as it did in *Gawain* and as it does in Vittoria Di Palma's study. Sometimes it was also used to name the behavior of waste, as in the waste of money or resources. But it did not mean what we most often mean when we use the word in its nominal form now: waste matter, refuse, garbage, ordure, filth.[6] That meaning comes roaring into English currency in the very late eighteenth century.[7] And that meaning of "waste" as garbage, refuse, ordure, or trash is by far the predominant in modern culture.

If I tell people I have written a book about waste in the Middle Ages, they almost inevitably respond by saying something like, "That makes sense. They threw their shit out the windows, didn't they?" Or "Were there even rules about garbage back then? Were there landfills?" And I almost inevitably disappoint them by saying "waste" didn't mean then what it does now. It didn't mean "garbage," nor did it mean "shit." The Industrial Revolution, with its huge increase in garbage production and in disposable goods, had to intervene before "waste" would really take on those meanings. And intervene it did.

Susan Strosser's *Waste and Want* gives a jaw-dropping account of early American practices of domestic order, consumption, and waste management.[8] She describes how clothing was recycled time and again, not just thrown away at the first appearance of wear: a dress that was stained or torn could be cut into strips that could then be refashioned into bows or trim for other clothes, perhaps even to cover up their stains. Broken pottery was not discarded but was smashed into finer powder and spread in yards and pigsties. Metal could be reused and repurposed time and time again. Food scraps were fed to livestock or dogs when they were past recycling into new meals for people. Tattered fragments of cloth could be sold to rag buyers, who roved from town to town collecting strips of ruined cloth to resell to paper makers. Shit had agricultural uses; urine had domestic uses. And, crucially, there was no plastic, no rubber, no Styrofoam, nothing truly single-use or disposable. Early Americans produced *some* garbage and *some* filth, but on nothing like the scale at which we produce waste nowadays. Similarly, in preindustrial England there was simply much, much less garbage produced. That's not to say none at all; as I mentioned earlier, urban London of the Middle Ages was quite clogged with trash in the streets and in the river. But the garbage that there was, well, it wasn't really *waste matter* in the sense we mean it now. It wasn't packaging. It wasn't an outdated toy. It wasn't a single-use object. It wasn't, in effect, the collective by-products of mass industry. Instead, it was something that was broken beyond repair, or so overworked as to be useless. Or else it was organic matter or bodily effluvia: blood, shit, vomit, animal offal, bones.

It was mass industrialization that created a true garbage-based human ecosystem, both in cities and, eventually, in towns and rural places. It was the rise of industrialization that shifted the nominal meaning of "waste" from an empty place, or an underuse or squandering of some kind, to the visible remnants of the marketplace. The Victorians, for instance, threw away pottery and metal goods that were only somewhat damaged, and sometimes even things that were intact or in working order—a material practice unthinkable in preindustrial times.[9] They discarded old toys, bottles, and other containers that in earlier centuries would have been reused until they were unrecognizable. In the postindustrial period "waste" usually means the unusable part of some commodity, the excess, the packaging, the bit that gets squandered in either the production process or in consumption. It's the unincorporated bit, the overflow, the excess, the by-product. And it's almost always material, though we do talk about wasted heat, light, and energy. But waste for us, now, almost always signals a concrete, measurable thing, something external to us but that we must deal with in some way as the undesirable residue of our participation in the marketplace. Waste is waste *matter*.

That is not to say this *idea* of waste as waste matter was totally unimaginable in the Middle Ages. We see a gesture toward this idea of waste qua garbage in *The Yeoman's Tale*. He doesn't call the superfluous materials of alchemy "waste" matter, but he does associate wasting and being wasted with those materials. We see a gesture, as I noted, in Langland's depiction of the puking Glutton—the word "waste" isn't used, but the puking is adjacent to passages focused squarely on waste. There is some sense, that is, that underproduction and overconsumption waste away the self, waste society's goods, and produce a certain kind of excess—think back to the sweating alchemists and their horses. Similarly, the *Middle English Dictionary*'s two mentions of the noun "waste" meaning something like "the rest," or "the excess" are meaningful anticipators of the idea of waste as garbage, though they lack that strong connotation of grossness, ordure, filth, or trash they come to have in later centuries.[10] What those two meanings record is the idea that when you overconsume something, when you *waste* it, whether it is crops or other material goods, there may still be some excess that has to be acknowledged and dealt with. Not disposed of, not thrown away, but accounted for, maybe even reincorporated.

In the modern day we know that consumption produces waste—eating produces feces, of course, as everyone in all of history has known, but also any act of marketplace consumption entails the production of by-product, or waste. Garbage is a natural outgrowth of large-scale industry. Waste results from consumption. For medieval people, wasting *was* consumption, and consumption was wasting. But two important medieval ideas about the nature of waste have been lost in the welter of both lexical and material change that the Industrial Revolution inaugurated. First, the medieval idea that wasting existed on a spectrum from the wasting of land to money, from goods to time, energy, words, life, and breath. Medieval poets demonstrate an awareness in the late Middle Ages that misusing your personal energy had real consequences in the material world, and that the two behaviors couldn't be perfectly separated. Second, medieval people had a profound sense that my own misuse of my own goods never really happened in isolation. That deep, old sense, derived from the Bible and from the Common Law, was that waste was something you did to someone else's land, that sense persisted in a particular way: if I wasted my words or wasted my money, or my energy, I might materially affect *your* bottom line, your ability to feed your children, your physical health. The choices I make with how to use my time, and especially the choices I make about whether or not to work collaboratively for the common profit, those have meaningful consequences for everyone. Waste, in Middle English, is a way for poets to think seriously and carefully about resource interdependence, about mutual precarity, and about ecosystemic interimplication. The poems about waste in the English Middle Ages show, in essence, that nothing is *exclusively* mine, and nothing is exclusively yours—not even the hours, minutes, and seconds of my day. Because if I misuse those seconds by, say, not working, I am hurting your own ability to thrive. I am being a bad farmer. A bad steward. A bad worker bee.

However painfully aware some people nowadays are about how their household waste might affect other people—might become trash islands in the sea, might produce estrogen in groundwater—that sense that our material acts of consumption *and* the choices we make about how to use our time, our words, our energy, and our labor are part of that ecosystem of waste, that has been lost. It seems to me that it's been lost, actually, since long before the Industrial Revolution, because by the seventeenth century there's already a sense that the resources of one's soul—time, words, breath, life, mind, wits, conscience, the works—although definitely still wastable, are also in some deep way *one's own*. The poet of *Winner and Waster* didn't think that way. Neither did Langland. Neither did Chaucer or the *Mum* poet. For them these spiritual resources were, in essence, occasions for either consumptive or productive practices. Put in contemporary economic terms, there were severe opportunity costs associated with the use of time, words, thoughts, and life, just as there were with the use of wood, money, and land. If all you do is play dice games, you miss the opportunity to labor for poor relief. If all you do is eat, you miss the opportunity to provide for your family and community. If all you do is play, you miss your chance to pray. If all you do is consume, you are condemned to lock yourself and your larger worlds into cycles of waste, where that waste then yields shortages, famines, plagues, pollution, and bad weather. As stewards, we are accountable not only to the lord, but to other people, and we are accountable not only for how we use our material resources, like our land or our money, but for how we use our immaterial ones like our time, our words, our souls.

EPILOGUE

Many people today understand that we are accountable to each other for how we use our material resources: the waste matter my household generates ends up in an ocean that everyone shares. The pollution from processing what you waste darkens the skies that everyone shares. So on some level we all know that our waste affects other people. But the piece of the medieval understanding of waste as a kind of antisocial arch-sin—in which they understood time, wits, words, will, the body, the mind, and breath to be wastable resources that implicitly belonged to everyone, just as they understood land and money and their misuse to constitute bad stewardship—strikes me as very important and not yet having come into popular consciousness. Or rather, not yet having returned.

Bruno Latour's *We Have Never Been Modern* moves toward this idea. Latour claims that modern consciousness is defined and characterized by our tendency to understand the three realms of scientific knowledge, political power, and language as discrete things, and therefore to understand lived reality as comprising natural things and cultural things. For Latour (and for the later adherents to what becomes known as actor-network theory), the world *really* comprises nature-cultures, hybrids of made things and natural things. The distinction between humans, who think of themselves as subjects or actors, and things, which we think of as objects or as acted-upons, is not as sharp as we might think. For Latour the natural world is meaningfully interdependent with the political world and the world of language—with culture. These dimensions have always been mutually constitutive.[1] But the rise of scientific discourse in the wake of the Industrial Revolution has blurred that mutuality. Latour's contention is that we are all "networked." We are interwoven with each other, with our "objects," with nature, with the political, with language. The core explanatory practice of modernity—to think of nature and culture as different—is a delusion; hence "we have never been modern."[2]

The argument I have been advancing resonates with Latour's in many ways. For medieval people the political world and the natural world are mutually constitutive; that resonates with Latour. The idea that nature and human behavior could never be meaningfully separate also resonates. The idea that the things of our world (objects like money, resources, goods, land) and the agents of our world (subjects like people), with all their time, thoughts, will, and words, are intimately interlinked? Yes, that too feels very modern, very contemporary, very now, and it will resonate for readers of Latour. The idea that what I do necessarily affects you, even if at an imperceptible scale? Yes, I think many people who are focused on ecosystemic crisis think in precisely those terms. So is it the case that Latour's book title, *We Have Never Been Modern*, could be revised as *We Have Always Been Medieval*?

Not quite. There is one very important difference between Latour's ideas (and how they are taken up) and what we've seen in medieval English ecosystemic thought. For Latour and many of his adherents, a significant element of actor-network theory is that people are not in any absolute way at the center of things. Although they exercise a great deal of influence on actor-networks, people are still ultimately just a part of the network. The vast, hybrid world of quasi-objects (which is most stuff, defined as comprising both "nature" and "culture") possesses agency. There are no pure objects, no pure subjects; humans aren't all *that* special. The element of reality that matters most for Latour is the *relationship* between actors—so, the relationship between you and this book, between me and my computer, between me and you, between people and dogs, between bookshelves and their books, between airplanes and the news. Ecophilosophies deriving from Latour—chiefly Object-Oriented Ontology—even further decenter the human, arguing for a "flat ontology," in which all beings and things, whether real or imagined, are construed as "objects" with potentially equal levels of agency, efficacy, and existence in the world.[3]

For the medieval ecosystemic theorists in this book, humans decisively *are* at the center of things. It is *human* thoughts, words, will, intentions, time, energy, money, behavior, resources, and relationships that matter most. Real estate factors in, of course, as a kind of starting point for wasting, but to say that the medieval ecosystemic understanding of waste decenters the human or sidelines human specialness in any way would be a mischaracterization. Although I agree with Jeffrey Jerome Cohen's elegant phrasing, "the world is not for us," it remains true that, for medieval people, the world is in some deep sense *about* us.[4] In medieval ecosystemic thought, humans are part of a system, yes, but they are a privileged part; they play not just a large role but a *determining* role. Humans have an outsized effect on that system, such that the wasting of land, money, goods, time, will, breath, life, or of course words *by humans* can affect not only other humans but also, as the Yeoman shows us, animals.[5] And the environment itself: let's not forget that medieval people seriously believed in anthropogenic climate change. But that belief originated in the deep conviction that humans were very special indeed—special to God—and would suffer special consequences if they wasted the material and spiritual gifts God gave them.

So to get back to something I began with: Why study medieval people's ecosystemic thought? To me it is first because of their insistence on the centrality of the human. Medieval people believed clearly and instinctively in what we would now call an integrated ecology, where plants, animals, economies, people, social structures, and the earth itself must all be taken into consideration when thinking ecosystemically. But they believed people were the most powerful players.[6] They were not wrong then, and they would not be wrong now. People *do* have an outsized effect on the functionality of the global ecosystem. We just do. We all know it: we are the ones putting airplanes in the sky to spew carbon. We are the ones causing sea level rise. We are the ones through whose actions methane will probably be released from under northern permafrost. It's not beavers. It's not rocks. It's not forks. It's not even the most powerful quasi-object of all, the internet. It's people. Moreover, the consequences of human action fall hard on the shoulders of other people. Animals and plants do suffer enormously through human industry—we are in the sixth extinction period already.[7] But medieval thinkers' awareness about and sensitivity to the idea of stewardship, and specifically to the idea of being a good steward, means worrying about *humans* in more precarious circumstances than our own, treating them as our interimplicated counterparts rather than as distant others. It means acting on their behalf *knowing* that their behalf is ultimately coterminous with our own.

The second reason to study medieval ecosystemic thought is to help us learn that even those parts of human life that seem to be private or personal (our time, our ideas, our energy) should be understood to be collective and social. Pope Francis sees this clearly in his *Laudato si'*, a papal encyclical on climate change. He says it is from the medieval Saint Francis of Assisi that we should take our ecobehavioral cues: "[Francis] shows us just how inseparable the bond is between concern for nature, justice for the poor, commitment to society, and interior peace."[8] Interior states, social engagement, and concern for nature exist on a spectrum. There is no hard boundary between my time and your money, or between your property and my breath. The way I choose to use my words cannot be segregated from the global economy, or from the land we live on. The resources of the spirit are coterminous with the physical resources of the human world.

In fact, when I read *We Have Never Been Modern*, one of the seeming dichotomies I kept expecting Latour to turn to, though he never really does, is the material/immaterial or even physical/spiritual one.[9] Medieval people were quite clear that dichotomy was false when thinking about ecosystemic interimplication. The world of things and the world of the soul were the *same world*, inextricably joined by deeds and by relationships between people, and were equally real. Medieval people understood the truth that scientists of symbiosis now seem to see clearly—that "we have never been individuals."[10] But medieval people included not only the biological entanglements that these twenty-first-century scientists focus on, but spiritual ones as well, as part and parcel of their denial of being truly individual—which is to say, separate, atomistic, unfettered.

Now, to start talking about a "spiritual" world will probably send shivers down the spines of many people reading this book, especially those who are avowedly atheistic and secular.[11] But I submit that that bias—the tendency to think of the immaterial world as somehow non-real, apolitical, naïve, or archaic—is extremely dangerous. It is dangerous because it allows us to continue quietly believing in the modern fantasy of separateness, of radical and undeniable individuality, with all its supposed rights and privileges.

"My time is my own," we say. But is it? At a minimum, isn't it also the time you share or perhaps even coinhabit with your friends, family, colleagues, and fellow commuters? Every time you sit and binge-watch television long after your children are in bed, you are using electricity. You are choosing not to engage with other human beings. You are choosing not to lobby for political change. You are not writing your book or think piece. You are not learning a foreign language. You are not beginning to compost food waste in your home. You are also guaranteeing that you will be tired the next day, which will have an impact on the people around you and on your own health. Your own health has an impact on the health-care system, which in turn has an impact on the health of other people—something Chaucer's *Yeoman's Tale* recognizes and insists upon.

We also say, "My money, my problem." But is it? Isn't it true that if you invest money in mutual funds that, in turn, invest in the fossil fuel industry, you are supporting fossil fuels with your money? If you are paying for the extraction of fossil fuels, aren't you contributing to global warming and to the exploitation of land and peoples elsewhere in the world? If you buy your children plastic toys for their birthdays, aren't you essentially saying you are OK with dumping plastics into the sea? That's the fate of most toys.

We say "I can only speak for myself." But we very often speak for others as well, without their consent, without even their knowledge. This is very obvious in families: we speak for our children, spouses, parents, and siblings all the time. But it also happens in organizations like universities and corporations. And it happens, of course, in the press, on the internet, and in government. Think of cyberbullying, where the words of one person have frequent and often devastating consequences for the body, psyche, or property of another. Presidents speak "on our behalf" in the eyes of the world. The US president's speaking for me has consequences for me as well as for the people listening to him speak for me. His speaking for me has consequences for my children. And yours. This is the nature of governance, but we don't think of it in terms of waste anymore, though some medieval writers and thinkers clearly did. When a ruler wastes "his" words, other people's material resources are laid waste to. We are afraid to acknowledge the connection between the immaterial and the material world, as though the precious edifice of the scientifically measurable world—the world of things—is endangered by the acknowledgment that unmeasurables and intangibles are still *real*.

It is a pervasive if often implicit principle of modernity that the world of spiritual or immaterial things is something to be embarrassed about and therefore to banish to the realm of the purely private. But as ecosystemically minded medieval people well recognized, God is not private. Faith is not private. Words are not private. Hopes are not private. Time is not private. Breath is not private. Thoughts are not private. There is no privacy to immaterial things. They are social, they are collective. Even beliefs are collective, and they have material consequences, because *people act* based on their beliefs. They derive their sense of entitlement or their resignation to their circumstances from their beliefs. Like the steward, we need to be rendering accounts, where our accounts include not only possessions and money, but time, words, intentions, energy, bodies, behaviors, and relationships. Medieval ecosystemic thinkers knew this, and we need to know it again. If we cannot learn this basic truth, COVID-19 will happen again, probably in worse form. The tundra will vomit forth uncontainable gases that make slowing climate change impossible. People will die by the millions—or more likely tens or hundreds of millions. If we cannot acknowledge that our thoughts and words and deeds are ecosystemic and economic resources, we're sunk. If we cannot acknowledge our own tendency to be wasters, the earth will simply cast us out of livable places and into waste spaces, as God cast Adam and Eve out of Eden. The earth will continue to exist, but we won't know it. *Sir Gawain and the Green Knight* understands this perfectly. If we don't mend our ways, we too will become earth, not just individually but as a species. All of us, forever, earth.

ACKNOWLEDGMENTS

This book has benefited from the help of many lovely people. First I'd like to thank Steven Justice, Maura Nolan, Lyn Hejinian, Geoffrey G. O'Brien, and Carol Clover at the University of California, Berkeley, for all their assistance in the earliest days of my thinking about this project—and Steve for a lot of extra help recently. Then I want to thank my supportive and brilliant colleagues (present and past) at Columbia University—Paul Strohm, Susan Crane, Chris Baswell, Tricia Dailey, Ezra Tawil, Jim Adams, Nick Dames, Aaron Ritzenberg, Edward Mendelson, Julie Crawford, Kathy Eden, Molly Murray, Hannah Weaver, Rachel Adams, Alan Stewart, Elisabeth Ladenson, and the inimitable Julie Peters. I am particularly grateful to Jean Howard and Jim Shapiro for bending over backward to help me frame this project the right way. I also thank my fantastic students, whose questions during lectures and seminars pushed this book to be much braver than it might have been. A special shout-out to Michael Dalby, my mentor of longest tenure; everything you ever said about this project ended up being right. Another shout-out to Brooke Holmes, my sympathetic coconspirator and stalwart writing partner, who smartens me by the week. A special thank you to Robert Michaels, whose impact on this book's finally getting finished cannot be overstated. I want to thank my almost impossibly excellent friends, who've been hearing me talk about this book for almost twenty years: Marie, Catherine, Sarah, Emily, Beth, Erin, Ellen, Mark, Olivia, and Julia. You are my oxygen, and I am so grateful for you all, always. I thank my parents for their dauntless support and love, as well as for listening to me talk through a hundred versions of how the book would look. And most of all, I thank my luminous children, Emlyn and Joanie: more than words, I love you. You make me grow every day, and you made this book grow too, by being your radiant selves and making me want to do what I can to fight for a beautiful world for you.

Earlier versions of portions of chapters 2, 3, and 4 appeared in "The Poetics of Waste: Medieval English Ecocriticism," *PMLA* 127 (May 2012): 460–76.

NOTES

INTRODUCTION

1   See F. Stuart Chapin, Pamela A. Matson, and Harold A. Mooney, *Principles of Terrestrial Ecosystem Ecology* (New York: Springer, 2002), 7–11.

2   *Oxford English Dictionary* online, "System," etymology.

3   Gillian Rudd also privileges "ecosystem" in her study of "green reading" in medieval literature. Rudd sees ecosystem as bespeaking a necessary interrelationality, whether large or small. "It is not possible to exist outside an ecosystem of some sort and all things necessarily partake of the largest one of the planet as a whole. Even on a local level, where it is possible to say that particular individuals (human or other) are not part of a given system, it is still the case that their being outside it helps to define it. . . . Every species is implicated in the fates of others." See Rudd, *Greenery: Ecocritical Readings of Late Middle English Literature* (Manchester: Manchester University Press, 2007), 7, 9.

4   Justin Barker's reading of *Piers Plowman* argues for using "ecological" as a central critical term: "An ecological reading of *Piers Plowman*, as I define it, emphasizes the interconnectedness of nature, humans and the divine. Specifically, to read ecologically is to read beyond the scope of the human and to be aware that all elements of the world interconnect." See Barker, "'Alle Kynnes Thynges': The Ecology of *Piers Plowman*," *Parergon* 33 (2016): 70. Barker's usage of "ecological," he notes, draws on Timothy Morton's idea that "ecological thought" is "a practice and process of becoming fully aware of how human beings are connected with other beings—animal, vegetable, or mineral." See Morton, *The Ecological Thought* (Cambridge, MA: Harvard University Press, 2010), 7.

5   Bruno Latour has questioned and destabilized the notion that "nature" and "culture" are (or could ever be) truly separate in his groundbreaking theoretical work on actor-network theory, which stipulates that any hiving off of culture from nature is artificial and fails to see that the two are

mutually interpenetrating. I will turn to Latour's theories in earnest later, especially in the epilogue. I don't use "actor-network" or even "network" as a term to ground my own study because, again, I want to foreground lexically the ideas of livability and organization—the ecosystem.

6 See Dipesh Chakrabarty, *The Climate of History in a Planetary Age* (Chicago: University of Chicago Press, 2021), 1–20, esp. 3 and note 5 to "Introduction," which references canonical writings on the Anthropocene such as Jeremy Davies's *The Birth of the Anthropocene* (Berkeley: University of California Press, 2018) and Simon Lewis and Mark Maslin's *The Human Planet: How We Created the Anthropocene* (London: Penguin, 2018).

7 The perplexity is of course less pervasive among medievalists than among others, since medievalists have become acutely interested in these issues in the past decade. There is in fact a growing trend of focusing on ecosystemic change and crisis in the Middle Ages. A new journal, *Medieval Ecocriticisms*, focuses its inaugural issue on weather, and scholar Shannon Gayk is completing a monograph titled *Apocalyptic Ecologies*. Jeffrey Jerome Cohen's brilliant and beautiful book *Stone: An Ecology of the Inhuman* (Minneapolis: University of Minnesota Press, 2015) helped prepare the way for work like this by focusing on stones as real entities that in the Middle Ages had the power to shape and affect the way people understood themselves in relation to the natural world. Two years before Cohen's book, Carolyn Dinshaw urged scholars to think more broadly and flexibly about nature and ecological philosophy in medieval art and literature. See Dinshaw, "Ecology," in *A Handbook of Middle English Studies*, ed. Marion Turner (West Sussex, UK: John Wiley, 2013), 347–62. Yet earlier, Lisa Kiser and Sarah Stanbury both called attention to ecological thought in medieval English literature. See Kiser, "Chaucer and the Politics of Nature," in *Beyond Nature Writing*, ed. Karla Armbruster and Kathleen A. Wallace (Charlottesville: University of Virginia Press, 2001), 41–56, and Sarah Stanbury, "EcoChaucer: Green Ethics and Medieval Nature," *Chaucer Review* 39, no. 1 (2004): 1–16.

8 For scholarly analysis of these phenomena, see Susan Crane, *Animal Encounters: Contacts and Concepts in Medieval Britain* (Philadelphia: University of Pennsylvania Press, 2012).

9 For extended treatments of how medieval people understood the physicality and materiality of their writing surfaces, see Sarah Kay, *Animal Skins and the Reading Self* (Chicago: University of Chicago Press, 2017). See also Bruce Holsinger's luminous new book *On Parchment: Animals,*

NOTES TO PAGES 4–8 : 179

Archives, and the Making of Culture from Herodotus to the Digital Age (New Haven, CT: Yale University Press, 2023).

10 Carolyn Dinshaw, "Ecology," in *A Handbook of Middle English Studies*, ed. Marion Turner (West Sussex, UK: John Wiley, 2013), 347—62.

11 One fascinating and unusual study of medieval ecopoetics looks at how Irish representations of the Otherworld—which is to say, supernatural and magical regions that connect in mysterious ways with the regular world of everyday life—express volumes about how medieval people understood their own relation to their actual environment, as well as their (and their environment's) relation to God and transcendence. See Alfred Siewers, *Strange Beauty: Ecocritical Approaches to Early Modern Landscape* (New York: Palgrave, 2009). Siewers points out the imaginative importance of the Otherworld to Ireland's own geographic and topographic relation to other real-world places: "The cultural combination of insular identity and connectivity parallels aspects of the doubled landscape of the Otherworld itself, as well as of the trope's geographical doppelgänger, archipelago" (Siewers, 8). Siewers sees the Irish landscape as, in effect, a reflection of the Otherworld itself—landscape and Otherworld are mutually interpenetrating spatial and temporal realities, and the presence of the Other in the Real has the effect of changing our experience of time and space in the here and now (Siewers, 18, 20–21, 29, 31, 41, 48). What I like most about Siewers's work is the way it insists on the immanence of the transcendent—the real-lifeness of the Otherworld. Although my own study doesn't focus so much on otherworldliness, it too will insist that spiritual matters are truly *matter*, in the sense of belonging to and affecting the ecosystemic world and its functionality.

12 Sophie Gee, *Making Waste: Leftovers and the Eighteenth-Century Imagination* (Princeton, NJ: Princeton University Press, 2010).

13 Pope Francis, *Laudato si': On Care for Our Common Home* (Huntingdon, IN: Our Sunday Visitor, 2015), 48.

14 Lynn White argued that the modern view of nature as something to pilfer and dominate is an inheritance from the Middle Ages. See Lynn White, "Historical Roots of Our Ecological Crisis," in *The Ecocriticism Reader*, ed. Cheryll Glotfelty and Harold Fromm (Athens: University of Georgia Press, 1996), 12. Working with, through, and beyond White's ideas, Jeffrey Jerome Cohen says, "Most medieval representations of nature strive to reinforce human domination of the earth rather than offer a mode of companionate dwelling." Cohen, *Stone*, 28–29.

CHAPTER ONE

1 Maria Rosa Menocal, *The Ornament of the World: How Muslims, Jews, and Christians Created a Culture of Tolerance in Medieval Spain* (New York: Little, Brown, 2002).

2 William Newman, "What Have We Learned from the Recent Historiography of Alchemy?," *Isis* 102, no. 2 (2011): 313–21.

3 Richard Hoffman, *An Environmental History of Medieval Europe* (Cambridge: Cambridge University Press, 2014), 149.

4 Hoffman, 150.

5 Hoffman, 160.

6 The poem (translated into Modern English) reads, "Antichrist came then, and all the crop of truth / turned upside down, and he overturned the roots / And made falsehood spring and spread, and speed men's needs." For the original Middle English, see William Langland, *Piers Plowman: A Parallel-Text of A, B, C, and Z Versions*, ed. A. V. C. Schmidt (New York: Longman, 1995), B 20, 722, 52–55.

7 Hoffman, 240.

8 H. Neilson, "Early English Woodland and Waste," *Journal of Economic History* 2 (1942): 54–62; D. R. Denman, *The Origins of Ownership* (London: Unwin, 1958), 125.

9 Hoffman, 252. Traditionally, historians have understood the period of intensive and damaging privatization of land to have been the Early Modern period, say from about 1500 to 1700. But by the fourteenth century, 25 percent of England's available land had been privatized through afforestation. The economic pressures of afforestation were extreme enough that in 1327 some forests were "disafforested" and returned to common use. That seems like a meaningful break for farmers and nonaristocrats, but that *some* land was disafforested points to the severity of the problem beforehand rather than to its being decisively resolved by the legislation.

10 Neilson, "Early English Woodland," 58, 61. See Denman, 103: "Land is assarted from the wild by taking new areas into the orbit of cultivation"; and *Black's Law Dictionary*, 7th ed., ed. Bryan Garner (St. Paul, MN: West Group, 1999), 109: "Assart: Hist. 1. The action of pulling up trees and bushes to make the land arable. This was a crime if done without a license."

11 The discourse of uselessness that Vittoria Di Palma rightly associates with the wastelands in later periods, and the correlative discourse of moral

NOTES TO PAGES 14–16 : 181

disgust that she also sees, are not present in the medieval context. See Vittoria Di Palma, *Wastelands: A History* (New Haven, CT: Yale University Press, 2014), 22–34. In the Middle Ages there was no sense that the wastelands needed to be "improved" (Di Palma, 43–83, esp. 44); that sense emerges later.

12 Oliver Rackham, *The History of the Countryside* (London: J. M. Dent, 1986), 291 ff.

13 Denman, 115.

14 McKechnie, *Magna Carta: A Commentary on the Great Charter of King John, with an Historical Introduction* (Glasgow: Maclehose, 1914), 175.

15 "Think of the activities you'd consider normal as a peasant living near a wood . . . digging turf for fuel or marl for fertiliser; carrying a strung bow; allowing your pigs to root freely for acorns (pannage); having or extending a common pasture for stock grazing; taking even small wood to repair your house or your hedges (housebote and haybote); building a new barn in an open space. Illegal under the definition of Common Law forest, these are criminous acts, subject to fines, and central authorities." Ralph Hanna, "'The Wilderness of Wirral' and Further Thoughts on 'The Gawain-Country': Literature, Landscape and Ideologies in the Later Middle Ages," presented at the University of York CMS and English conference, June 25, 2005.

16 Hanna, n.p.

17 Denman, 176, 177.

18 Selden Society, *Select Cases of Trespass*, 376 ff.

19 See Jean Birrill, "Common Rights in the Medieval Forest: Disputes and Conflicts in the Thirteenth Century," *Past and Present* 117 (1987): 22–49. "To quote two examples, a dozen people threw dozen hedges and ditches round legally rented purprestures in the New Forest in the 1330s, and a band of forty armed men from five villages threw down enclosures and burned hedges in the forest of Galtres in 1348" (48)

20 Selden Society, *Select Cases of Trespass*, 303. A similar case is recorded on the following page from the year 1345, and again in 1383.

21 Selden Society, *Select Cases of Trespass from the King's Courts, 1307–1399*, ed. Arnold Morris, vol. 103 (London: Selden Society), 280.

22 For a fascinating historicizing of the very idea of "immemorial time" in English law, see M. T. Clanchy, "Remembering the Past and the Good Old Law," *History* 55 (1970): 165–76, at 174.

23 In this case from 1382 the abbot responds by producing a document in

which William's ancestor quitclaimed his commons rights to certain areas. William and the others respond by saying the covenant in question did not pertain to the lands in which they committed their potential trespass, and which they hold in common. Ultimately, following the general trend toward validation of private ownership in this period, William and his allies were convicted, and the abbot's right to enclose the former commons was upheld (Selden Society, *Select Cases of Trespass*, 338).

24 Lynn Staley has written compellingly about "the anxieties of enclosure" throughout late Middle English literature, focusing with special care and sensitivity on *Piers Plowman, Winner and Waster*, and the *Canterbury Tales*. See Staley, *The Island Garden: England's Language of Nation from Gildas to Marvell* (Notre Dame, IN: University of Notre Dame Press, 2012), 75–90. My own *PMLA* article (2012) on *Piers* and *Winner* traversed some of the same ground about waste, which I will come back to in chapter 5. See Eleanor Johnson, "The Poetics of Waste: Medieval English Ecocriticism," *PMLA* 127 (May 2012): 460–76. But Staley goes into great detail about the phenomenon of enclosure and how it was represented in medieval literature, with attention to the traumatic nature of enclosure for people going back to the early fourteenth century. See Staley, 121–76.

25 *Parlement of the Thre Ages*, ed. Warren Ginsburg (TEAMS, 1992), line 94. Translation mine.

26 Denman, 114. Assarting was particularly prevalent during the thirteenth century and up until the plague years of 1349 and following, during which time the development and assarting of lands tapered off because of a decrease in population. Oliver Rackham, *Trees and Woodland in the British Landscape* (London: J. M. Dent, 1976), 171.

27 Birrill, "Common Rights in the Medieval Forests," 117.

28 Rosemary Hopcroft, "The Social Origins of Agrarian Change in Late Medieval England," *American Journal of Sociology* 99 (1994): 1563. Resulting in part from this gradual assarting, the concentration of individual wealth in the southwest and east of England compared with the northern areas of the country grew enormously up until the late fifteenth century. These areas were characterized by "irregular open fields and enclosures," which meant, effectively, more privately held land than in more northerly reaches of the country, which had "open [commonly held] fields" and a more traditionally manorial socioeconomic structure (1581–82). The irregular fields and enclosures, and the abolition or near abolition of common property that they bespeak, enabled a relatively early concentration of

wealth and tailoring of local agricultural production to the demands of national and international trade.

29 As Hoffman puts it, "Any consideration of the sustainability of medieval northern agroecosystems must acknowledge that something went quite wrong during the first part of the fourteenth century" (166).

30 Hoffman, 324.

31 William Chester Jordan, *The Great Famine: Northern Europe in the Early Fourteenth Century* (Princeton, NJ: Princeton University Press, 1996), 8. Other factors contributing to the Great Famine were the massive increase in European population in the generations before the shortages, which could not be met by available agricultural resources and technology; distribution problems attendant on chronic warfare; and unwise domestic practices in advance of coming shortages. England's population is thought to have increased from about 1.5 million in 1100 to about 5 million in 1300. See Jordan, 12–13.

32 William Rosen, *The Third Horseman: A Story of Weather, War, and the Famine That History Forgot* (New York: Penguin, 2014), 133. The estimated fatality rate is between 5 percent and 12 percent of the population of all of Northern Europe.

33 Rosen, 150.

34 Jordan, 32.

35 Rosen, 151–52. See also Brian Fagan, *The Little Ice Age: How Climate Made History* (New York: Basic Books, 2000), 40.

36 Jordan, 37.

37 Jordan, 36–37.

38 Jordan, 37.

39 Fagan, 40.

40 Jordan, 38.

41 Jordan, 37.

42 Jordan, 17.

43 Hoffman, 325.

44 J. A. Galloway, "Coastal Flooding and Socioeconomic Changes in Eastern England in the Later Middle Ages," *Environment and History* 19 (2013): 173–207, at 184.

45 Galloway, 186.

46 Galloway, 187.

47 Galloway, 188–92.

48 J. A. Galloway, "Marine Flooding in the Thames Estuary and Tidal River c.

1250–1450: Impact and Response," *Area* 39, no. 3 (2007): 370–79, at 373.

49 Galloway, "Marine Flooding," 373–74.

50 James A. Galloway, "'Tempests of Weather and Great Abundance of Water': The Flooding of the Barking Marshes in the Later Middle Ages," in *London and Beyond: Essays in Honor of Derek Keene*, ed. Matthew Davies and James A. Galloway (London: Institute of Historical Research, 2012), 75.

51 Galloway, "'Tempests,'" 77, 78.

52 P. F. Brandon, "Late Medieval Weather in Sussex and Its Agricultural Significance," *Transactions of the Institute of British Geographers* 54 (1971): 1–17, at 5.

53 Hoffman, 328, 332.

54 Hoffman, 342.

55 This quotation is from Jordan's book, which he translates from Curschmann, *Hungersnöte*, 215. The original reads, "inundatio tanta aquarium facta fuit, quod quasi particulare diluvium videretur." See Fritz Curschmann, *Hungersnöte im Mittelalter: Ein Beitrag zur deutschen Wirtschaftsgeschichte des 8. bis 13. Jahrhunderts* (Leipzig: Leipziger Studien aus dem Gebiet der Geschichte, 1900).

56 Jordan, 24.

57 Lines 451, 450.

58 *Wynnere and Wastoure*, ed. Warren Ginsburg (TEAMS, 1992), 12–13.

59 Morton Bloomfield, "*Piers Plowman* as a Fourteenth-Century Apocalypse," *Centennial Review* 5 (1961): 281–95; Douglas Bertz, "Prophecy and Apocalypse in Langland's 'Piers Plowman,' B-Text, Passūs XIV to XIX," *Journal of English and Germanic Philology* 84 (1985): 313–27.

60 William Langland, *Piers Plowman: A Parallel-Text of A, B, C, and Z Versions*, ed. A. V. C. Schmidt (New York: Longman, 1995). Passages from this poem will be cited in this chapter by version, passus, page, and lines, so: A, 5, 177, 14–20.

61 *Piers*, A, 7, 315, 302–7.

62 "Piers the Plowman's Crede," ed. James Dean, from *Six Ecclesiastical Satires* (TEAMS, 1991), line 432.

63 Line 435.

64 Line 440.

65 Bonnie Millar, "*Richard the Redeles* and the Concept of Advice," *Reading Medieval Studies* 24 (1998): 54–77, at 54.

66 See also James Dean, "Introduction," *Richard the Redeles* (TEAMS, 2000).

NOTES TO PAGES 24–29 : 185

67 *Richard the Redeles*, ed. James Dean (TEAMS, 2000), 124, 125, 127.

68 *Richard the Redeles*, 131.

69 *Richard the Redeles*, 133–34.

70 Geoffrey Chaucer, *Canterbury Tales*, lines 1–18. Translation mine. This and all other quotations from Chaucer are taken from *The Riverside Chaucer*, ed. Larry Benson (Boston: Houghton Mifflin, 1985).

71 Hoffman, 291; William H. TeBrake, "Air Pollution and Fuel Crises in Preindustrial England, 1250–1650," *Technology and Culture* 16, no. 3 (1975): 337–59, at 355.

72 There are data to suggest that mortality rates were higher among frailer portions of the population and that the first waves of Black Death were so severe compared with later waves, because the first major die-off ended up leaving alive only the heartiest people in a given age bracket. See Sharon DeWitte, "Mortality Risk and Survival in the Aftermath of the Medieval Black Death," *PLoS One* 9, no. 5 (2014): e96513.

73 E. A. Bond, ed., *Chronica Morasterii de Melsa*, 3 vols., *Rolls Series, 1866–1886*, 3:35–37, 40, 72. Cited in Rosemary Horrox, *The Black Death* (Manchester: Manchester University Press, 1994), 68.

74 William H. TeBrake, "Air Pollution and Fuel Crises in Preindustrial England, 1250–1650," *Technology and Culture* 16, no. 3 (1975): 337–59, at 355.

75 Hoffman, 291.

76 John Kelly, *The Great Mortality: An Intimate History of the Black Death, the Most Devastating Plague of All Time* (New York: Harper Perennial, 2005), 219.

77 Kelly, 292.

78 Rebecca Carol Noel Totaro, *Suffering in Paradise: The Bubonic Plague in Literature from More to Milton* (Pittsburgh: Duquesne University Press, 2005), 26.

79 In *Piers*, Reason prays for the people: he "preyede the peple haue pite on hemselue, / And prouide that thise pestilences was for pur synne" (prayed the people have pity on themselves, / and argued that the pestilences were the result of pure sin) A, 5, 177, 12–13.

80 Horrox, *Black Death*, 95.

81 Giovanni Boccaccio, *Decameron*, trans. John Payne (New York: Walter J. Black, 1935), from "Day the First," accessed online at Project Gutenberg.

82 Boccaccio, *Decameron*.

83 Margery Kempe had at least fourteen.

186 : NOTES TO PAGES 29–33

84 David Coley, *Death and the Pearl Maiden* (Columbus: Ohio State University Press, 2019), 9.

85 Boccaccio says, "I say, then, that the years [of the era] of the fruitful Incarnation of the Son of God had attained to the number of one thousand three hundred and forty-eight, when into the notable city of Florence, fair over every other of Italy, there came the death-dealing pestilence, which, through the operation of the heavenly bodies or of our own iniquitous dealings, being sent down upon mankind for our correction by the just wrath of God, had some years before appeared in the parts of the East and after having bereft these latter of an innumerable number of inhabitants, extending without cease from one place to another, had now unhappily spread towards the West." Boccaccio, *Decameron*, trans. John Payne (New York: Walter J. Black Inc., 1935), from "Day the First," accessed online at Project Gutenberg.

86 E. M. Thompson, ed., *Robertus de Avesbury de Gestis Mirabilibus Regis Edwardi Tertii*, Rolls Series, 1889, 406–7; British Library, Cottonian MS, Faustina B V fols. 86v–101. Cited in Horrox, *Black Death*, 64 and 70.

87 Antonia Gransden, ed., "A Fourteenth-Century Chronicle from the Grey Friars at Lynn," *English Historical Review* 72 (1957): 274. Cited in Horrox, *Black Death*, 63.

88 Lynn Perrigo, "Plagues and Pollution in Medieval England," *Social Science* 46 (1971): 133–38, at 138.

89 Coley, *Death and the Pearl Maiden*, chap. 1.

90 Coley, *Death and the Pearl Maiden*, chap. 2.

91 "Kynde came after hym, with many kene sores, / As pokes and pestilences, and muche peple shente . . . Many a louely lady and hir lemmans knyghtes / Swowned and swelted for sorwe of Dethes dyntes," *Piers Plowman*, B, 20, 724, 97–98; B, 20, 105.

92 Chaucer, *Canterbury Tales, The Pardoner's Tale*, 675.

93 *The Pardoner's Tale*, 679, 688.

94 Calendar of the Patent Rolls, Edward I, 1281–92, 207, cited in William H. TeBrake, "Air Pollution and Fuel Crises in Preindustrial England, 1250–1650," *Technology and Culture* 16, no. 3 (1975): 337–59, at 339.

95 TeBrake, 340.

96 Hoffman, 204.

97 Maryanne Kowaleski, "Medieval People in Town and Country," *Speculum* 89, no. 3 (2014): 573–600, at 589–90.

98 Perrigo, "Plagues and Pollution in Medieval England," 133–38.

NOTES TO PAGES 33–38 : 187

99 Dolly Jørgensen, "Running Amuck? Urban Swine Management in Late Medieval England," *Agricultural History* 87, no. 4 (2013): 429–51, at 434.

100 Perrigo, 133–38.

101 John Lydgate, *Troy Book*, ed. Robert R. Edwards (TEAMS, 1998), book 2, 731–36.

102 "The Blacksmiths," in *Fourteenth-Century Verse and Prose*, ed. Kenneth Sisam (Oxford: Clarendon Press, 1921), 169, at lines 2, 3, 5, 7, 19, and 22. This poem survives in one manuscript, British Museum MS Arundel 292, dating to the early fifteenth century.

CHAPTER TWO

1 And also in military narratives, which I'll talk more about shortly. All quotations from the Bible are drawn from the Latin Vulgate, and the translations are my own. *Biblia Sacra Vulgata*, ed. Robert Weber and Roger Gryson (Deutsche Bibelgesellschaft, 1983).

2 This distinction is sometimes minimized or overlooked even by thorough and insightful scholarship. Vittoria Di Palma's path-breaking cultural history of the wastelands lumps together the biblical categories of wasteland, desert, and solitary place, effacing the difference between a naturally uninhabited place and a place that was once inhabited but was emptied out—*terra vastata* (Di Palma, *Wastelands: A History* [New Haven, CT: Yale University Press, 2014]). She sees wasteland's emptiness as its "core characteristic" but does not register that the emptiness is created and produced rather than natural (Di Palma, 3). She sees wastelands as places of "lack," whereas they are actually, at least in biblical discourse, places of privation and destruction (Di Palma, 4). A desert is a place that never had a city; a wasteland is a place that once *was* a city. Later Di Palma says, "In the Old Testament, the westen was the place to which the Israelites were banished" (Di Palma, 16); but in Latin Bibles the wastelands were usually the places various peoples were banished *from*. Di Palma does note that in Middle English the word "wasteland" came to denote "devastation" (17); but in biblical discourse, devastation was always part of the meaning of waste. And she eventually notes, too, that "wasteland" does have a subtle distinction from wilderness and desert, precisely because of its association with devastation (Di Palma, 18). This is absolutely right, but it's important to further emphasize that wastelands aren't just associated with devastation; they *are* devastation.

3 All biblical citations originate in *Biblia Sacra Vulgata*, ed. Robert Weber

188 : NOTES TO PAGES 39–43

and Roger Gryson (Stuttgart: Deutsche Bibelgesellschaft, 1983). All translations are my own.

4 Instances of this kind of wasting are frequent in the Old Testament. See Numbers 24:17 and 24:24, and Joshua 10:36–43.

5 I noted earlier that wasting (as *vastare*) occurs in the Bible as well as in military narratives; to elaborate on that briefly here, waste comes up *when* the Bible enacts military narration *and* in classical epic and classical military narratives.

6 For those not versed in the technicalities of medieval English law, unlike other medieval European countries, England had a bizarre arrangement of legal jurisdictions. Ecclesiastical jurisdiction encompassed, essentially, what is now family law, the law that pertains to movable property, and to a decreasing extent, the law of covenants, serfs, and torts. Manorial jurisdiction was local justice, doled out by local manorial lords. The King's Bench oversaw significant criminal behaviors. The so-called Common Law was a jurisdiction that pertained primarily to the law of property. The Common Law dealt with things like inheritance, the alienation of property, infractions against a neighbor's lands, tenancy, and rights to land use.

7 S. F. C. Milsom, "Legal Introduction," in *Novae Narrationes*, ed. Elsie Shanks and S. F. C. Milsom (London: Selden Society, 1963), vols. 100 and 103, cxci.

8 K. J. Kesselring, "Felony Forfeiture in England, 1170–1870," *Journal of Legal History* 30, no. 3 (2009): 201–26.

9 *Statutes of the Realm*, vol. 1, 1215–1713 (London: Eyre and Strahan, 1810, repr. 1963), Magna Carta, p. 9. "Custos terre hujusmodi heredis qui infra etatem fuerit, non capiat de terra heredis nisi racionabiles exitus, et racionabiles consuetudines, et racionabilia servitia, et hoc sine destructione et vasto hominum vel rerum."

10 Milsom claims that the Great Charter's provisions against waste apply only to royal wardships, whereas the first statute of Westminster, c. 21, extends the protection against waste to all chivalric wardships (Milsom, cxci). T. F. T. Plucknett assumes, likewise, that Magna Carta applied only to tenants-in-chief. See Plucknett, *Statutes and Their Interpretation in the Fourteenth Century* (Cambridge: Cambridge University Press, 1922), 74.

11 Medieval legal historian Henry Bracton writes, in about 1235, that the guardian functions merely to guard the land for the future inheritance of the heir, and that any profits the guardian takes from the land should serve only to defray the costs of the wardship. If the guardian exceeds these

profits, he commits waste. See William Pollock and F. W. Maitland, *The History of the English Law, before the time of Edward I*, vol. 1 (Cambridge: Cambridge University Press, 1898), 326.

12 "Provisum est & quod si terra que tenetur in socagio sit in custodia paren-tum heredis, eo quod heres infra etatem exstiterit, custodes illi vastum facere non possint neque, vendicionem neque, aliquam destruccionem de hereditate; sed salvo eam custodian ad opus dicti heredis: ita quod cum ad etatem pervenerit, sibi respondeant per legitimam computacionem de exitibus dicte hereditatis; salvis ipsis custodibus rationabilibus misis suis" (*Statutes of the Realm*, vol. 1, p. 24, c. 17) (It is Provided, That if Land holden in Socage be in the Custody of the Friends of the Heir, because the Heir is within age, the Guardians shall make no Waste, nor Sale, nor any Destruction of the same Inheritance; but safely shall keep it to the use of the said Heir: so that when he cometh to his lawful Age, they shall answer to him for the Issues of the said Inheritance by a lawful Accompt, saving to the same Guardians their reasonable costs.)

13 See *Black's Law Dictionary*, 7th ed., s.v. "socage," p. 1395. See also D. R. Denman, *The Origins of Ownership* (London: George Allen and Unwin, 1958), 118.

14 Paul Brand has demonstrated that the Statute of Marlborough represents not a radical innovation at law, but rather the culmination of continual intermittent legislative amendments to the 1259 Provisions of Westmin-ster. Indeed, Brand finds that one of the French rewritings of the Provi-sions actually includes a clause condemning waste in socage. But the 1267 Marlborough was the first truly mainstream, Latinate, authoritative text to concretize the legal developments that had been in the works since 1259. See Paul Brand, "Drafting of Legislation in Mid-Thirteenth-Century England," in Brand, *The Making of the Common Law* (London: Hamble-don Press, 1992), 352–53, 364.

15 "Et si fecerint & super hoc convincantur dampna plene refundent, & gaverit per merciam puniantur" (*Statutes of the Realm*, 1:24, c. 23). (Which thing if they do, and thereof be convict, they shall yield full Damage, and shall be punished by Amerciament grievously.)

16 *Statutes of the Realm*, 1:24, c. 23. "Item firmari tempore firmarum suarum vastum, vendicionem, seu exilium non faciant, in domibus, boscis, hosi-bus, neque de aliquibus ad tenementa que ad firmam herent spectantibus, ni specialem habuerint concessionem per scripturam sive convencionis mencionem quod hoc facere possint" (Also Fermors, during their Terms,

190 : NOTES TO PAGES 45–47

shall not make Waste, Sale, nor Exile of House, Woods, Men, nor of any Thing belonging to the Tenements that they have to ferm, without special License had by Writing of Covenant, making mention that they may do it).

17 *Statutes of the Realm*, 1:48, c. 5. "Ensement purveu est qe len eit desoremes bref de Wast en la Chauncelrie, [fet de ceo sur] home qi tient par la ley de Engleterre, ou en autre manere a terme de vie, ou a terme de annz, ou femme en doweire, e celui qi serra ateint de Wast perde la chose [qil ad] wastee e estre ceo face gre del trebble de ceo qe le Wast serra taxe. E Endreit de Wast fet en garde seit [fet] solom ceo qe il est contenu en la graunt chartre. E par [la ou il est contenu] en la graunt chartre, qe celui qi avera fet wast en garde, perde la garde, acorde est qe il rende al heir les damages del wast, si issi ne seit qe la garde perdue ne soffise my a la value des damages avaunt le age del heir de mesme la garde" (It is provided also, that a Man from henceforth shall have a Writ of Waste in the Chancery against him that holdeth by law of England, or otherwise for Term of Life, or for Term of Years, or a Woman in Dower; and he which shall be attainted of Waste, shall leese the Thing that he hath wasted, and moreover shall recompense thrice so much as the Waste shall be taxed at. And for Waste made in the Time of Wardship, it shall be done as is contained in the Great Charter. And where it is contained in the Great Charter, that he which did Waste during the Custody, shall leese the Wardship, It is agreed that he shall recompense the Heir his Damages for the Waste, if so be that the Wardship lost do not amount to the Value of the Damages before the Age of the Heir of the same Wardship).

18 Brand, *Making of the Common Law*, 96.

19 T. F. T. Plucknett, *The Legislation of Edward I* (London: Cambridge University Press, 1949), 83.

20 For a full discussion of this important fiction at common law, see Bruce R. O'Brien, *God's Peace and King's Peace: The Laws of Edward the Confessor* (Philadelphia: University of Pennsylvania Press, 1999).

21 See Plucknett, *Statutes and Their Interpretation in the Fourteenth Century*, 22.

22 *Statutes of the Realm*, 1:109–10.

23 By the middle of the fourteenth century, in Plucknett's assessment, "Butler's case [1292] is on the way to being regarded as a statute. . . . contemporaries fully recognized its legislative effect, while two centuries later the early printers boldly entitled it Statutum de Vasto." *Statutes and Their Interpretation*, 23.

24 See *Black's Law Dictionary*, 7th ed., 564. The *Oxford English Dictionary* online specifies the etymology of the term as follows: "Escheat: [ME.

NOTES TO PAGES 48–52 : 191

eschete, a. OF. *eschete, eschaete, escheoite*, n. of action (orig. fem. pa. pple.), f. OF. *escheoir* (mod.F. *échoir*):—late L. **excadēre* (class. L. *excidēre*) to fall to a person's share, f. L. *ex* out + *cadēre* (vulg. L. *cadēre*, OF. *cheoir*) to fall. In continental OF. the n. meant succession, inheritance, esp. collateral inheritance; in England the etymological sense received a different application. As in many other words (cf. *exchange*) the prefix *es-* was in the 16–17th c. often replaced by *ex-* after L. analogies.] . . . An 'incident' of feudal law, whereby a fief reverted to the lord when the tenant died without leaving a successor qualified to inherit under the original grant. Hence, the lapsing of land to the Crown (in U.S., to the state), or to the lord of the manor, on the death of the owner intestate without heirs."

25 "Into perjury against the king fall escheators who make waste in the wardships or fees of the king, or take venison, or fish" (*Mirror of Justices*, ed. F. W. Maitland [London: Selden Society, 1895], 7:77). See Jennifer Jahner, "The *Mirror of Justices* and the Art of Archival Invention," *Viator* 45 (2014): 221–46.

26 14 Edw. III, 1, c. 13. See *Statutes of the Realm*, 1:290. The statute, further, sets up a commission whereby, in situations of escheatorial waste, the heir's closest relative takes the lands into his possession until the heir reaches his majority. In addition to this added protection, once he comes of age, the heir can sue the escheator for wastes done during his minority and prior to the relief afforded by the transfer of possession to his collateral relative.

27 14 Edw. III, 4, 4. *Statutes of the Realm*, 1:294.

28 1362 Statute of Purveyances, 36 Edw. III. The statute claims that escheators have been committing "wast et destruccion" (*Statutes*, 374) in lands of wards within age. It then insists that an escheator has no rights of wood, fish, or venison and must answer to the king for issues and profits yearly until the majority of the heir, at which point the escheator must "rende al heir les damages au treble." cf. Gloucester.

29 Capitula Escaetrie, *Statutes*, 238–41.

CHAPTER THREE

1 Augustine of Hippo, *Sermon 9: Evangelio Luc. XVII* (Patroloia Latina, ed. J.-P. Migne, online edition, vol. 46, col. 1000).

2 Rabanus Maurus, *Expositionis super Jeremiam Prophetam Libri Viginti* (PL, 111, col. 1118).

3 Aelred of Rievalux, *Sermones de oneribus* (PL, 195, cols. 455–56).

192 : NOTES TO PAGES 52–59

4   Aelred, *Sermones*, 462–63.

5   Aelred, *Sermones*, 485–86.

6   Hugh of Saint Victor, *Adnotationes elucidatoriae in Joelem Prophetam* (PL, 175, cols. 323–24).

7   *Glossa ordinaria*, "Evangelium Secundum Joannem" (PL, 114, col. 397).

8   See *Middle English Dictionary*, s.v. "wasten." *Middle English Dictionary*, ed. Robert E. Lewis, et al. (Ann Arbor: University of Michigan Press, 1952–2001), Online edition in Middle English Compendium, ed. Frances McSparran et al. (Ann Arbor: University of Michigan Library, 2000–2018), http://quod.lib.umich.edu/m/middle-english-dictionary/, accessed 26 January 2023.

9   Dan Michel, *Ayenbite of Inwit*, ed. Pamela Gradon (London: Oxford University Press, 1965), prologue: "This boc is ywrite / uor englisse men, thet hi wyte / hou hi ssolle ham-zelue ssriue, / and maki ham klene / ine thise liue" (This book is written for English men, that they may know how they shall shrive themselves and make themselves pure in this life).

10 See Mannyng, *Handlyng Synne*, ed. F. J. Furnivall, Early English Text Society, original series (London: Oxford University Press, 1901, 1903), lines 37–56.

11 Michel, *Ayenbite*, 18–19.

12 Frère Laurent, *La somme le roi*, ed. Edith Brayer and Anne-Françoise Leurquin-Labie (Paris: Société des anciens textes français, 2007), chap. 32, 209–13, 117.

13 Another Middle English translation of this passage from *La somme* reads "waastid and dispended it in folies and in outrages byfore his lordys ighen ne nought purueieth him of his acounte. And wel he wot that he muste acounte straitly." See *Two Middle English Translations of Friar Laurent's Somme le Roi: Critical Edition*, ed. Emmanuelle Roux (Turnhout: Brepols, 2010), 5, 11, 109–10. A third Middle English translation of the same passage is very similar, emphasizing wasting and misspending as equivalent sins against God: "Wastith and dispendith in folies and in outrages beforn the sight of his Lord the goodis that be nought his owne, but ben the goodis of his Lord of wiche hymm bihoweth streytliche to yelde acounte and rekening." Ibid., 69, 11, 103–6.

14 See also Laurent, *La somme*, chap. 38, 61–62, and specifically 70–71, 153.

15 See Laurent, *La somme*, chap. 38, 152–58, at 155. "La quarte branche est li pechiez de ceus qui trop noblemen veulent vivre, qui despendent et gastent por leur gueules ampler ce dont cent povres porroient estre sou-

fisament peu" (The fourth branch of this sin is of those who want to live too nobly, who spend and waste to fill their gluttony from what could have sufficed for a hundred poor people).

16 *Wycliff Bible*, ed. Josiah Forshall and Frederic Madden (Oxford: Oxford University Press, 1850), 201.

17 The parable of the prodigal son also often features treatments of waste, as when the prodigal son wastes his heritage in ribaldry and lechery. See Laurent, *La somme le roi*, chap. 53, 11–12, 238, and Michel's translation of that passage in the *Ayenbite*, 128: "Ase dede the guode mannes zone thet his eritage wasted and dispendede ine ribaudie and leuede lecherusliche / alhuet him behouede to loki zuyn. Ase oure lhord ous maketh thise uorbysne ine his spelle" (As did the good man's son who wasted and mis-spent his inheritance in ribaldry and lechery, so that he had to take care of swine, as our lord makes the example in his gospel).

18 *Selected Works of John Wyclif: Sermons on the Gospels*, ed. Thomas Arnold (Oxford: Oxford University Press, 1869), 34.

19 *Wyclif: Sermons on the Gospels*, 23–24.

20 See Stephen A. Lahey, *Philosophy and Politics in the Thought of John Wyclif* (Cambridge: Cambridge University Press, 2003), 59.

21 Chaucer built his comic career around critiquing that social paradigm. See Jill Mann, *Chaucer and the Medieval Estates Satire* (Cambridge: Cambridge University Press, 1973).

22 Mann, *Chaucer*, 66.

23 Mann, *Chaucer*, 66.

24 Mann, *Chaucer*, 69–70.

25 Mann, *Chaucer*, 76–77.

26 Bernard of Clairvaux, *Sermones in Cantica canticorum*, PL, 183, col. 891.

27 Bernard of Clairvaux, *Sermones*, 80.

CHAPTER FOUR

1 May McKisack, *The Fourteenth Century: 1307–1399* (Oxford: Oxford University Press, 1991), 313, 333–36; J. M. Bennett and C. W. Hollister, *Medieval Europe: A Short History* (New York: McGraw-Hill, 2006), 326; Charles Ackerman, "The Rural Demography of Medieval England," *Ethnohistory* 23, no. 2 (1976): 105–15.

2 McKisack, 163–66.

3 McKisack, 154–57.

4 McKisack, 335.

5 McKisack, 257.

6 McKisack, 336, 411.

7 Bennett and Hollister, 326; Ackerman, 105–15; Eona Karakacili, "English Agrarian Labor Productivity Rates Before the Black Death: A Case Study," *Journal of Economic History* 64, no. 1 (2004): 26–27; Margaret Schlauch, "The Revolt of 1381 in England," *Science and Society* 4 (1940): 414–32, at 417.

8 Personification allegories are not much more popular in the twenty-first century than are dream visions, but they do play a key role in how poetry does philosophy in the Middle Ages. Personification allegories personify abstract concepts as agents who participate in the action of the poem. For example, a personification allegory might feature a character named Truth. Or Virtue. That character would bop around, interacting with the other characters in the poem, who might also be personifications or might be regular people.

9 Morton Bloomfield, "A Grammatical Approach to Personification Allegory," *Modern Philology* 60, no. 3 (1963): 161–71.

10 Stephanie Trigg, "Introduction," in *Wynnere and Wastoure and The Parlement of the Thre Ages*, ed. Stephanie Trigg (Oxford: Oxford University Press, 1990), xiii–lii, at xxiv–xxv.

11 Morris Arnold, "Introduction," *Select Cases of Trespass from the King's Courts, 1307–1399* (London: Selden Society, 1984), ix; S. F. C. Milsom, *Natural History of the Common Law* (New York: Columbia University Press, 2003), 82; A. W. B. Simpson, *History of the Common Law of Contract* (Oxford: Oxford University Press, 1975), 202.

12 Maura Nolan reads the poem as a staging of a court of chivalry (Nolan, "'With Tresone Within': *Wynnere and Wastoure*, Chivalric Self-Representation and the Law," *Journal of Medieval and Early Modern Studies* 26 [1996]: 1–28).

13 Waste became fully actionable in trespass with the 1292 Statute of Waste (*Statutes of the Realm*, 109–10; Plucknett, *Statutes and Their Interpretation in the Fourteenth Century*, 22–23; Shanks and Milsom, cxcvi).

14 See Arnold, *Select Cases*, xvii. S. F. C. Milsom gives a fuller treatment of trespass law and how it relates to other late medieval legal developments (Milsom, 25–50).

15 Arnold, *Select Cases*, xxvi–xxix.

NOTES TO PAGES 74–81 : 195

16   Indeed, Magna Carta uses "destruction" and "waste" of lands interchangeably, as does Bracton (*Statutes*, 22; Bracton, 410).

17   Since lumber is a key source of revenue, the "wasting" of trees from a piece of property is a paradigmatic type of criminal waste. See the 1382 case of William Brook, in which he and others are accused of cutting trees down *vi et armis* and *contra pacem* (Arnold, *Select Cases*, 38).

18   "Wyse words and slee, and icheon wryeth othere" (*Wynnere and Wastoure*, 6) (Clever words and slick ones, and each one overlays the next).

19   See lines 450–51 in the poem as well as my discussion of these lines in chapter 1.

20   "For almost no one was reckoned worse than a hoarder, a person who profited from the misery of fellow human beings or reserved the earth's bounty for himself while the wretched went hungry." Jordan, *Great Famine*, 3 ("Prologue"). Jordan gives an example of this by citing a medieval tale of children dragging the corpse of a miser around the streets until they eventually flung it into a river and pelted it with rocks. So Waster's critique of Winner would not have struck anyone in the straitened agricultural landscape of midcentury England as unreasonable.

21   Jordan, 19–21.

22   Jordan, 114.

23   *Piers Plowman* is frequently taken as witness to a literature of social protest that existed in late fourteenth-century England. See Steven Justice, *Writing and Rebellion* (Berkeley: University of California Press, 1994), 102–40; Anne Hudson, "Comment: Senses of Censorship," *Journal of British Studies* 46 (2007): 758–61; Kathryn Kerby-Fulton, *Reformist Apocalypticism and "Piers Plowman"* (Cambridge: Cambridge University Press, 1990), 766–73; David Lawton, "Lollardy and the *Piers Plowman* Tradition," *Modern Language Review* 76 (1981): 780–93; Anne Middleton, "Narration and the Invention of Experience: Episodic Form in *Piers Plowman*," in *The Wisdom of Poetry: Essays in Honor of Morton Bloomfield*, ed. Larry Benson and Siegfried Wenzel (Kalamazoo, MI: Medieval Institute Publications, 1982), 94–114; Alan Fletcher, "The Social Trinity of *Piers Plowman*," *Review of English Studies* 44 (1993): 343–61; Andrew Cole, "Trifunctionality and the Tree of Charity: Literacy and Social Practice in *Piers Plowman*," *ELH* 62 (1995): 1–27; Andrew Galloway, "The Making of a Social Ethic in Late Medieval England: From *Gratitudo* to Kyndenesse," *Journal of the History of Ideas* 55 (1994): 365–83.

196 : NOTES TO PAGES 83–86

CHAPTER FIVE

1   This chapter will focus on the first version of the poem, the so-called A-text, but I will address the two later versions—B and C—toward the end of the chapter. The A-text was probably written in about 1362, ten years after *Winner and Waster*.

2   Matthew Giancarlo, "*Piers Plowman*, Parliament, and the Public Voice," *Yearbook of Langland Studies* 17 (2003): 135–74. Langland registers the equivalence of "transgression" and "trespass" in the first passus of his poem: "And taken transgressores and teighen hem faste / Til treuthe hadde termined here trespas to the ende" (And take transgressors and tie them tight, until truth had determined their trespass to its full extent) (37, 94–95).

3   *Piers Plowman*, 4, 149, 37–46, and 65–66. Unless I note otherwise in the chapter, all quotations taken from Schmidt's edition refer to the A-text of the poem, and they will be cited by passus number, page number, and then lines. When I refer to the later versions they will be cited parenthetically by version, passus, page, and lines, as in (B, 19, 710, 355–57).

4   In comparing the two poems' treatments of waste, Lynn Staley has argued that *Piers* shifts focus from how landholders affect the land to how laborers do. See Staley, *The Island Garden: England's Language of Nation from Gildas to Marvell* (Notre Dame, IN: University of Notre Dame Press, 2012), 76–82.

5   Langland's emphasis on the social importance of labor has long been recognized, though the correlation between this labor-oriented emphasis and Langland's ecological consciousness has not been much explored. For examples of this scholarship, see especially Steven Justice and Kathryn Kerby-Fulton's collection *Written Work: Langland, Labor, and Authorship* (Philadelphia: University of Pennsylvania Press, 1997).

6   William Rhodes calls this agrarian ecology in *Piers Plowman* "an ecology of interdependence from which no one may withdraw." See Rhodes, "Medieval Political Ecology: Labour and Agency on the Half Acre," *Yearbook of Langland Studies* 28 (2014): 107. Of course, part of the problem in *Piers Plowman* is that potential workers routinely *do* withdraw from this ecology, which Rhodes elsewhere calls a "political ecology of food production . . . from which no one may withdraw" (117), so that ecosystemic contracture and peril *do* ensue. Langland's vision of ecosystemic interimplication is always balanced on a knife's blade: though no one is supposed to withdraw, people constantly do.

NOTES TO PAGES 87–101 : 197

7   See *La somme le roi*, chap. 53, 33, p. 239: "'Reguarde, cheitis, ta vie ça arrieres, car tu vienz de la taverne au deable ou tu as ta vie gastee et perdu tout ton tens et touz les biens que Diex t'avoit donné'" ("Look, wretch, at your life behind you, for you come from the devil's tavern, where you have wasted your life and lost all your time and all the goods that God had given you"). Dan Michel translates this very precisely: "'Loke, wrechche this lif arrieres / uor thou comst uram the tauerne of the dyuele / huer thou hest / thi lif y-wastid / and y-lore thine time / and alle the guodes that god the hedde y-yeue.'" Dan Michel, *Ayenbite of Inwit*, ed. Richard Morris, rev. Pamela Gradon (London: Oxford University Press, 1965), 129.

8   William Rhodes has brought medieval writings to bear on animal husbandry, suggesting that Langland is broadly concerned with how best practices of agrarian management are on display (and often violated) in the poem. See Rhodes, "Medieval Political Ecology," 117–23.

9   As J. A. Burrow has demonstrated, the later versions of *Piers Plowman* that Langland wrote, the B and C versions, show increasing anxiety about the use of time. See Burrow, "Wasting Time and Wasting Words in *Piers Plowman* B and C," *Yearbook of Langland Studies* 17 (2003): 191–202.

10 Anne Middleton suggested that the assertion of one's lack of habit for working is a reference to a technical way of opting out of the labor economy under the terms of the Statutes of Laborers. See Middleton, "Acts of Vagrancy," in *Written Work: Langland, Labor, and Authorship*, edited by Steven Justice and Kathryn Kerby-Fulton (Philadelphia: University of Pennsylvania Press), 208–317.

11 Those familiar with the work of Bruno Latour will find a resonance here: Latour urges us, following Clive Hamilton, to let go of hope and accept the reality of climate disaster as "definitive." See Latour, *Facing Gaia: Eight Lectures on the New Climatic Regime*, trans. Catherine Porter (Cambridge: Polity Press, 2017), 13. I'll be returning to Latour in the epilogue.

12 William Rhodes sees Hunger as a disciplinary figure and a "manifestation of Adam's curse." See Rhodes, "Medieval Political Ecology," 126.

13 Burrow, 191–202.

14 See Anne Middleton, "Narration and the Invention of Experience: Episodic Form in *Piers Plowman*," in *The Wisdom of Poetry: Essays in Honor of Morton Bloomfield*, ed. Larry Benson and Siegfried Wenzel (Kalamazoo, MI: Medieval Institute Publications, 1982), 91–122.

15 Vittoria Di Palma notes this dialectical tension in writings about forest land in the Early Modern period. John Manwood wrote at the end of

198 : NOTES TO PAGES 103–110

the sixteenth century that wasting the forest was both an overuse and an underuse; as Di Palma puts it, "Hinging on the dual connotation of the word 'waste' as both 'to neglect to use' and 'to use up,' a waste of the forest was a use that undermined its wildness, a use that went counter to the forest's own nature" (Di Palma, 184).

CHAPTER SIX

1 *The Canon's Yeoman's Tale* has had a checkered history in Chaucer scholarship, with some scholars famously insisting that it was not an authentic Chaucerian production but instead was put together by the "editorial committee" that pieced together the Ellesmere order of the *Canterbury Tales* overall. See N. F. Blake, "Introduction," *The Canterbury Tales by Geoffrey Chaucer*, ed. N. F. Blake (London: Edward Arnold, 1980), 9. The tale is viewed as inferior to many of Chaucer's works, despite the extraordinary poetic virtuosity it displays, which I will go into later. Since Blake's edition, however, many scholars have pushed back on the notion that the Ellesmere order is inferior to other manuscripts and on the notion that *The Canon's Yeoman's Tale* is anything other than Chaucerian. See Jill Mann, "Chaucer's Meter and the Myth of the Ellesmere Order," *Studies in the Age of Chaucer* 23 (2001): 71–107.

2 Some of the best work on the Yeoman's physicality and his alchemical work, particularly in connection with the tale's position in the *Canterbury Tales*, is that of Joseph Grennen. See Grennen, "The Canon's Yeoman and the Cosmic Furnace: Language and Meaning in the 'Canon's Yeoman's Tale,'" *Criticism* 4, no. 3 (1962): 225–40; and Grennen, "The Canon's Yeoman's Alchemical Mass," *Studies in Philology* 62, no. 4 (1965): 546–60.

3 Horrox, 100.

4 Of course droves of people died of plague in the countryside, but as Boccaccio's famous Florentines realized in the *Decameron*, cities were more dangerous than rural areas.

5 John Arderne, *Treatises of Fistula in Ano, Haemorrhoids, and Clysters*, ed. D'Arcy Power (Oxford: Oxford University Press and Early English Text Society, 1910), 74.

6 Arderne, 86–87.

7 Arderne, 38, 49.

8 Lanfranco of Milan, *Lanfrank's "Science of Cirurgie," Edited from the Bodleian Ashmole MS. 1396 (ab. 1380 A.D.) and the British Museum Additional*

MS. 12,056, ed. Robert Fleischhacker (London: EETS, 1894), 206.

9 For a more extensive treatment of the often surprisingly close proximity of animals to humans in the medieval imagination, see Susan Crane, *Animal Encounters: Contacts and Concepts in Medieval Britain* (Philadelphia: University of Pennsylvania Press, 2012).

10 For an overview, see Jill Mann, "Chaucer's Meter and the Myth of the Ellesmere Editor," *Studies in the Age of Chaucer* 23 (2001): 71–107.

11 Morris Halle and Samuel Jay Keyser, "Chaucer and the Study of Prosody," *College English* 28 (1966): 187–219. A few years later W. K. Wimsatt followed up on the Halle-Keyser theory to argue that it is too rigid, and that Chaucer's commitment to a ten-syllable line can allow us to read his verse as regular even when the stress patterns are not. See Wimsatt, "The Rule and the Norm: Halle and Keyser on Chaucer's Meter," *College English* 31 (1970): 774–88. There have been other scholars who see in Chaucer's meter a more decisive adherence to a hendecasyllabic line and even consider later scribes' adjustments to manuscripts to be evidence of their having registered and sought further to regularize this meter. See Derek Pearsall, *The Canterbury Tales* (London: Allen and Unwin, 1985), 10.

12 Mann, "Chaucer's Meter and the Myth of the Ellesmere Editor," 101.

13 See again Blake, "Introduction," *Canterbury Tales*.

14 That first line could also be stressed to minimize the stress at the end of arsenic: "ARsenyk, SAL arMONyak and BRYMSTOON." That would result in a five-stress line. Then again, the line could be read, "ARsenYK, SAL ARmonYAK and BRYMSTOON," or "ARsenYK, SAL arMONyAK and BRYMSTOON," both bringing it up to seven stresses, or six if we de-stress the end of "arsenyk."

15 Mann notes that in some cases a strong stress in a weak position can be canceled by adjacent stresses; she cites the line from *The Knight's Tale* that reads, "He felt a coold swerd sodeynliche glyde," in which coold, swerd, and sod- should all take stress but, she argues, the stress on swerd is muted. Mann, 101.

16 See *Middle English Dictionary*, s.v. "doten."

17 See James Dean, "Dismantling the Canterbury Book," *PMLA* (1985): 746–62.

18 For more on the dangers of wonder in the medieval imagination, see Eleanor Johnson, "Critical Poetics: A Meditation on Alternative Critical Vernaculars," *postmedieval* 6, no. 4 (2015): 375–84. For a broader introduction to wonder in general in medieval culture, see especially Carolyn Walker

200 : NOTES TO PAGES 126–127

Bynum, *Metamorphosis and Identity* (New York: Zone Books, 2005), and Bynum, *Wonderful Blood* (Philadelphia: University of Pennsylvania Press, 2007).

CHAPTER SEVEN

1 For an overview of what we know about the manuscript the poems appear in, see the introduction to the critical edition by Malcolm Andrew and Ronald Waldron, *The Poems of the Pearl Manuscript: Pearl, Cleanness, Patience, Sir Gawain and the Green Knight* (Exeter: University of Exeter Press, 2007), 1–12. For a strong advocacy of common authorship, see also William Vantuono, "*Patience, Cleanness, Pearl,* and *Gawain*: The Case for Common Authorship," *Annuale Medievale* 12 (1971): 37–69. For a thematically based argument for the authorial coherence of the manuscript, see Lynn Staley Johnson, *The Voice of the* Gawain-*Poet* (Madison: University of Wisconsin Press, 1984). For a treatment of the manuscript as a unified authorial production, based on how the poet deploys the gaze, see Sarah Stanbury, *Seeing the* Gawain-*Poet: Description and the Act of Perception* (Philadelphia: University of Pennsylvania Press, 1991). See also Robert Blanch and Judith Wasserman, "The Miracles of God and the Conventions of *Kynde*," in *From Pearl to Gawain* (Gainesville: University of Florida Press, 1995). For a slightly more skeptical treatment of everything we know about the "author" and the texts in the manuscript, see Malcolm Andrew, "Theories of Authorship," in *A Companion to the* Gawain-*Poet*, ed. Derek Brewer and Jonathan Gibson (London: D. S. Brewer, 1997), 23–33. More recently, Cecilia Hatt has argued for the unity of the manuscript and its single authorship through a thematic study of the poem's Thomistic theology. See Hatt, *God and the* Gawain-*Poet: Theology and Genre in "Pearl," "Patience," "Cleanness," and "Sir Gawain and the Green Knight"* (Cambridge: Brewer, 2015). Piotr Spyra makes a similar argument for authorial and textual coherence based on its Augustinianism. See Spyra, *The Epistemological Perspective of the Pearl-Poet* (Surrey: Ashgate, 2014). Sarah Sprouse sees the poems of the manuscript as unified by their common interest in stone imagery; see Sprouse, "Lady Bertilak's Pearls," *Arthuriana* 28 (2018): 25–45.

2 Carolyn Dinshaw, "Ecology," in *A Handbook of Middle English Studies*, ed. Marion Turner (Oxford: Wiley Blackwell, 2013), 347–62. As Gillian Rudd puts it, "*Sir Gawain and the Green Knight* is a text which apparently

NOTES TO PAGES 128–134 : 201

cries out for a green reading." Gillian Rudd, "'The Wilderness of Wirral' in *Sir Gawain and the Green Knight*," *Arthuriana* 23 (2013): 52–65. Michael Twomey notes, however, that the Green Knight himself should not be the sole focus in ecological readings of the poem, since the poem is actually concerned to represent an entire ethos of land management and curation. Michael Twomey, "How Green Was the Green Knight? Forest Ecology at Hautdesert," *Arthurian Literature XXX*, ed. Elizabeth Archibald and David Johnson (Cambridge: Brewer, 2013), 27–53. Twomey sees the Green Knight as a "settled, managed environment—part of civilization, rather than apart from it" (38).

3   From Malcolm Andrew and Ronald Waldron, eds., *The Poems of the Pearl Manuscript* (Exeter: University of Exeter Press, 2007).

4   Victoria Flood seems to recognize an affinity between the two poems, but she ascribes it to a larger cultural awareness of the Galfridian model of English prehistory rather than to a direct relationship between the two poems. See Flood, "*Wynnere and Wastoure* and the Influence of Political Prophecy," *Chaucer Review* 49 (2015): 427–88.

5   The Old English poem *The Ruin* testifies to the profound cultural burden of living in a place of *enta geweorc* (the work of giants)—giants who are long gone and whose lives are erased but for the presence of their broken structures.

6   *Sir Gawain and the Green Knight*, trans. Simon Armitage (New York: Norton, 2008), line 86, p. 26, and line 86, p. 27.

7   Lynn Staley says, "The word 'childgered' is not laudatory: it connotes childishness and thoughtlessness and would not have been applied to a king as a form of praise." For her too the young king's recklessness seems to invite in the moral challenge of the Green Knight. See Lynn Staley Johnson, *The Voice of the* Gawain-*Poet* (Madison: University of Wisconsin Press, 1984), 49.

8   As Gillian Rudd points out, "wildernesses" are places conspicuous both for their lack of habitation and, usually, for their adjacency to more "hospitable" places—a point that will become important later. Rudd, "'Wilderness of Wirral,'" 55.

9   Lynn Arner, "The Ends of Enchantment: Colonialism and *Sir Gawain and the Green Knight*," *Texas Studies in Literature and Language* 48 (2006): 79–101, at 79.

10 Arner, 84.

11 Jeffrey Jerome Cohen's beautiful reading of this scene focuses on the rocks

Gawain sleeps among and how they seem to participate in his vulnerability and also accentuate it: "In *Sir Gawain and the Green Knight*, the
wasteland of 'naked rokkes' among which the wandering hero must sleep
manifests the precarity of his life. Hung with icicles, devoid of shelter,
these cold crags are the elements at their most uncaring, a stony indifference to human suffering." See Cohen, *Stone: An Ecology of the Inhuman*
(Minneapolis: University of Minnesota Press, 2015), 17.

12 Geraldine Heng has argued that what matters most about the girdle is
not so much its color as its knottedness, the sign of Gawain's entrapment
by and partially as a feminine figure. See Heng, "Feminine Knots and the
Other *Sir Gawain and the Green Knight*," *PMLA* 106 (1991): 500–514.

13 Cohen, *Stone*, 56.

14 This designation of the place as "ugly" resonates with what Vittoria Di
Palma says about wastelands as an environment perhaps uniquely capable
of inspiring disgust. See Di Palma, *Wastelands*, 5–11, 93–95, 165–74. On
disgust as a "defense reaction" against unacceptable sensory content,
see Aurel Kolnai, *On Disgust*, ed. and trans. Barry Smith and Carolyn
Korsmeyer (Chicago: Open Court, 2004), 30, 31, 34. For Kolnai, disgust
is almost always a biological reminder of our own mortality; the Green
Chapel—distinctively biological in its greenness—certainly does remind
Gawain of his mortality. See Kolnai, esp. 54–62; here, and in general, for
Kolnai the biological is also the acutely bodily. In *Gawain* individual mortality is fascinatingly conflated with what I would call cultural mortality,
so that the Green Chapel portends not only Gawain's bodily death, but
eventually the death of Camelot when nature reclaims it. So in essence
this poem offers an expansion of Kolnai's theory by suggesting that not
only can physical rot or bodily excess be disgusting, because of how it
flags our physical vulnerability, but so can a certain kind of intractable
naturalness be disgusting, because of how it flags the vulnerability of our
civilizations.

15 Cohen, *Stone*, 56.

16 Di Palma notes that "wasteland leaves no place 'over there' that is
untouched by human presence, but posits all places, all categories, as
interconnected" (Di Palma, 244). I think that is entirely correct, and I
would simply add that in *Gawain* it is also all *times* that are connected. In
our daily lives we are sitting on a dead, buried past, and our future will
eventually sit on us, equally dead, equally buried in the wasteland.

17 Lynn Staley sees the poem as manifesting "degenerative time" in a manner

similar to what I see here, where Troy anticipates the fall of Camelot, and Gawain's test involves a certain kind of fall too, but for her the poem ends in rebirth and redemption. See Staley, *Voice of the* Gawain-*Poet*, 96. I see the poem's ecotheology as far more fundamentally pessimistic.

18 A significant amount of scholarship has tried to pin down the place the *Gawain* poet is talking about here. Michael Bennett has suggested that the poem is referring to the sparsely populated but not totally wasted Wirral area, probably subsequent to its disafforestation in 1376; Ralph Elliott has tried to locate possible Green Chapel analogues in the contemporary landscape of North Wales, the Wirral, and Cheshire. In my own view, the *Gawain* poet is not at all eager to have us precisely locate the Green Chapel on a map; quite the contrary, we are meant, I think, simply to feel lost, alone, and abandoned by all legible markings. See Bennett, "The Historical Background," and Elliott, "Landscape and Geography," both in *A Companion to the* Gawain-*Poet*, edited by Derek Brewer and Jonathan Gibson (London: Brewer, 1997), 71–90 and 105–18.

19 Scholars have read the Green Chapel itself in a number of ways, from relic of pagan past to evidence of diablerie. See Larissa Tracey, "A Knight of God or the Goddess? Rethinking Religious Syncretism in *Sir Gawain and the Green Knight*," *Arthuriana* 17 (2007): 31–56; Malcolm Andrew, "The Diabolical Chapel: A Motif in *Patience* and *Sir Gawain and the Green Knight*," *Neophil* 66 (1982): 313–19.

20 As Lynn Staley notes, "The Camelot of *Sir Gawain*, like Troy, is a city whose brilliant and glory, though real, rest upon shaky foundations." Lynn Staley Johnson, *The Voice of the* Gawain-*Poet* (Madison: University of Wisconsin Press, 1984), 45. Staley also points out that the poem embodies "degenerative time" in its representation of Camelot—it shows a young Camelot, the decay of which was a historical certainty (46–49).

21 Gillian Rudd calls it a "mortality lyric." See *Greenery*, 23.

22 *The Middle English Poem Erthe upon Erthe*, ed. Hilda Murray (Oxford: EETS, 1964). This edition assigns the poem an approximate date of composition of 1307.

23 Eleanor Johnson, "Horrific Visions of the Host," *Exemplaria* 27 (2015): 150–66.

24 Charlotte Morse, "The Image of the Vessel in *Cleanness*," *University of Toronto Quarterly* 39 (1970): 202–16.

25 See also Sacvan Bercovitch, "Romance and Anti-romance in *Sir Gawain and the Green Knight*," *PQ* 44 (1965): 30–37.

204 : NOTES TO PAGES 143–144

26 What Richard Neuhauser says about the poem is still technically true, that "unlike the [rest of the poems in the manuscript], *Sir Gawain and the Green Knight* owes very little to the Bible by way of direct paraphrase." See Neuhauser, "Scriptural and Devotional Sources," in *A Companion to the* Gawain-*Poet*, edited by Derek Brewer and Jonathan Gibson (London: Brewer, 1997), 269. "By way of direct paraphrase" seems right; the spirit of what Neuhauser says, namely that *Gawain* is a poem not very concerned with staging or exploring the Bible, strikes me as inaccurate. *Gawain* is a profoundly biblical poem; it just does not announce its affinities anywhere near as explicitly as do *Cleanness* or *Patience*.

27 *Pearl*, line 12, from Andrew and Waldron.

28 As editors Andrew and Waldron note in their critical introduction, a summary of the poem "will clearly indicate that *Sir Gawain* is a romance. It reflects many of the principal characteristics of the medieval genre: a glittering and idealized chivalric background, a quest in an unknown country, a trial of courage, an attempted seduction by a beautiful woman, and elements of the mysterious and marvelous." *The Poems of the Pearl Manuscript: Pearl, Cleanness, Patience, Sir Gawain and the Green Knight*, ed. Malcolm Andrew and Ronald Waldron (Exeter: University of Exeter Press, 2007), 23. Andrew and Waldron do note, however, that the romance material is at moments used ironically, to provide a framework for testing those chivalric ideals (23). Even essays that seek to foreground the role of the divine in the manuscript often have a hard time incorporating discussions of *Gawain*; Robert Blanch and Judith Wasserman give a splendid overview of miracles and covenantalism in the first three poems, but when they turn to *Gawain* they tend to read it comically and ironically, even if in the end the poem seeks "to remind us of the laws of *kynde*." See Blanch and Wasserman, "The Miracles of God and the Conventions of *Kynde*," in *From Pearl to Gawain* (Gainesville: University of Florida Press, 1995), 45–64, at 64. W. A. Davenport calls Camelot in the poem a scene of "idealized luxury" and the poem overall "a combination of romance and realism." See Davenport, *The Art of the* Gawain-*Poet* (London: Athlone, 1978), 144.

29 Larry D. Benson, *Art and Tradition in "Sir Gawain and the Green Knight"* (New Brunswick, NJ: Rutgers University Press, 1965), 208.

30 John Bowers, *An Introduction to the* Gawain *Poet* (Gainesville: University of Florida Press, 2012), 28.

31 On the Christian symbology and meaning of the shield, see Robert Ackerman, "Gawain's Shield: Penitential Doctrine in *GGK*," *Anglia* 76 (1958):

NOTES TO PAGES 144–146 : 205

254–65. See also Richard Green, "Gawain's Shield and the Quest for Perfection," *ELH* 29 (1962): 121–39.

32 As M. Mills puts it, "It is worth noting at the outset that even the most purely 'secular' romances are in some respects well adapted to support a Christian meaning." Mills, "Christian Tradition and Romance Tradition in *Sir Gawain and the Green Knight*," *Modern Language Review* 60 (1965): 483–93, at 483.

33 See Andrew and Waldron, 23–24. Lynn Staley does note, however, that the poem's internal calendar of events has a carefully designed relation to the liturgical calendar. See Lynn Staley Johnson, *The Voice of the* Gawain-*Poet* (Madison: University of Wisconsin Press, 1984), 50–69.

34 Nicholas Watson, "The *Gawain*-Poet as a Vernacular Theologian," in *A Companion to the* Gawain-*Poet*, ed. Derek Brewer and Jonathan Gibson (Cambridge: Brewer, 1997), 293–313, at 294 and 296.

35 Watson, 296.

36 Indeed, Watson says, "*Pearl, Cleanness*, and *Patience* are thus part of a broad contemporary movement in which religious ideas of all kinds were quickly becoming accessible to vernacular readers," but he doesn't include *Gawain* in that list. For him the earlier poems offer a motivation for reading the final scene of *Gawain* with a stronger sense that Gawain is truly meant to embody a devotional and practical ideal of aristocratic devotion (Watson, 295, 294).

37 J. Stephen Russell, "Sir Gawain and the White Monks: Cistercian Marian Spirituality and *Sir Gawain and the Green Knight*," *Journal of Medieval Religious Cultures* 39 (2013): 207–26.

38 Karen Cherewatuk, "Becoming Male, Medieval Mothering, and Incarnational Theology in *Sir Gawain and the Green Knight*," *Arthuriana* 19 (2009): 15–24.

39 Cecilia Hatt, *God and the* Gawain-*Poet: Theology and Genre in "Pearl," "Patience," "Cleanness," and "Sir Gawain and the Green Knight"* (Cambridge: Brewer, 2015).

40 Spyra, *Epistemological Perspective of the Pearl-Poet*.

41 Hautdesert has been claimed as the radical moral other of Camelot, though as a sort of dark, jaded place as against the "moral faith" of Camelot. See Bonnie Lander, "Convention of Innocence and *Sir Gawain and the Green Knight*'s Literary Sophisticates," *Parergon* 24 (2007): 65–66.

42 See Patricia Dailey's work on dwelling places in Old English poetry, "Questions of Dwelling in Anglo-Saxon Poetry and Medieval Mysticism:

Inhabiting Landscape, Body, and Mind," *New Medieval Literatures* 8 (2006): 175–214, at 187.

43 The gorgeous Old English poem "The Ruin" uses "westen," the wastes, to signal precisely the conversion of a city place to an empty space: "wurdon hyra wigsteal westen statholas" (their war-halls became waste places). This Old English term "westen" "signals a becoming-uninhabitable of the habitable" (Dailey, 188–89). Moreover, as Dailey notes, the Old English term *westen* often denotes "what remains of the past in the present" and can signal a place "marked by solitude, lawlessness, and separation that borders on the monstrous."

44 As Dailey notes of Old English translations from Latin, the tendency is to take the words *solitudinis* and *deserta* and convert them into "westen." The lexical differentiation between kinds of uninhabited places is erased, and that erasure seems to carry over into Middle English. See Dailey, 189, esp. note 23.

45 *Middle English Dictionary*, s.v. "waste."

46 Ann Martinez sees Lord Bertilak as an embodiment of an ecologically minded mode of land stewardship; as, in fact, a model for the aristocracy about how to manage land. See Martinez, "Bertilak's Green Vision: Land Stewardship in *Sir Gawain and the Green Knight*," *Arthuriana* 26 (2016): 114–29. That reading strikes me as somewhat compatible with my own, although to me, if Bertilak is modeling something for others, it is a willingness to recognize the inevitable and ineluctable movement of nature toward a nihilistic reclamation of human spaces.

47 J. J. Anderson calls him "a spectacular and complex version of the challenger figure of romance literature." See Anderson, *Language and Imagination in the* Gawain *Poems* (Manchester: Manchester University Press, 2005), 172.

48 Some scholars even see Morgan as part of a violent lineage originating in Troy, having no discernible redeeming qualities. See Evelyn Reynolds, "Kynde in *Sir Gawain and the Green Knight*," *Arthuriana* 28 (2018): 41–42.

49 One of the hardest-charging readings of Morgan as a maleficent witch, associating her with the "goddess of discord," comes in Albert Friedman's "Morgan le Fay and *Sir Gawain and the Green Knight*," *Speculum* 35 (1960): 260–74, at 271. The entire article is written to combat another reading that tried to construe Morgan as a positive, healing figure in the poem.

50 Michael Twomey, "Morgan le Fay, Empress of the Wilderness: A Newly

NOTES TO PAGES 147–151 : 207

Recovered Arthurian Text in London BL Royal 12.C.ix," *Arthurian Literature* 25 (2008): 69.

51 A similar argument was advanced decades ago, when a study argued that Morgan's testing of Gawain serves to bring into being and indeed crystallize the chastity that is the poem's eventual point—a chastity that is meant actually to discipline Guinevere. Morgan thus, is essentially a beneficial character. See Devner Baughn, "The Role of Morgan le Fay in *Sir Gawain and the Green Knight*," *ELH* 17 (1950): 241–51, at 251. Baughn sees Morgan as a holy enchantress whose job is to be a moral healer in the poem, a healer of the moral depravity of Arthur's court.

52 This reading chimes with Larissa Tracey's reading that Morgan embodies a certain cultural syncretism between Christianity and pre-Christian pagan culture. To me, however, Morgan is less a holdover from an ancient pagan world than an ongoing manifestation of the naturalness—in the sense of nature orientedness—of Christianity itself. See Tracey, "A Knight of God or the Goddess? Rethinking Religious Syncretism in *Sir Gawain and the Green Knight*," *Arthuriana* 17 (2007): 31–56.

53 Decades ago, Morton Bloomfield noted the pervasiveness of Christian themes in the poem but insisted that those themes don't seem to amount to an adequate account of what the poem is aiming at. See Bloomfield, "*Sir Gawain and the Green Knight*: An Appraisal," *PMLA* 76 (1961): 7–19, at 15.

54 Read in this way, *Gawain* proves a marked counterexample to Barbara Newman's compelling observation: "In tracing Natura's trajectory from the twelfth century through the early fifteenth, we have ovserved a progressive secularizing of the goddess [Natura] and her concerns" (136). I do not want to collapse Morgan with Natura; if anything she seems to be specifically the goddess of one particular ecosystem, not of some personified nature overall. But still, *Gawain* seems to push back against the oversecularization of a feminine "natural" goddess figure. See Newman, *God and the Goddesses: Vision, Poetry, and Belief in the Middle Ages* (Philadelphia: University of Pennsylvania Press, 2003).

CHAPTER EIGHT

1 Of course, there is a long tradition of showing this kind of analogic relation between the natural world and the political world. Sometimes that relation is demonstrated through beast fables. *Piers Plowman*, for example, contains a beast fable where the dreamer encounters a group of

rats and mice that run in "to a council for the common profit" (Pr. 146). It's well established in scholarship and fairly clear from the poem itself that the rats represent the parliamentary House of Lords and the mice represent the House of Commons. The broader tradition that suggests nature is in an analogical relation to human society is in part classical: Vergil's *Eclogues* and his *Georgics* both thematize the natural world—and mankind's relation to it—in order to understand political economy. And the tradition is in part biblical: in Job the order of the natural world serves as a reminder of the supervening power and justice of God; the order of the natural world is a mark of God's providence, which encompasses us all and should comfort us, providing we act in virtue and righteousness. Boethius's *Consolation of Philosophy* stitches together the classical and biblical understandings of political economy in relation to the natural world by consistently emphasizing the order of nature as an epiphenomenon of God's providence and suggesting that mankind would do well to model its economic and political conduct after a well-ordered natural example.

2   Lynn Staley has argued for the shaping force of the garden image on medieval understanding of England as a nation. See Staley, *The Island Garden: England's Language of Nation from Gildas to Marvell* (Notre Dame: University of Notre Dame Press, 2012), esp. 16–70.

3   See W. W. Skeat, *Piers Plowman* (Oxford, 1886), vol. 2, lxxxiv-v, and Alcuin Blamires, "*Mum and the Sothsegger* and Langlandian Idiom," *Neuphilologische Mitteilungen* 76, no. 4 (1975): 583–604.

4   Helen Barr, *Socioliterary Practice in Late Medieval England* (Oxford: Oxford University Press, 2001), 165–66.

5   Barr, 172.

6   This poem chimes, then, with what Vittoria Di Palma sees in later periods, when the wastelands were universally slated as places for "improvement." Although *Mum* does not stipulate that this wonderful garden used to be a wasteland, in need of improvement, the general dynamic is the same as what Di Palma sees: industrious labor can stand as a bulwark against waste, here construed as a bad behavior rather than as a particular landscape type. See Di Palma, 43–83.

CHAPTER NINE

1   The Tudor poet Thomas Wyatt (fl. 1530s–40s) writes in his poem "Lament my Losse, My Labor, and My Payne" that his "boddye quakes, [his] wyttis

begynne to waste" (20). Elsewhere he says, "My lute awake performe the last / Labour that thou and I shall waste" (1–2). See Wyatt, *Collected Poems of Sir Thomas Wyatt* (Liverpool: Liverpool University Press, 1969). The pragmatic poetry of John Lyly, in particular his poem about his waiting at court for attention, uses "waste" to describe the misuse of time: "to loose good dayes, that mighte be better spent, / to waste longe nights in pensiue discontent" (6–7). John Lyly, *The Complete Works of John Lyly Now for the First Time Collected and Edited from the Earliest Quartos with Life, Bibliography, Essays, Notes and Index*, ed. R. Warwick Bond (Oxford, 1902). The poet Angel Day notes in a love poem that "the sighs I spend are else but waste, and vaine is all my sute" (10). Angel Day, "Ye heauens (if heauens haue power to iudge of things amisse)," in *Daphnis and Chloe* (London, 1587), accessed online at ABELL. Robert Parry says in 1597 in a mode of self-reproach, "Eu'n thus I weare and waste away the time, / Declining when I haue most minde to clime" (11–12). Robert Parry, "Passion XL, Rest I at home, remembrance rackes my minde," *Sinetes: Passions Vppon His Fortunes, Offered For an Incense At the Shrine Of the Ladies Which Guided His Distempered Thoughtes* (London, 1597), accessed online at ABELL.

2   The term "waster" is frequently coupled with terms like "prodigality" and "liberality" or used in contexts of critiques of how supposed "wasters" do their "spending." Alexander Barclay's translation *The Myrrour of Good Maners*, written in 1523, says, "For often in the world / This thynge prouydyd we se / That whan the prodygall / and waster hath all spent, / He beggyth, or steleth, by ways fraudulent" (1327–29), accessed online at ABELL. John Fisher's *Three Dialogues* (1558) orders obedience to one's parents, saying, "Your Father, Mother, and Maister / Loue, feare, serue, and gently obay: / Of their goodes be ye no waster / with truthe helpe to gette that you may" (410–13), accessed online at ABELL. T. A. writes in 1602, "Nor you the sonne of carelesse diffluence, / Brother to loosenesse and intemperance, / Waster of thrift, maister of large expence, / Whose wealth is of an houres continuance. / No more thou marshall vnto diffluence, / Feed leaudnesse in so bounteous a measure; / No more be waster of such great expence, / Nor fondly throwe abroad Pecunia's treasure" (425–36), accessed online at ABELL.

The late sixteenth-century play *Misogonus* juxtaposes "waster" with "spendall"; Angel Day in 1586 warns of the difference between being "liberall" and being a "waster." *Misogonus*, in *Early Plays from the Italian*

210 : NOTES TO PAGES 163–164

(Cambridge: Clarendon Press, 1911), 185. Angel Day, *The English Secretorie* (1586), 225. See also Edward Sharpham, *The Discouerie of the Knights of the Poste* (1597), 3. All accessed online at ABELL.

3   Richard Johnson's 1612 "A New Sonnet, of a Curst Wife and Her Husband," embodies this idea: "At night I make to her account / what monny I haue spended. / Or else my pockets she will search, / And say I am a waster" (19–22), accessed online at ABELL. John Davies's 1617 work "Wits Bedlam" includes an epigram that denigrates "Brute," which seems to mean something like man's own brutal physical senses and tendencies, by calling Brute "the Waster." As such, Brute must make account of all his misexpenditures, his "expences," including his culinary excesses, his sartorial excesses, his libational excesses, and his love for toys and gambling. Davies's Brute, then, is very much like Winner's characterization of Waster: he spends too much money on riotous partying. Though it's not entirely clear that Brute's wasterliness hurts anyone other than Brute himself. John Davies, "Against the Prodigall Brutes Excessiue Riotousnesse," in *Wits Bedlam* (London, 1617), 108, accessed online at ABELL. Seeming to lean back toward medieval senses of "waste," John Stradling's 1625 poem "The Fift Classis" uses the term "waster" in the direct context of the unjust steward parable. "The wicked Steward, poore (it seemes) by birth, / Liu'd brauely on the substance of his Master, / His time he spent in jollitie and mirth: / Found-out at last to be a lauish waster, / His subtle wit suggest to him a shift, / To helpe at need: though 'twere a knauish drift" (895–900).

Poor stewardship qualifies as wastefulness for Stradling as much as it did for John Wycliffe and his followers two hundred years earlier. But what's most striking about this poem is that the "shift" Stradling talks about, when the unjust steward redistributes wealth to the needy ("to helpe at need"), is characterized as "knavish" rather than redemptive. Something about the logic of how to redeem oneself from greedy, spendthrift wasterliness—that is, in the Middle Ages, to redistribute wealth to the broader social ecosystem—seems to have vanished. Now the unjust steward is unjust, period. His wasteful habits are unredeemable. John Stradling, "The Fift Classis," *Divine Poems* (London, 1625), accessed online at ABELL.

4   Di Palma, 4–5, 11, 17–18, 24, 43–83, 89–110, 137–43, 186–91, 210–20.

5   *OED*, s.v. "waste," verb.

6   There is one meaning of "wast" as garbage cited in the *OED* from 1430,

more than three hundred years before the next citation. See *OED*, s.v. "waste," noun, III, 11, a. This long preindustrial citation is drawn from a manuscript of *Libeaus Desconus*, and the line reads, "Full gore, and fen, and full wast / that was out ykast." But the manuscript that provides that transcribed line seems to contain a scribal error: the correct reading, the one cited in the *Middle English Dictionary*, seems to be "Full gore, and fen ful faste, that er was out y-cast." The first clear usage of "waste" in this sense in the *OED* is from 1764.

7 See Sophie Gee, Making Waste: Leftovers and the Eighteenth-Century Imagination (Princeton, NJ: Princeton University Press, 2010). See also A. C. Turner, *The Salvaging Disposition: Waste and the Novel Form*, forthcoming. The introduction to this book asserts that "waste" as "garbage" is a distinctly modern category, a distinctly modern usage. According to Gee, the noun form of waste has to do with the material excesses of large-scale industrial production: by-products and how they must be disposed of.

8 Susan Strosser, *Waste and Want: A Social History of Trash* (New York: Picador, 2000).

9 Tom License, *What the Victorians Threw Away* (Oxford: Oxbow Books, 2015), 5, 31.

10 *Middle English Dictionary*, waste n. 1, def. 7.

EPILOGUE

1 Jeffrey Jerome Cohen says of Latour's actor-network theory, "ANT offers a mode of understanding inhuman agency that insists nature and society are not preexisting, separate, and self-evident realities, so that no human/world duality exists." Cohen, *Stone*, 42.

2 Bruno Latour, *We Have Never Been Modern*, trans. Catherine Porter (Cambridge, MA: Harvard University Press, 1993).

3 Levi Bryant, *The Democracy of Objects* (Ann Arbor, MI: Open Humanities Press, 2011), 245–46.

4 Cohen, *Stone*, 63.

5 Cohen notes that Latour-inspired object-oriented ontology, named by Graham Harman, "attempts a careful account of the autonomy and materiality of the world and is not satisfied with analyses that disperse things into language, as if human words had sovereign power." Cohen, *Stone*, 45. But in a Christian, medieval European imagination and ecosystemic

212 : NOTES TO PAGES 171–172

worldview, words *did* have sovereign power, if only because people accepted that *logos* is the starting point of creation.

6   For more on medieval advocates of integrated ecology, see Pope Francis, *Laudato si'*, 12–13.

7   Elizabeth Kolbert, *The Sixth Extinction: An Unnatural History* (New York: Picador, reprint 2015).

8   Pope Francis, *Laudato si': On Care for Our Common Home* (Huntington, IN: Our Sunday Visitor, 2015), 12.

9   Although he does not address immaterial resources like energy, words, wits, or will as part of the nature-culture hybrids he theorizes, Latour does talk about how "modernity" scuttles the idea of divine presence as an element of the hybridizing he sees among other elements of social networks. He says that the premodern God (or gods) evolves into what he calls the "crossed-out God" of Protestantism: "A wholly individual and wholly spiritual religion made it possible to criticize both the ascendancy of science and that of society, without needing to bring God into either. The moderns could now be both secular and pious at the same time" (33).

10 See Scott Gilbert, Jan Sapp, and Alfred Tauber, "A Symbiotic View of Life: We Have Never Been Individuals," *Quarterly Review of Biology* 87, no. 4 (2012): 325–41. Gilbert, Sapp, and Tauber focus on the "bionts," nested living organisms within a person's body, and their interactions with that person's putative "individual" self, to argue that people should properly be understood as "holobionts"—aggregations or, perhaps better, confederations of microscopic organisms with the large host organism that thinks of itself as an individual.

11 Indeed, there has been a strong trend in past decades to attempt to demystify and secularize our understanding of nature or the world or Gaia and our relationship with it. As Latour says in *Facing Gaia*, following James Lovelock, "the concept of Gaia . . . may be called *wholly secular.*" Latour, *Facing Gaia: Eight Lectures on the New Climatic Regime* (Cambridge: Polity Books, 2017), 87, italics in original. Latour recognizes the limitations of this term—secular—being precisely that it calls up the spectral other of "religious." He also calls Gaia "the anti-system," which is quite opposed to how the medieval ecotheorists in this book saw things (87).

INDEX

accountability, ecosystemic or ecological, 4, 42, 46, 49, 64–65, 71, 80, 168–69
actor-network theory, 169–70, 177n5, 211n1
Adam and Eve, 151, 174
Aelred of Rievaulx, 52
afforestation, 13–15, 17, 180n9, 203n18
agrarian ecology, in *Piers Plowman*, 196n6, 197n8
alchemical procedure, ingredients and tools, 114–16, 123
alchemists, 103, 158, 166; recognized by their stink, 107–8
alchemy, 11, 105–8, 112, 119, 121; and greed, 108, 113; and medicine, 110; natural, of the earth, 116; as plague, 109, 112; wasteful, 119, 122; as a wasting sickness, 111, 113
allegory, 52, 79, 95, 151, 155. *See also* personification allegory
anaphoras, 119–20
Anderson, J. J., 206n47
Andrew, Malcolm, 204n28
Anthropocene era, 2, 178n6
Antichrist, as ecosystemic collapse, 99–100
apocalypticism, in *Piers Plowman*, 21, 23, 31
Apostles' Creed, 23
Arderne, John, *Treatise on Fistula in Ano*, 109–10
Armitage, Simon, 131
Arner, Lynn, 133
art, in the absence of vocabulary, 4
Arthur (king), and his court, 131–32, 147, 149, 154. *See also* Camelot
assarting, 14–15, 17, 21, 157, 180n10, 182n26, 182n28
atonement, 62

Augustine, 52
Ayenbite of Inwit, The, 55–59, 66, 87, 192n13

Barclay, Alexander, 209n2
Barker, Justin, 177n4
barn breaking, 83
Barr, Helen, 155
Baughn, Devner, 207n51
bees, exemplifying saving the world from waste, 153–55, 158
Bennett, Michael, 203n18
Benson, Larry, 144
Bernard of Clairvaux, 66–67
Bertilak de Hautdesert, 134, 142, 145–49, 205n41, 206n46
Bible, 7–8, 23, 37–42, 50–52, 94, 100, 126–27, 167, 187n1, 187n2, 188n5, 204n26. *See also* Vulgate Gospels; Wycliffite Bible
biblical commentaries, on waste, 51, 53. *See also* sermons
Birrill, Jean, 181n19
Black Death, 27–28, 31–32, 69–70, 112, 185n72. *See also* plague
"Blacksmiths, The" (poem), 35
Blake, N. F., 198n1
Blanch, Robert, 204n28
Bloomfield, Morton, 71–72, 207n53
Boccaccio, *Decameron*, 28–29, 186n85, 198n4
body politic, 107
body. *See* human body
Boethius, *Consolation of Philosophy*, 208n1
books, fleshiness of, 4, 178n9
Bowers, John, 144
Bracton, Henry, 188n11
Brand, Paul, 189n14
brimstone, 107

214 : INDEX

Brook, William, 16, 182n23
Burrow, J. A., 96, 197n9

Camelot, 137–138, 147, 149, 154, 202n14,
  203n17, 203n20, 204n28, 205n41
Canterbury Tales, 25–27, 31–32, 101–2, 114;
  Ellemere order, 198n1; rhythm and
  meter, 113–16; *The Canon's Yeoman's
  Tale*, 36, 103–25, 149, 150, 157, 164, 166,
  173, 198n1; *The Merchant's Tale*, 102;
  The Pardoner's Tale, 102; *The Parson's
  Tale*, 102; *The Tale of Melibee*, 102
capitalism, 2, 113, 157
Capitula Escaetrie, 49
case law, fourteenth-century, 15, 181n20,
  181n23
castle, paper, 134–37, 142–43, 145
chastity, 207n51
Chaucer, Geoffrey, 102–4, 106, 160, 167,
  193n21; on work, 103–4
Cherewatuk, Karen, 145
children, in leadership roles, 131–32
chivalry, 133–34, 137–39, 148, 188n10,
  194n12, 204n28
Christ, 60–61, 143–44, 155
Christianity, 8, 54–55, 138, 144, 161,
  205n32, 207n52, 207n53
Chronicles of the Grey Friars of Lynn, 30
Cistercian writings, 145
Cleanness (poem), 30, 126, 140, 142–45,
  205n36
clear-cutting, of trees, 12, 21, 75, 157,
  195n17
clergy, misuse of material public goods,
  65–68
climate change, anthropogenic, 3, 36,
  124, 145, 152–53, 157, 171, 174. *See also*
  Anthropocene era
climate change: deniers, 8; in the Middle
  Ages, 18, 20–21, 26, 35–36, 125. *See also*
  weather: in the Middle Ages
climate disaster (crises), 25, 151. *See also*
  ecosystemic catastrophe (change, collapse, crisis, disaster, imperilment)
Cohen, Jeffrey Jerome, 136, 171, 178n7,
  179n14, 201n11, 211n1, 211n5
Coley, David, 30–31
collective landholding. *See* common land
collectivity, 14, 78, 85, 97, 142, 156–58, 161,
  172, 174

colonization, 39–40, 129, 161
common land, 13–14, 17, 182n23; rights
  to, 15–16
Common Law, 41–42, 45, 49, 51, 54, 56–
  57, 67, 72–74, 78, 81, 83, 86, 161, 167,
  188n6. *See also* waste law
consumption (being consumed, evaporative), and wasting, 109–10, 122
consumption, excessive or wasteful, 13,
  85–89, 92–93, 131, 142, 155–56, 160,
  165–67
contagion, 104, 107, 109, 124–25, 160;
  understood by medieval people, 28–29
contamination, 109; industrial, 124
corruption, 24, 107, 111, 123; political or
  juridical, 151, 154
courtliness, 133, 135, 137, 139, 142–44, 148
COVID-19, 28, 174
criminality, inadequate legal vocabulary
  for, 86
cyberbullying, 173
cyborg, 106, 112

Dailey, Patricia, 206n43, 206n44
damages, as the penalty for the crime of
  waste, 45–46, 49, 84
Davenport, W. A., 204n28
Davies, John, 210n3
Day, Angel, 209n1, 209n2
Death, 31
demurrer, 73, 77, 88
desert, 37–38, 146–47, 149
devotion (devotional writings), 50, 57, 59,
  68, 144–45, 205n36
*Diagnostic and Statistical Manual of Men-
  tal Disorders* (*DSM*), 54
Dinshaw, Carolyn, 178n7
Di Palma, Vittoria, 163–64, 180n11, 187n2,
  197n15, 202n14, 202n16, 208n6
discourse, penitential. *See* sermons
disease, 29, 35; as industry, 149; spread
  by animals, 28; wasting, 110. *See also*
  wasting sickness
disgust, 136, 163, 181n11, 202n14
disturbing the peace, 46, 54, 72
dominion, 8
Do-Well, personification of willpower,
  94–95
dowry, 45
dream vision genre, 71

drought, 19
dumping, 33

earth, 136, 138–40, 142–43, 160, 174
ecocriticism, 1, 9
ecological disaster, 3
ecology, 1, 171
economy, of England in the Middle Ages, 70
ecophilosophies, 170
ecopoetics, medieval, 161, 179n11
ecosystem: definition, 1–2, 177n3; and the economy, 70, 101, 158; garbage-based human, 165; medieval, 12; socioeconomic, 63–65, 67, 80; urban, medieval, 34, 103–4, 160; of waste, 167
ecosystemic anxiety, contemporary, 91
ecosystemic catastrophe (change, collapse, crisis, disaster, imperilment), 5, 123, 126, 157–58, 170, 197n11; complicated by war, 81; embracing it, 92; in the Middle Ages, 11–12, 130, 150, 156, 161, 178n7
ecosystemic discourse, 4; waste-based, 6
ecosystemic fatalism, 138
ecosystemic interimplication, 4, 79, 101, 104, 113, 120, 150, 167, 172
ecosystemic thought (ecological thought, ecosystemic awareness), in medieval England, 2, 8, 125, 160, 162, 170–72, 174, 177n3
ecotheology, 145, 148, 156
Eden, 151–52, 158, 161, 174
Edward III (king), 69
Elliott, Ralph, 203n18
enclosure, 182n24
English landscape, littered with ruins, 130
English law, medieval, 13, 42, 188n6. See also Common Law; specific statutes and documents
English prehistory (Trojan backstory), 34, 127–30, 137–38, 201n4
environment, 1, 7; in the Middle Ages, 11–12; natural, 2
erosion. See soil, and soil depletion
"Erthe toc of erthe" (lyric), 138–39
escheat, 47–49, 190n24
estates, or classes, in medieval social structure, 63–64, 89
Exodus, 38

famine, 13, 18, 23, 35–36, 70, 78, 82, 88–89, 92–95, 99–100, 151, 153, 156, 160. See also food precarity (scarcity, insecurity)
fatality rate. See mortality rates
Fisher, John, 209n2
Flood, Victoria, 201n4
floods and flooding, 19–20, 23, 126, 157; historical accounts, 20
food economy, as zero sum, 59
food precarity (scarcity, insecurity), 13, 17–20, 36, 93, 96, 125, 152, 156
forest, wasting of, 197n15
forest law. See case law, fourteenth-century
fossil fuels, 12, 173
Francis (pope), 8; Laudato 'si, 172
Friar Laurent, 58
Friedman, Albert, 206n49
fuel shortage, 18
futility, in Piers Plowman, 98–99

Gaia, 212n11
garden, 151, 153, 157–59, 161, 208n2
Gawain, vulnerable to nature, 132–34
Gayk, Shannon, 178n7
Gee, Sophie, 211n7
giants, 201n5
Gilbert, Scott, 212n10
girdle, green, 134–35, 137, 139, 145–47, 202n12
global trade, 12, 29–30
global warming, 7, 12, 173
Glossa ordinaria, 53
gluttony, 58, 86–93, 96, 98, 140, 166, 193n15
God, 171, 174, 212n9; as beekeeper, 155; belief in by medieval Europeans, 3; displeasure with sinful mankind, 28, 38–41; ecosystemic power, 38–40, 149; punishing, 3, 22–23, 28, 37–40, 42, 52–53, 93–94, 126, 140–42, 156, 161; wasting of disobedient peoples' lands, 42. See also nature: and God
grace, 151, 157; in Piers Plowman, 99
grain shortages (grain yields), 13, 18. See also food precarity (scarcity, insecurity)
Great Famine, 18, 183n31
greed, 78, 86, 88, 108, 113, 149, 160, 210n3

Green Chapel, 136–38, 202n14, 203n18, 203n19
Green Knight, 126, 132, 135, 137, 139, 145–47, 154; as God's wasting agent, 142
Grennen, Joseph, 198n2
guardianship, profit, and waste, 43–46, 48, 188n11

Halle, Morris, 114, 199n11
Hamilton, Clive, 197n11
Handlyng Synne, 55
Hanna, Ralph, 15, 181n15
Harman, Graham, 211n5
Hatt, Cecilia, 145
Hautdesert. *See* Bertilak de Hautdesert
health, of medieval people and exposure to urban toxins and pollutants, 32
hendecasyllabic line, Chaucerian, 114, 199n11
Heng, Geraldine, 202n12
Henry IV, 24
heroism, 133
hoarding, 6, 73, 77–79, 86, 88–89, 160
Hoffman, Richard, 13, 183n29
holobionts, 212n10
Horrox, Rosemary, 28, 107–8
Hugh of Saint Victor, 52
human body: corruption of, 107; porous, 106
human culture (society, civilization), wastable or vulnerable, 41, 127, 130–31, 137–40, 147, 163
humans, at the center of things, 170–71
Hundred Years' War, 69, 80
hunger, personified, 92–94, 98–100, 154
hypermetricality, 119–20, 123–24

ideas, ecosystemic entities, 124
idleness. *See* sloth
individuality, 172–73
industrialization, mass, 2, 165
Industrial Revolution, 3, 12, 164, 166–67, 169
industries, proto, in medieval Europe, 3
infection, 106–7, 112
interspecies contact, 4
Isaiah, prophecy, 40
Islam, 151

Jeremiah, 93–94

Jesus, teachings of, 51
Job, 156, 208n1
Johnson, Richard, 210n3
Jonah, 126, 141–42, 145
Jordan, William, 20, 78, 81, 184n55, 195n20
Jørgenson, Dolly, 33
Judaism, 151

Keyser, Samuel Jay, 114, 199n11
king bee, 153–55, 158
Kiser, Lisa, 178n7
knowledge, corporeality of, 4
Kolnai, Aurel, 202n14
kynde, various translations, 31

labor: economy, 69, 103, 197n10; social importance of, 154–58, 160–61, 196n5. *See also* work
land: agricultural, as the ecosystem of late medieval England, 100; arable, loss of, 3, 19–20, 35, 76, 151, 153; having financial value, 45; management and curation, 201n2; and monetary wealth, interconnected, 76; nonarable, value of, 14; as a resource, 75–76,168; shortage, in the Middle Ages (land contraction), 12–18, 36, 69, 125, 160. *See also* stewardship
Lanfrank, *Science of Surgery*, 110
Langland, William, 28, 88, 95, 102–3, 167; condemning waste, 85, 90, 160; dire vision, 93, 196n6; influenced by *Winner and Waster*, 69; personifying sin, 86–87; skeptical about the power of law to regulate waste, 91; three versions of *Piers Plowman*, 23, 95–97
language, 169–70; poetic, 4
La somme le roi. See *Ayenbite of Inwit, The*
Latour, Bruno, 169–70, 172, 177n5, 197n11, 211n1, 211n5, 212n9, 212n11
law: inadequate, in *Piers Plowman*, 84–85; natural, 145
lead (base metal), 106
Libeaus Desconus, 211n6
literacy rates, 20
Little Ice Age, 18, 25, 134, 137
liturgical calendar, 205n33
livability, 2–3, 35
livestock, under stress, 18–19
Lovelock, James, 212n11

INDEX : 217

Lydgate, John, *Troy Book*, 33–35
Lyly, John, 209n1

Magna Carta, 43–45, 74, 188n10, 195n16
malnutrition, 18
Mann, Jill, 114, 120, 199n15
Mannyng, Robert, 55
Manwood, John, 197n15
Martinez, Ann, 206n46
Maurus, Rabanus, 52
medical manuals, medieval English, 109–10, 122
metaphor, in medieval poetry, 24–25
meteorology, 3
meter, Chaucerian, 113–14, 117
Michel, Dan, 55–58, 61
microbiology, 28–29
Middle Ages: characterized as medieval, 11; scholarship on, 4–5
Middleton, Anne, 197n10
military narrative, 39–40, 80
Mills, M., 205n32
Milsom, S. F. C., 188n10, 194n14
Mirror of Justice, The, 48
Moab, 38, 52, 93
modernity, 170, 174, 212n9
money, 45, 75–79, 122, 160–64, 167–68, 173
morality, 99–100, 144, 147–48, 180n11, 201n7, 205n41, 207n51; Christian, 38, 55, 57, 138, 140–41; and law, 48; and personification allegory, 71–72, 77, 85; of waste, 5, 43, 81
Morgan le Fay, 147–49, 206n48, 206n49, 207n51, 207n52, 207n54
mortality, 30, 134–35, 139, 147, 202n14
mortality rates, 18, 27–28, 183n32, 185n72
Morton, Timothy, 177n4
Mum and the Sothsegger, 36, 151–62, 164, 167

Natura, 207n54
natural climate, 126, 130, 132, 139
natural world, 1–7, 36, 111, 125–27, 132, 140, 143–45, 149–50, 160, 169–170, 178, 207n1; analogic relation to the political world, 207n1
nature: and culture, 169–70, 177n5, 212n9; and ecological philosophy, 178n7; as the enemy, 133, 136–37; and God, 3, 22–23, 38–39, 208n1

Neuhauser, Richard, 204n26
Newman, Barbara, 207n54
Noah, 23, 140, 156
Notre Dame, 11

object-oriented ontology, 170, 211n5
Old Law (old, green law), 145, 149
Old Testament, 51; as a military and colonial narrative, 39–40
Otherworld, Irish representations of, 179n11
overconsumption. *See* consumption, excessive or wasteful
overfishing, 20
ownership, 7, 47

packaging, 165–66
pagan culture, 203n19, 207n52
parable: of the prodigal son, 193n17; of the unjust steward, 57, 59–63, 65, 67
Parlement of the Thre Ages (poem), 17
Parry, Robert, 209n1
Pater Noster prayer, pissing, 87, 96
Patience (poem), 30, 126, 140–45, 205n36
Pearl (poem), 30–31, 126, 143–44, 205n36
Pearl-manuscript, 30, 126. *See also four poems by title*
Peasants' Rising of 1381, 21
penitential manuals, 53–55, 59, 78, 81, 86; in the vernacular, 54–55, 59
Perrigo, Lynn, 33
personal energy, misspent, 77, 86, 96–97, 167
personification allegory, 71–72, 76, 81–85, 103, 150, 194n8
pestilence, 28–31, 70, 151, 154, 186n85
pharmaceutical industry, 12
Piers Plowman, 13, 20–24, 26, 31, 36, 81–101, 150, 157, 160, 164, 180n6, 185n79, 195n23, 207n1; compared to *Mum and the Sothsegger*, 154; discontinuous logic, 98; ecological reading of, 177n4
Piers the Plowman (character), 23–24
pig manure, in medieval cities, 33
plague, 27–29, 31, 36, 104, 110–12, 126, 153–57, 160; cultural trauma in the aftermath, 31–32; Eastern origins, 29–30; English literary writing on, 30; transmission, 107; understood as an ecosystemic event by medieval

218 : INDEX

plague (*continued*)
  people, 29–30; an urban phenomenon, 108; vocabulary for, 30. *See also* Black Death
Plucknett, T. F. T., 188n10, 190n23
poaching, 17
poetic archive, and broad cultural awareness, 21
poetic form, and ecosystemic critique, 70–72
poetry: in late medieval England, 5, 7, 20–21, 101, 113–14; skepticism about its value, 121; and waste, 121
political behavior, prosocial, 157
political catastrophe, 25
political unrest, in England in the Middle Ages, 69–70
political world, and nature, 151, 169–70, 208n1
pollution, 32, 35–36, 104, 107, 123–25, 153–54, 157, 160, 169; alchemical, 109–11; noise, 35; from plastics, 12, 92, 124, 165, 173
population levels, 28, 35, 183n31
precarity, ecosystemic or ecological, 3, 7–8, 104, 112–13, 123, 167. *See also* ecosystemic catastrophe (change, crisis, collapse, imperilment, disaster)
pride, 56–57, 97, 99, 142, 145–47
privacy, 174
privatization, of land, 13–17, 180n9
Promised Land, 39
property, 61, 75, 78–79
property rights (property law), 42, 44, 112
prophets, in the Bible, 40
purgation, 38–42, 51–54, 58, 93–94, 104, 111, 137, 139–41, 161

resistance, to restrictions placed on land use, 15–17, 181n19
Rhodes, William, 196n6, 197n8, 197n12
rhyme, indicating emphasis, 27
Richard II (king), 24–25
Richard the Redeles (poem), 24–25
rivers, polluted, in medieval cities, 33
Robert of Avesbury, 30
romance, conventions of, 143–44, 148, 204n28, 205n32
Rudd, Gillian, 177n3, 200n2, 201n8, 203n21

"Ruin, The" (poem), 201n5, 206n43
Russell, J. Stephen, 145

Saint Francis of Assisi, 8
salt, price of, 18
Sapp, Jan, 212n10
scientific discourse (vocabulary), 5, 169
sea coal, 32
Second Statute of Westminster, 15
secularity, 52, 61–65, 91, 144, 172, 207n54, 212n9, 212n11
sermons, 86, 89, 161; and ecological critique, 59, 64–65; on the *Song of Songs*, 66–67; and waste, 60–63, 78
Siewers, Alfred, 179n11
sin, 127, 140, 142, 146, 154, 169; perceived by medieval Christians as a disorder, 54; personified, 86; seven deadly, 54, 56, 87, 97. *See also* waste: as sin; *personified sins by name*
Sir Gawain and the Green Knight (poem), 4, 30, 36, 126–50, 156–57, 160, 163–64, 174; ecological readings, 201n2; its secularism and theology, 144–45. *See also* ecotheology
sloth, 58, 86–90, 96–98, 100
socage tenure, 44, 189n14
social justice, 61–62, 65, 161
Sodom and Gomorrah, 142, 145
soil, and soil depletion, 12–13, 17, 19, 35–36, 157
soul, as an ecosystem, 52, 172. *See also* waste: and the soul
special traverse, 73
spiritual diagnosis, 55–56
spiritual world, 172, 174
Spyra, Piotr, 145
squandering, 6, 37, 42, 53–56, 58, 68, 161–62, 165–66
Staley, Lynn, 182n24, 196n4, 201n7, 202n17, 203n20, 205n33, 208n2
Stanbury, Sarah, 178n7
starvation, 18, 94–95, 100
statutes, English, 161; Statute of Gloucester, 45–46, 49; Statute of Laborers (1351), 70; Statute of Marlborough, 44–46, 189n14; Statute of Merton (1236), 15; Statute of Treasons, 70–72; Statute of Waste of 1292 (lawsuit), 46–

47, 56, 194n13; *Statutes of the Realm of England*, 41
stewardship, 79, 169, 171–72, 206n46, 210n3; biblical notion of, 8, 59, 62–64; a two-way obligation, 62, 65. *See also* accountability, ecosystemic or ecological
stones, 178n7
Stradling, John, 210n3
streets, polluted, in medieval cities, 33
Strosser, Susan, 164
sustainability, of medieval agroecosystems, 183n29
sweating profusely, 105–6, 110–11, 119, 122, 166; by animals, 111
symbiosis, 172

T. A., 209n2
Tauber, Alfred, 212n10
taverns, as location for waste, 87, 102
tenancy, 45–46
Thames River, 19–20, 34–35
theology, 145
time, 162, 167–68, 173–74; degenerative, 202n17, 203n20; immemorial, 16, 181n22; misspent, 82, 102, 209n1. *See also* wasting: of time
topical allusions, in *Winner and Waster*, 71
Tracey, Larissa, 207n52
trade routes. *See* global trade
transcendent, immanence of, 179n11
treason, 70
trespass, 16, 46, 76, 81, 83–84, 86, 194n13, 194n14, 196n2
trial format: in *Piers Plowman*, 83–84; in *Winner and Waster*, 73, 76, 81
Troy, 33–34, 128–30, 138, 203n20, 206n48
truth telling, 151
Twomey, Michael, 201n2

urban environment, 29; in the Middle Ages, 32–35, 103–5, 165
urbanization (urban society), 5, 70, 108, 112, 158

vastare, 38–39, 51, 53, 59, 67
vastator, biblical, 52, 93–94, 100, 108, 140, 142, 145, 147
vastitas, 37, 127, 135, 146
venerye, 135

Vergil, *Ecologues* and *Georgics*, 208n1
Vulgate Gospels, 51, 58–59, 93, 146
vulnerability, 104–7, 133, 135, 139, 142, 147, 202n11, 202n14; ecosystemic, 2, 4, 8, 76, 149; of human culture, 130, 142, 202n14

Waldron, Ronald, 204n28
warfare, 80–81; chronic, 183n31
Wasserman, Judith, 204n28
waste: as a behavior, 6, 85, 98, 101, 164; in the Bible, 37–41, 50, 51, 161; both economic and ecosystemic problem, 82; of both energy and material goods, 96–97; as a by-product, 166; as a crime against the future, 47, 49; as dissipation or squandering, 53–54, 58; ecosystemic (as ecosystemic behavior), 59, 63, 102–3; escheatorial, 48–49, 191n26, 191n28; etymology, 37, 146; as evil, 78, 90, 150, 153; as garbage, refuse, ordure, or trash, 164–66, 210n6, 211n7; household, 167, 169; as a keyword, 6, 41, 101, 150, 161; linked to proxy misuse, 45, 48–49, 56, 67; as a management problem, 50, 165; in the Middle Ages, 5–7, 36–37; as misspending or overspending, 53–54, 56–59, 61, 74–78, 162–63; as misuse of both spiritual and material goods, 59–60, 162–63, 167; monetized, 45–46, 49; moral valence, 81; of personal energy, 8, 37, 58, 77–80, 86, 97–100, 108, 123, 167, 171–72; personal, linked to socioeconomic problem of waste, 97–98, 100; as punishment for a crime, 42–43; and redistribution of wealth, 74; as a right of the upper class, 44; shift from verb to noun, 162–65; as sin, 53–55, 79, 86; sociality, 68; and the soul, 51–59, 77, 96, 162, 168; as trespass, 46, 51, 73, 194n13
waste and wasting: as a crime, 42–45, 48–49, 54, 79; as ecosystemic crisis or problem, 38, 46, 75, 82, 100, 161; in military narratives in the Bible, 37, 39–40, 188n5
wasteland, 6, 14, 16, 41, 133–37, 146–47, 149, 163–64, 180n11, 202n14, 202n16, 208n6; distinct from deserts or

220 : INDEX

wasteland (*continued*)
  wilderness, 37, 187n2
waste law, 41–42,47–49, 72, 74, 161;
  expanded, 44–46; statutory, 75
wasters: clergy as, 66; defined, 23, 46,
  86, 88, 91, 93–95, 100, 162, 209n2;
  necessary for the economy, 77; as a
  threat, 154
wastes, in the Bible. See *vastitas*
wastes, meaning wastelands, 127
wasting: as an act of colonization or
  nation-building, 39–40; in the Bible,
  causing fear and confusion, 41; of
  blood or other humors, 110; by the
  environment on the human body, 106;
  the goods of the Lord/lord, 56–57; of
  immaterial goods, 51–53, 55, 102; key
  to ecosystemic thought in medieval
  English, 41; for land acquisition or
  resettlement, 39, 188n4; in Middle
  English, 77; of material goods, 68, 102;
  as purification, fortification, or distillation, 109–10; systemic infraction, 79;
  of time, 77–78, 89, 94, 96, 164, 197n9
wasting and winning, 72, 77, 88, 129
wasting body, 103–6, 123–24, 198n2
wasting sickness, 111–12
wasting verse, 119, 123
Watson, Nicholas, 144, 205n36
wealth: concentrated, 17,182n28; equitable distribution, 78–79, 88, 158, 160;
  redistributed as a remedy for waste,
  62, 210n3
weather, 2, 126, 143, 149, 160; in the Middle Ages, 18–25, 35, 156; as a threat, 28,
  35, 133–34, 140–41, 154

westen, 146, 206n43, 206n44
White, Lynn, 179n14
wilderness, 133–34, 136–37, 146–47, 201n8
Wimbledon, Thomas, 63–67, 89, 91, 102
Wimsatt, W. K., 199n11
Winner and Waster (poem), 13, 21, 36,
  69–82, 102–3, 150, 157, 160–164, 167;
  compared to the *Gawain*-manuscript,
  129–32, 137
winning: in fourteenth-century English,
  76; and misexpenditure of energy, 77
Wirral, 133–34, 136–37, 144, 203n18
wonder, 122, 129
words (speaking): as ecosystemic entities,
  124, 173–74; having sovereign power,
  211n5; wasted, 53, 55, 58, 78–79, 96–97,
  124, 163, 167–68, 174
work, 104, 167; agricultural (working the
  land), 89–90, 100; being wasted by,
  105–8; refusal to or failure to, 85–86,
  88, 90–91, 94, 97–98, 100, 197n10; as
  salvation, 95, 99, 157–58; of the wrong
  kind, 103–4
work ethic, Protestant, 157
world, immaterial and material, 172, 174.
  See also spiritual world
wrath, God's divine, 40, 93, 146, 186n85
wrath, sin of, 54, 86
Wyatt, Thomas, 208n1
Wycliffe, John, 210n3
Wycliffite Bible, 59–62, 65–66, 91
wynne, 122, 129

Yeoman (the character), 103–4; his lists,
  113–20; his poetry, 118

Printed and bound by CPI Group (UK) Ltd, Croydon, CR0 4YY
25/11/2024
14598834-0001